YOGMAYA & DURGA DEVI
REBEL WOMEN OF NEPAL

YOGMAYA & DURGA DEVI

REBEL WOMEN OF NEPAL

B. Nimri Aziz

*For poet/novelist and Marxist activist Parijat, and for geographer,
writer and intellectual Harka Gurung—friends
and outstanding Nepali patriots.*

*Along with an unremitting commitment to their nation,
both Parijat and Gurung imbued their humour
and their joy of life into everyone
who gathered with them.*

Journalism provides answers while fiction provides questions.
South American journalist /
novelist Karina Sainz Borgo, 2019

*I always think I'm at some archeological site and I find a shard,
a little piece of pottery, and then I have to invent the rest.
But first I have to go to the place, move the dirt and
find out why I am there.*
Novelist Toni Morrison, 1995,
"The Site of Memory"

*The problem is… the poor get admired, or pitied. They are also
not considered knowledgeable, and that there is nothing
interesting about their economic existence.*
2019 Nobel laureates,
Esther Duflo and Abhijit Banergee

Contents

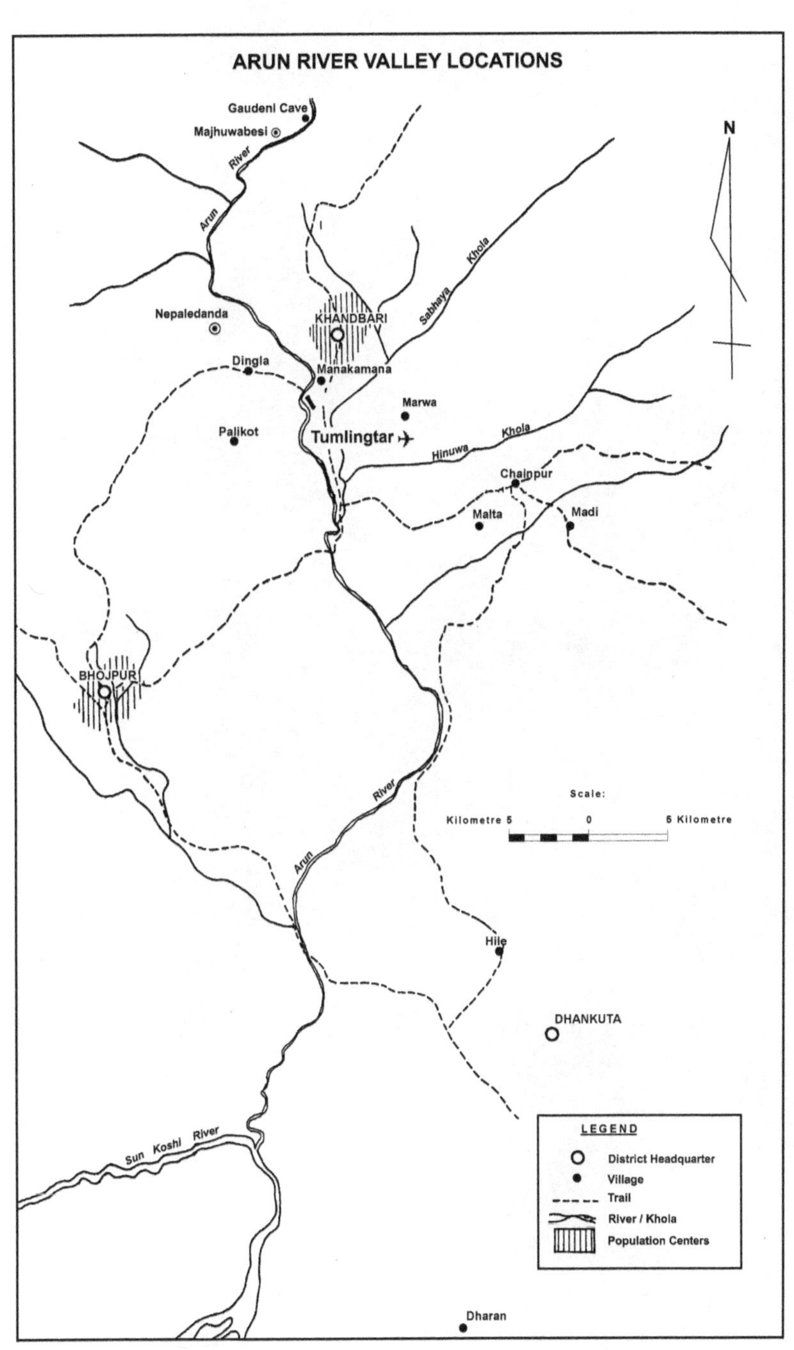

ARUN RIVER VALLEY LOCATIONS
N
Gaudeni Cave
Majhuwabesi
Arun River
Sabhaya Khola
KHANDBARI
Nepaledanda
Dingla
Manakamana
Marwa
Palikot
Tumlingtar
Hinuwa Khola
Chainpur
Malta
Madi
BHOJPUR
Arun River
Scale:
Kilometre 5
0
5 Kilometre
Hile
DHANKUTA
Sun Koshi River
LEGEND
District Headquarter
Village
Trail
River / Khola
Population Centers
Dharan

Foreword

Like many Nepalis I wasn't very knowledgeable about Yogmaya until recently. Only after winning the Padma Shree prize, on a return visit to Nepal from America, I heard her name. My guru and colleague Dahal Yagya Nidhi at Radio Nepal spoke about her with such awe, and he urged me to write Yogmaya's story.

Where should I begin? I wondered. My Google search was of little help to me. Next, I turned to Kathmandu bookstores and started at Nepal's oldest and best-known shop Ratna Pustak Bhandar where I was able to find a single volume on Yogmaya. It was by Dr. Govinda Man Singh Karki. Maybe this is when my real pursuit of Yogmaya started. When I located him he told me about a few writers who'd begun researching Yogmaya's history. Among them was an anthropologist, Barbara Nimri Aziz, whose book I was able to find in Kathmandu as well—in a bookstore in Thamel. As soon as I began to read her book, I felt I had to meet Barbara.

She was living in USA, so with an introduction from Dr. Karki, I phoned her as soon as I got back there. When I told her my plans to write about Yogmaya, she was so happy, and she encouraged me wholeheartedly. She felt that Nepali women had to take up the challenge of Yogmaya, and she explained that up to then none had seemed interested. She believed fiction was a perfect way to explore the life of a special woman like Yogmaya.

Barbara's approach had been different from Janak Lal Sharma and Gayan Mani Nepal who had written about Yogmaya earlier. Barbara was the first person ever to go in-depth with field research and describe our Nepali revolutionary in such detail. I was determined to do as she did—to wander around the places in Nepal where Yogmaya had carried her campaign and to meet people there who might remember her. This is how I prepared myself to write my novel, *Yogmaya*.

In the 1980s when Barbara carried out her first investigations at historical sites connected to Yogmaya, travel and communication in Nepal was difficult. Political discussion was risky then too. But Barbara was able to complete a lot of work and that eventually sparked wide interest in our Nepali ancestor. Now people in Kathmandu valley are reciting and translating yogbani verses created by Yogmaya a hundred years ago.

At the same time that Barbara was collecting facts about Yogmaya from the women living at Manakamana, she learned about a second activist, Durga Devi, a child widow whose courageous social work many decades ago was unique. In this book Barbara focuses her attention on Durga Devi, another Bhojpur woman who she believes is as important as Yogmaya. Barbara writes that there's much work to be done to study Durga Devi's life and to bring greater prominence to her accomplishments at an early period of Nepal's history. Just as Barbara paved a path that makes it easier for others to learn more about Yogmaya, she again points the way to uncover Durga Devi's social and political contributions.

As early as 1970, Barbara traveled to Nepal for her educational research. Even after she completed her studies in this country and although she branched out to learn and write about other parts of the world, to me it seems that through Yogmaya and Durga Devi, Barbara remains deeply invested in Nepal.

When writing my novel, I would regularly contact and refer back to Barbara, sending her questions. She responded with helpful in-depth answers. Then, when my book was released in Kathmandu in

2018, Barbara was in Nepal and kindly postponed her departure so that she could attend my book launch.

This goes to show Barbara's unceasing dedication to Yogmaya and Durga Devi. Now Yogmaya is a figure written about by many authors, and the Nepali government is opening Yogmaya University; but the pioneering work that allowed Yogmaya to come to such prominence can only be attributed to Barbara.

Neelam Karki Niharika
North Carolina, March, 2020

List of Illustrations

YOGMAYA & DURGA DEVI

REBEL WOMEN OF NEPAL

Chapter 1

After Yogmaya

Preparing this new edition in the wake of a very welcome rising interest in Yogmaya Neupane is an exciting task. Along with five edited and updated chapters from the original is my commentary on this early pioneer's legacy today. I also take this opportunity to re-reflect on my portrayals of the two rebel women from Bhojpur and how things evolved to the present.

Yogmaya's character is summarized by my colleague Padma Tara Tuladhar as sahasi—daring. Our Yogi from Bhojpur was indeed daring... and so much more.

Yogmaya was perhaps the most resolute and profound of Nepal's advocates for justice during a politically very dangerous period. So it's a challenge to write about her and, if I may, include renewed appeals for her contemporary sahasi—Durga Devi Karki Ghimire. Inevitably, Karki Ghimire's career will attract greater interest and offer new possibilities to anyone pursuing the history of woman and the struggle for justice.

Many questions confront us today at the beginning of a new era of political and social awareness in Nepal, a democratic republic barely twelve years old. Where do Yogmaya's audacious demands of a century ago stand now, when Nepal has become an open democracy with new freedoms? Human rights along with women's rights are common idioms of public life today.

Yogmaya and Durga Devi were not only courageous women; concern for all women was in the forefront of their calls for responsible leadership long ago. That was a radically different era in Nepal. Their campaigns were launched when the nation was a dictatorship ruled first by the Rana dynasty and then the Shah monarchy, both maintained in partnership with Hindu religious authority. Opposition to those who governed did not exist then; neither did freedom of association. Even with an elected parliament working within a constitutional monarchy in 1990, possibilities were limited. Under those circumstances, could dissenting voices have any impact? At that time, true democracy in Nepal was an ideal embodied in an underground movement whose leaders were forced to seek protection abroad.

Eighty years have passed since Yogmaya's death. A ban imposed at the time suppressed all reference to her and her work. With its dissolution we can now learn more about her. Still, we wonder in what form her pioneering spirit could survive at all, subjected to half a century (1940 to 1990) of enforced silence. Can that once potent message be revived and become effective, joining a wider democratic agenda in modern Nepal?

Whatever was permissible, legal or practical then, what about now? Can a campaign for social justice so long ago hold any relevance to contemporary Nepal? What do inequalities and injustices today have in common with issues these women championed during their lifetimes? Sati, widow sacrifice, was outlawed during Yogmaya's and Durga Devi's time; so was indebted slavery.

Both women were villagers and essentially addressed common discriminatory practices where they lived. Could their proposals be applicable to urban life and law as well? Are they pertinent today?

Unarguably Yogmaya's call to her community to disregard caste boundaries was close to heresy. Such a proposal not only challenges deeply held values; it defies a sacred and inviolate pillar of Hindu society—the authority of Brahmin priests.

Across Nepal, especially in the new era, women and men want to believe oppressive social barriers are weakening; reformers and writers are tempted to reach outside Nepal for support in their struggle to overturn entrenched discriminatory practices at home. Outside heroes seem so accessible. Others may say: No, let's look to Nepal's past—to Yogmaya and Durga Devi for example—to draw inspiration for the hard work of reform within our borders. Maybe these women offer historical evidence that within Nepal, we may find principles of justice. Does a longstanding Nepali concept of justice, one that we can revive and on which we can build, exist?[1]

Significant reforms have been instituted across the country over the past quarter century. But serious inequities remain; we find them in cosmopolitan, educated circles as well as in rural communities. Reflect for example at modern women's parity with men in the family: between husband and wife or between siblings. Are we treated equally in our rights to family property, in our marriage choices, in birth and funerary observances, in how family decisions are made, in how we address each other?

Those who grow up in cites and imbibe international values may believe everyone's equal in their family; we assume that caste barriers, exploitation of women (including physical abuse), multiple wives, and men's claims to their sisters' share of family property are rural phenomenon and if found in the city, they are the backward ways of migrants from the villages. Social inequities, we think, persist mainly in towns where progress is slow and schools are inferior. But such ideas are out of date; 'remote' villages now have schools; many homes there are served by local hydro-electric plants allowing inhabitants to watch news on television and their cell phones.

In private and in government spheres, social changes have accompanied Nepal's move to a democratic republic. Free speech, free association, compulsory education, and the rise of women's voices in public life are universal. Did Yogmaya's and Durga Devi's work contribute to this? What new ways of thinking—what social and political liberties—resulted from their advocacy programs?

Then too, reforms may be attributed to today's democratically elected government and the secularization of Nepal. Where would Yogmaya's religious idioms fit into this? She was a highly spiritual woman, reported to have accomplished extraordinary feats through severe austerities and meditation. And she uttered her edicts in spontaneous verse.

That spiritualism seems to be a foundation of Yogmaya's power to confront the authority of an absolute ruler and corrupt bureaucrats and priests. At the same time, religious persona offered her some protection because of the prohibition on Brahmin murder. (According to Hindu law, even a tyrant should not harm any Brahmin, this priority caste being particularly immune.)

Today in Nepal's current secular system with the Hindu kingdom dissolved and the priesthood somewhat tempered, one wonders: would Yogmaya's religious idioms be less effective in motivating public support for reform? Thus we ask: does she appear to young Nepalis as simply poor yogi invoking an obsolete religiously-based strategy because other means of redress may have been unavailable at that time?

Corruption among Rana officials and extortion by the Brahmin priesthood were targets of Yogmaya's criticisms. (She was accused of diluting essential religious observances.) It was anathema to charge priests for disingenuousness and to question their demands. (In Chapter 5, you will find examples of her poignant metaphors targeting the corrupt system.) [2]

It is hard to know if any of Yogmaya's tactics would work today. Take corruption for example; only she and Durga Devi dared point the finger at culprits in early times. Today, corruption is widely reported in the press; it's so common in contemporary Nepal that it's not even a topic of reform. (Corruption may have even infected government projects on behalf of this remarkable woman, a point we'll return to.)

In East Nepal where Yogmaya conducted her campaign, government funded projects and programs are now being planned in her name. The Communist and Maoist-led governments have been particularly generous in recent years. But if this is because leftist parties have genuinely adopted (or co-opted) her as a symbol of their ideals, we are uncertain.

A century ago her critics derisively labelled her 'communist', but that may have been a handy term of derision. Actually one finds no specific communist or socialist ideology underlying her philosophy and her strategy. She fought to end discrimination, enslavement by debt, priestly domination and caste biases. She appealed to a ruler who wielded his authority by hereditary primacy and priestly sanction. However, she made no effort to protect vulnerable minority citizens and it appears that she expected the omnipotent leader to check exploitation.

Durga Devi Karki, born in nearby Palikot in the district of Bhojpur, grew up not far from Yogmaya's theatre of activity in the forested hills overlooking the Arun River. The two women shared a commitment to justice. But they were not associates. They differed widely in their character and in their lifestyles too. I was told by women who knew both rebels that Durga Devi actually disapproved of Yogmaya's tactics. Yet, that didn't completely exclude her being influenced by the older woman's ideas.

From what I was able to learn about Durga Devi she seems to have more in common with modern-day feminists. In Durga Devi's character I perceive a more realistic model for advocates for gender parity. However, whether today's generation of Nepali feminists will recognize this and champion her remains to be seen.

Contemporary women possess a host of skills and technologies unavailable to our earlier reformers. Can conditions of 100 years ago, even fifty years earlier, offer a model for a society led by modern, school-educated citizens imbued with international concepts of justice? Is their example even practical in today's democracy?

Yogmaya and Durga Devi might be viewed as 'simple' or naïve villagers. If so, this is a mistake. Anyone without a formal education who accomplished what they did surely demonstrates that education and cosmopolitanism are not essential for political sophistication. These women were in no way simple; neither were they normal.

A Good Time to Review

I am not approaching these questions from foreign retirement. Nor am I evaluating these women through the prism of agendas in the U.S., across Europe or in other parts of Asia. My interest in these women stems from my own personal search for heroines starting when I was at college. As I became increasingly aware of biases underlying western education I was compelled to look eastward. In my case, I became aware of how my Arab identity was being devalued and obscured— one could say stunted—overwhelmed by the dominant White European culture and polity. Like other immigrant children, I knew little about the lands of my parents, in my case, the Arab world.

Many of the world's people's histories are filtered out by the western educational structure, a system and culture dominated by European institutions so that only those pioneers and defenders of justice who are allied to and approved by their colonial powers might receive mention in our school texts. Those esteemed European institutions, also heavily misogynist, kept us ignorant of women's achievements through time and across continents. European women's history was hardly written about or taught; until recently even less was available about women from across Asia, Africa and South America. Today, we are only beginning to understand how riddled with prejudice and racism our school history lessons are. (We'll pick up this theme in the next chapter.)

Growing up and receiving my education in Canada and the U.K., from grade school through graduate studies, I did not escape these biases. As for any personal political ambition, in fact I had no political inclination until I began to work on this project with Nepali women, starting with Yogmaya and Durga Devi in 1980, then with poet and leading dissident Parijat, followed by my contacts

The author with Nepali poet and Yogmaya enthusiast, Parijat; 1982.

with two experienced, savvy Nepali colleagues—Manjula Giri and Sukanya Waiba.[3]

I've remained in regular touch with Nepal over the 19 years since this book first appeared, 25 years since I published my first reports about both rebel women—altogether 40 years extending back to my arrival in the Arun River Valley when I began learning about them.

As I assimilated what I gathered from the bhaktini I worked with at the Manakamana hermitage—these women were among the remaining living devotees of Yogmaya—and then imbibed what Parijat exposed me to, I watched a serious challenge to the monarchy erupt in 1990. I became more politically attentive and involved as Nepal grappled with a rising (and unstoppable) Maoist insurgency. Eventually a cease-fire ended military conflict and free elections opened the way for dialogue between widely opposing parties, eventually ousting the monarchy, and drawing up a democratic secular constitution in 2015. I've seen massive advances in communications, from road construction and universal cell phone use to an explosion in free media. I've witnessed people from across the economic spectrum leave the country, among them women and men I worked with on earlier projects in Nepal. When I now visit Colorado, Toronto, or New York, I meet Nepalis whom I first encountered in their villages near Khandbari, Jomsom, Therathum and in distant Sherpa monasteries. Some of my dearest friends, Parijat for example, are no more.

In 2002 I revisited the Arun River Valley to reunite with anyone who had assisted me seventeen years earlier. (Among them only Vishnumaya Dahal remained; both of us were thrilled to meet again.) Solu Khumbu was also on my agenda, reconnecting me with nuns and monks whom I'd earlier known when they were teenagers.

Encouraged by friends whom you'll meet in the following pages, I resumed visits to Nepal on a regular basis; then I unexpectedly found myself in a new community, a group of researchers and writers as intrigued and inspired by Yogmaya as I was.

By 2010 Yogmaya Neupane began to arouse the serious attention of historians and journalists.[4] These men and women keep me abreast of on-going projects, proud to share their thoughts and research findings.

Our rebel women's histories are now in their hands. I've since met more and more Nepali fans of Yogmaya across the country and in the U.S. as knowledge about her spreads—mainly from newspaper accounts. Yogmaya-related projects seem to expand year by year.

The reign of King Mahendra and his son Birendra was not so long ago. Many Nepalis can recall the atmosphere then; they will testify how before 1990, no political discussion or publication critical of the administration were possible. A singular newspaper carried official news along with royal declarations. Older citizens can appreciate today's open political landscape—even though their freely elected government seems incompetent and corrupted, and progress is slow.

I follow Nepal's emergence with undiminished hope. (Perhaps because I don't live in Nepal for more than two months a year I may be less pessimistic.) Alternatively optimistic and dismayed, I gather material for articles I regularly publish.[5] I talk to people who believe things will improve, who see new opportunities here; others I speak to have abandoned Nepal.

Having been engaged with Tibetan nuns and monks since the earliest years of my experience in Nepal, I am a witness to the extraordinary evolution of the Buddhist landscape, especially in and around Kathmandu Valley. I watch with admiration interrupted by moments of anxiety, the rising pride and daring of various Nepali communities —Newar, Manangi, Rai, Tamang and Thakali who with scores of others have begun identifying as Janajati (see p.19, below). This political and cultural movement was once a disconnected, individualized and marginalized population. (Labelled by anthropologists as minorities, 'tribes', or simply 'a language group'.)

This introduction is an opportunity to address some of the questions noted above, following which I'll revisit the time and places of my original research.

I dare to offer this summary assessment without drawing on any of thousands of commissioned socio-economic reports and publications. I know that anyone needing empirical data on Nepal can easily access the substantial body of documents assembled from countless studies completed, underway and proposed. So extensive are those investigations that they constitute a thriving business—it's called 'development studies', a barely digestible, costly and ponderous body of information accumulating in data bases year after year with weak signs of progress on the ground. One doubts if it could possibly accommodate the personalities and controversies of Durga Devi Karki Ghimire and Yogmaya Neupane. This presentation is more anecdotal but no less valid.

Allow me to begin with comments on four chapters from the 2001 edition. Chapter 5, "Yogmaya: Poet, Teacher, Insurgent", stands largely as I wrote it in 2001; any new thoughts are included here and in Chapter 5 which take into account some ideas from subsequent books and articles written about her, and where I share re-evaluations based on my political maturation and new perspectives.

Three semi-fictional portraits—"A Girl Named Laxmi", "Manu, the Basket Carrier" and "Maya, a Little Weaver Girl"—are slightly edited and represent portraits from Nepal as I witnessed it travelling across the country in the 1970s and 1980s. The chapter on Durga Devi Karki Ghimire is an historical biography which I'll address here first because, although I have little new information about her (only a postscript in Chapter 3, based on my November 2019 visit to Marwa village), she is a worthy and brave Nepali leader. Karki Ghimire deserves as much attention as Yogmaya by anyone concerned with social justice and women's history. Knowing how these women, in their individual ways, approached injustices helps us to appreciate women's potential and what was possible in the past. Durga Devi offers plenty of drama too!

Briefly, Karki Ghimire was a reformer of extraordinary courage and skill who chose an independent approach to injustice. She adroitly applied a remarkable familiarity of the laws of the last century, however limited they were, and through the courts she was able to exact some justice. Her first goal was to win her own rights as a widow; then she assisted wronged women and children; she secured the release from jail of her father; finally she brought charges against people who physically threatened her. We must take care not to assume that her more personalized campaign for justice means Durga Devi is less worthy of an honoured place in the history of Nepal. While Durga Devi confined her work to her neighbourhood, her efforts hold implications for anyone afflicted by similar injustices. Legal steps she took on her own behalf were not based on

Framed photo at Manakamana Kuti of their patron and civil rights advocate, Durga Devi Karki Ghimire, circa 1960s.

greed; they were political. That is, she fought for property that was legally hers but which culturally was denied her. Women's property rights were an issue when Ghimire was a young widow; today, denial of their property continues to plague women across Nepal. The injustices she highlighted affect people living in towns and cities as well as in villages.

Almost everything I know about Durga Devi's activities is reproduced as it appeared in *Heir to a Silent Song*. Still I will have more to say about Karki Ghimire's significance for us in the following chapter. At this point, I want to raise the question: why has she not captured the attention and respect she deserves, attention which would expand our picture of what women were capable of at that time. Perhaps understandably, she is eclipsed by the almost mythical revolutionary, Yogmaya Neupane. But she will no longer remain in the shadow of her predecessor.

Now, about the semi-fictional portraits in this book: "A Girl Named Laxmi" and "Maya, a Little Weaver Girl" I based on anecdotes gathered from first hand experience moving through the countryside. Staying in villagers' homes overnight—sometimes for days—I was a guest but also a witness. I heard how the servant girl was roused to light the fire and refill the water pot before anyone else stirred. I saw these children hunched over and silent, scrubbing pots and sweeping the floor, the last person to take food. As for daughters, they rarely faired as well as their brothers. While boys gather together to play board games, girls and women toil in the garden and kitchen—collecting water, weeding, scrubbing, winnowing, cooking, feeding the house animals—all while caring for a younger child. They often sit out of sight waiting, roused by an order from others while boys and adults cluster around the hearth eating and joking.

I often overheard young women gossip about their miserable peers. I listened to unhappy mothers grumble about daughters-in-law, the everyday tension between them undisguised. I heard brothers quarrel over their duties in the family; I listened to women moan and weep about their husband's second wife; I witnessed eight-year-olds working at looms in dusty, dim sheds for 10–12 hours a day.

It was impossible not to notice discrimination operating, not only in public places but also within families. Human rights and social inequalities were not the subject of my research, so the only record I kept of these scenes was in my soul. My written portraits are therefore composites drawn from recollections, anecdotes of many of those hapless men and women. They're presented here to serve as a backdrop illustrating some conditions that motivated the two rebel women who emerged as champions for social change and for women's rights. They also offer flashbacks to life in the 1980s for readers to compare with what they know of present-day Nepal.

It was because of what I'd already witnessed moving through Nepal during the course of a decade (1970–1980) that I was receptive to what I would hear about Durga Devi and Yogmaya. It was easy to make the link between their campaigns and the daily life I observed not so very long after their passing—caste boundaries, loss of land, accumulating debt, incompetent selfish officials, youngsters sent away to work, men taking a second wife, unwanted widows. If I, a casual visitor, grasped some of the problems, then every Nepali must have been all too familiar with these conditions, and more. Why did so few dare challenge the status quo? Therein lays the exceptionality of those who did take action and who appealed for justice.

To a degree the fates of blind Laxmi and of Maya the weaver tell the story of children across the country, today and in the past. The notorious carpet factories employing thousands of child workers in reprehensible circumstances closed twenty years ago, the result of a vigorous campaign by child welfare advocates. Today Maya may not exist in that context. "Maya, a Little Weaver Girl" nevertheless still epitomizes the fate of many Nepalis, perhaps a little older than Maya. Forced to work in exploitative conditions and under debt, these young workers represent the only opportunity for countless 21st century families to escape the cycle of poverty and harsh village conditions.

A few years of education does not guarantee a job. Nine-year old Maya was packed off to toil in a factory far from home. Today an older Maya would be among countless women who strike out on their own in search of work, who run away to India, who are smuggled abroad to unknown fates. An older Maya is succeeded by her son, one of millions of Nepali men (and some women as well) forced to seek work abroad. His migration reflects the same family pressures on youths, the same vulnerabilities, the same limited choices.

"A Girl Named Laxmi", blind and left in a field, was defenceless against a sexual predator. Today, if lucky, she may be enrolled in a special school. But blind and other disadvantaged children remain in danger of abuse. A press report of the rape of a seven-year-old blind girl (Himalayan News Service, Dec. 18, 2018–the same time that demonstrations were on-going across Nepal to the demand the government rigorously pursue efforts to find the murderer of 13-year old Nirmala Panta.[6]) is just one of numerous rapes we read about, reported in Nepal's English language dailies in the span of a month. (We'll return to this issue.)

"Manu, the Basket Carrier" also appears here in its original form. The story of Manu is about inequality and human haulage, but it's also about the invisibility of the poor against a fantasy landscape maintained for tourists.

I encountered many Manus in the course of my walks from town to town. He's not just a basket carrier. He's a son, a brother, a father and a husband with a house and fields somewhere on an earth-sculpted hillside. Manu was not ferrying supplies for his family or fodder for his animals. He was on contract with a dealer to haul goods to a retailer in an interior market town.

I created Manu out of my compassion for the many men I witnessed working as porters—all of them farmers—forced into cash-paying jobs. Viewed from afar, these porters involuntarily serve the imaginary bucolic landscape of Himalayan hill life featured in coloured travel brochures and websites. Trudging doggedly along paths in stained shirts and thin shorts, sometimes shoeless, these village sons served as Himalayan transport vehicles until the 1990s. Farmers pressed for cash left their fields for months each year to carry merchants' supplies into the mountains.

Here again my familiarity with rural life helps me understand what so many villagers face; even farmers cannot escape the need for cash. Personal tastes, changing household needs and market relations in rural Nepal were rapidly changing by the mid-20th century; families wanted materials and produce they could no longer barter or grow in their fields:—cotton goods, processed foods, sugar, rice and kerosene. Those have to be imported from the plains and from India, shipped by truck to a road-head from where they're transferred to the backs of men like Manu. Transport was one of the few labour markets for muscle power.

During my work in the 1970s and 1980s roads in Nepal were confined to strategic hill routes and across the plains. So I encountered many of these men on hilly pathways over which I too moved from place to place. We did not speak much on the road, but I knew their home-life. I saw how they shoulder responsibilities for their elders, their wives and their children, maybe their brother's children as well— usually a large household. Their social and ritual obligations weigh as heavily as an 80 kg. load on their shoulders.

I merge my witness of porters moving along northbound trails with personalities I encountered in farmhouses where I stopped, and at the teashops where we rested on the side of the path and sipped the same five-rupee tea from small glasses.

Today, long distance haulage by human power is largely a thing of the past. Extensive road construction allows trucks and jeeps to reach deep into Nepal's interior with supplies. Plodding figures, once wistfully portrayed in photos of rural Nepali life, are almost absent from major trails. This does not mean families do not need cash incomes. No; cash is in greater demand than ever; in fact pressures to take up wage labour have increased.

Where a man with a load travelled between Dharan and Bhojpur and beyond or from the road-head at Lamsango to Jiri and deeper into Solu-Khumbu, today his son or brother or grandson leaves the village altogether, expecting to be gone for an extended period. He'll set out by bus for the capital or Biratnagar or another border town where he'll seek a labour broker. If someone sets up a job for him in Malaysia or Qatar, he'll feel fortunate.

"Migration Studies" is a body of research that now includes a range of disciplines and employs experts working for agencies that garner hundreds of thousands of dollars to execute and publish. You can read accounts in the daily press or peruse exhaustive reports generated by research institutes. (The self indulgence of aid agencies and their value or worthlessness is poignantly captured in Manjushree Thapa's 2016 novel, *All of Us in Our Own Lives*.) From those inexhaustible reports, you can decide to what degree Manu may represent what Nepali villagers face today and if little weaver girls have really been rescued. You yourself can judge whether their drudgery is a thing of the past. Indeed, in 1980 Manu was possibly better off than his 2019 counterpart. Manu may have earned enough in 3 or 4 months to satisfy the family's cash needs and did not leave his fields unploughed or his children fatherless for long.

By contrast with the last century, today farms are lost to another kind of debt. (Villagers often offer their fields as collateral to borrow cash needed to arrange overseas work.) Countless fields lie uncultivated when men depart to take up employment abroad. Their parents, wives and children find themselves unable (or unwilling) to continue farming and they move to cities where they rent rooms, all their needs met with the remittances sent home by their toiling men. Families may find city life more comfortable although their living expenses surely reduce any savings from overseas wages. More serious is the concomitant decline in farming due to migration to cities and loss of land due to debts incurred in the search for overseas employment. Domestic production of food across Nepal has severely declined in the past decade, necessitating more food imports and thereby greater reliance on cash.[7]

Besides those loads of migration studies, one can find ample documentation of women's hardships in gender-focused reports accumulated over the past quarter century after women became the focus of development programs in Nepal as elsewhere. Hundreds, perhaps thousands, of non-governmental organizations and government bureaus in Nepal are devoted to women. The daily press, in Nepali and English, offers vivid victim testimonies on a dizzying scale, along with the remedial work of agencies devoted to their plight. I dare not compete with their reports or summarize them, or even evaluate them. I can only try to assess changes and conditions I witness and learn about in the context of Yogmaya's and Durga Devi's work. My limited aim here is to help evaluate these two women's extraordinary efforts.

Fundamental Realities

The major transformation from Yogmaya's and Durga Devi's time unarguably is the replacement of the absolute monarchy with a democracy. Second, many more people, women and men, are educated. A large middle class with strong international ties enjoys conveniences —from brain surgery to fresh trout and imported fruit, global satellite broadcasts and authentic pizza—like anyone in their class anywhere in the world. Changes extend to a rise of women's demands for equality, in part due to Nepal's participation in the international feminist movement.

More people are aware of their human rights. Abundant reports of social conditions appearing in the Nepali press foster open discussion of abuse, crimes and injustices. The number of women in public office[8] and in teaching, engineering, medicine, journalism and law is considerable. Due to public pressure the Nepal constitution fixed a quota for women in public office and many women were recruited to run in the 2017 national election. Women are active in all political parties although men still dominate, and one increasingly hears reports from once-aspiring women that their party leadership is marginalizing them year-by-year.

We'll find increasing numbers of inter-caste couples among urban families although their unions are not without obstacles. (Often, after encountering parents' initial objections to an unconventional marriage, differences are forgotten and harmony is restored.)

Almost everyone, educated or not, rural or urban, owns a mobile phone. Few Nepali children are unfamiliar with computers. And however remote a village, its inhabitants have likely travelled by bus and jeep and by air as well. (Mountain airstrips provide essential links nationwide.)

Past hardships associated with rural life are greatly reduced by the arrival of hydro and solar power. Electrification no longer relies on long distance transmission lines. Television, viewed mainly for dramas and music videos, still provides news coverage of issues facing the country. With new press freedoms available after 1990, besides television channels, hundreds of locally run private radio stations emerged, broadcasting to all of Nepal's rural and urban areas. In the cities newspapers are flourishing.

The arrival of more democratic rights eventually gave rise to what's called Janajati Mahasangh.[9] This umbrella organization of 59 'nationalities' was established in 1991 but effective ethnic group identity blossomed only in the past decade. It now represents serious political and cultural implications for the Hindu caste hierarchy, which it views as separate but cannot altogether exclude. Janajati's rise corresponds to the expansion of democratic freedoms in Nepal and debates in the constituent assembly before the constitution was finally promulgated in 2015. Thirty years on, a cultural renaissance is underway in many of these communities. Rai, Sherpa, Limbu, Magar, Tharu, Gurung, Manangi are among 59 small and large ethnic peoples mobilizing members politically and through revitalized ritual observations. These also include the traditionally marginalized people populating the plains of Nepal adjacent to India who collectively identify themselves as Madhesi-Janajati. As these newly empowered ethnic groups gain economic clout and enter mainstream society, Nepal's centuries-old status quo is sure to change.

Meanwhile ethnic movements are stimulating the rebirth of languages once completely eclipsed by Nepali (the national language). Local festivals, literature, rituals and marriage celebrations and more are being redefined. Emerging interest groups are strengthening ties with overseas Nepalis of similar backgrounds. Gurung expatriates from Australia and the U.S. are linked, as are Newar across the globe. This in turn revitalizes religious and family activities. Economic success and ease of travel allow expatriates to regularly revisit Nepal and in turn influence life in the homeland. To what degree these developments actually alter basic injustices or discrimination within Nepal remains to be seen.

Buddhism, whose members had been underrepresented in the Nepali census, has become more mainstream. The economic success of Newar, Sherpa and Tibetan Buddhist families is manifest in the preservation and expansion of their religious centres. Witness the support for Lumbini, birthplace of Gautama Buddha. Declared a paramount heritage site and tourist centre, it will soon be served by an international airport.

With the creation of the Republic, the 'Hindu' definition of the Nepali state officially ended. The monarchy was dissolved. But was the status of Hinduism correspondingly diminished? Hardly. Hindu values still dominate Nepali life; Hindu priests retain considerable authority, perhaps bolstered by the rise of the BJP, the Hindu nationalist party in nearby India.

Even with the entry of Janajati into Nepal's public life the dominance of the Bahun (high caste) class does not seem threatened. One finds a preponderance of Bahun in all spheres of life—education, journalism, accounting, politics, finance, and political parties across the political spectrum. Most party leaders (past and present), ministers, and high-ranking civil servants are Bahun. Elected officials favour members of their own caste when naming directors to head semi-governmental institutions. Their grip on the bureaucracy and in education seems unassailable.

Though Yogmaya was Bahun, she emerged as one of the fiercest critics of Bahun exploitation which not only subjugated Bahun caste members but all others as well. Yet, from what we've been able to ascertain Yogmaya was unable to or did not try to attract oppressed lower castes into her movement. This ought to raise a question about the limits of her concept of justice. Thus far no one has taken up this possible flaw in her agenda.

Even now, Janajati members appear to be less excited than Bahun are by the two women's histories. They are not found among today's scholars and social activists celebrating Yogmaya's abilities and her struggle. Rather it is Bahun who seem to be the most committed advocates of her work.

What Can These Daring Women Teach Us?

This brings us back to the impact of these women.

During their lifetime these two Nepalis were outstanding characters and personalities, unrivalled in the history of dissenters and critics. There's general agreement that their advocacy and their readiness to face adversity and risk has no parallel in Nepal. First, they were creative innovators—geniuses really. Second, they were from rural Nepal and chose to carry out their campaigns there. Third, they continued with their mission despite encountering resistance and public opprobrium from some quarters. They faced banishment, if not death.

I will do my best to assess their long-term impact although I recognize that only further reflections and serious debate will arrive at anything definitive on this question.

At a meeting I attended in Biratnagar recently, a well known teacher in the city, Shanta Ghimire, shared three points about the importance of these historical figures. She asserts first that education while essential is not the only basis for women to advance; second, she emphasizes how Nepali culture itself embodies values to responsibly guide its people. Ghimire confidently addresses her third point too:

"Nepal does not need people from beyond its border to define the direction of our struggle." She was doubtless referring to the western-led feminist movement which proposes that others adopt the aims and tactics defined by Western advocates. I expect too that Ghimire and her colleague Kabita Chapagain (co-founders of Biratnagar's Yogamaya Memorial Foundation) are alluding to the many women-centred programs imported into Nepal from outside. One wonders: Is the history of these two Bhojpur rebels known to other gender-focused projects in Nepal?

Shanta Ghimire's remark is highly pertinent. Too often Nepalis seek out foreign agencies ready to locate yet another fanciful project to further their own global agendas (and provide generous outside funds to do so). In general, Nepal's administration and the staff of these projects, unwittingly or not, sell peoples' victim-hood and poverty. They are usually successful, so foreign support continues to flow into the country. (Again, see Manjushree Thapa's *All of Us in Our Own Lives*.) Thus the chain of humanitarian programs for 'needy' citizens continues. Conferences lead to more conferences, further reports are commissioned, additional staff are recruited, and on and on. Their agendas become self-serving and their wards become a permanent feature of the social landscape.

"You are enough!"

I am reminded how Black poet and philosopher Maya Angelou (1928–2014) so affirmatively advised an audience of young Black American women. Angelou spoke to them years ago when she was beginning to gain recognition as a talented writer. "You Are Enough", she repeats—a refrain captured in a clip in the 2017 film biography *Maya Angelou: And Still I Rise*.

What does Angelou mean by this injunction?

She is exhorting those young people to believe in their own past: "You have it in you, in your heritage and your self respect, in your history". It's a powerful petition, one among Angelou's abundant pithy wisdoms quoted as frequently as her poems. Knowing so well the experience of Black Americans, Angelou insisted her people cease looking beyond, that they rid themselves of the notion that others have more, that others possess an exclusive knowledge of solutions, that others have a right to claim dominance over them.

Perhaps within the exhortations of Yogmaya and the victories of Durga Devi, Nepal has "enough" to establish true justice. Like many countries, Nepal—even with its distinctive personality, its charm, its rich diversity, its architecture and its fertile fields—is blighted by a fixation with celebrity, by an eagerness to import what's fashionable beyond its borders, too keen to adopt foreign innovations. Unreasonably critical of each other, eager to dismiss our neighbours' successes, we eagerly seek outside approval, thus submit to outside guidance. Perhaps that accounts for Nepalis' excessive regard for foreign brands and stars, their deference to India. Yes, they adore their deities, their Gorkha regiments, their lamas and priests. But textbooks devote insufficient attention to Nepal's own heroes.

It's a dilemma. Nepal is swamped by Indian cinema and politics, by Korean boy-bands and by Chinese-made gadgets and household products. True, Nepal can boast how it was never colonized, militarily. Yet, while looking beyond its borders to answer its needs, the country seems to neglect its own talent. The Janajati movement and the success of Nepal's Buddhist leaders could counter this trend. So would a heightened celebration of its own citizens.

Dharma Raj: The Cost of Justice

Both our Bhojpur-born women identified injustice and devised ways to struggle against its many manifestations. Yogmaya called for a "Dharma Raj". The Dharma Raj she articulated is a powerful concept. After meditating on the phrase for a very long time, I finally translated Dharma Raj as "justice". Others may prefer "human right" or "social justice"; for me "human right" is insufficiently inclusive whereas "justice" embraces economic and sexual exploitation, corruption, land theft, and more.

Has anyone in Nepali history other than Yogmaya devoted her life for a principle like her "Dharma Raj"? Has any woman shown how she could fight for herself in the courts (and win) on a scale comparable to Durga Devi?

In articulating "Dharma Raj" around gender imbalance, property theft or exploitative priestly authority, Yogmaya undoubtedly awakened hope in the thousands of people who heard her. People sympathetic to her message felt an alternative social standard was possible.

Durga Devi too showed that women have an alternative to submission. Onlookers must have been astonished by her readiness to fight for her rights. No wonder the men whom these women challenged, from an unassailable national ruler to a family patriarch, found them not only threatening but imponderable. Could they even grasp the idea of "Dharma Raj"?

We should not be surprised how such champions might threaten any authority: religious authority, inherited caste authority, patriarchy in the family, kingly authority. Such threats had to be neutralized. That was accomplished by ridicule, by lies, by banishment or by charging them with madness. Did these women's adversaries succeed?

It seems so.

If we believe Yogmaya prevailed, it may be only through her martyrdom. To enter the roiling, engulfing current of the Arun River with her followers was as shocking as it was extreme. Not unexpectedly, the authorities had to erase this shameful episode by imposing a total legal ban on her and her movement, destroying or suppressing any related documents, terrifying survivors, and applying other intimidating tactics. No one spoke publicly about her passing for years. A colleague with a keen interest in this history recalls her 1992 stay in Nepaledanda, Yogamaya's birthplace: she was in this village on an economic development project; yet, she reports, she heard no mention whatsoever by villagers about their illustrious, 'lost' ancestor.

But Yogmaya was not forgotten; this is assured by vigorous research underway and by some of today's elders—mainly men—

speaking to journalists and researchers combing through local history, swell with pride as they recount incidents.

What morsels they conjure up to applaud their resurrected local hero! As we move further and further from her lifetime the lionization of Yogmaya could become a problem; how do we sort out fact from fiction—an issue I shall return to—especially at this nation's time of need for genuine Nepali heroes?

Concerning authorities' agendas to banish Yogmaya, I add my hitherto unreported experience with a priest, the only man in that kuti, who lived among the women at Manakamana when I worked there in the 1980s. A local man, although he was educated in India, he enjoyed authority as a 'learned' figure there. (I do not know if he received a salary, and if so, from whom. But the bhaktini cooked his food and washed his clothes.) Seeing how keenly the women were assisting me in my research, he informed Mata, the head bhaktini, of his disapproval of my inquiries. She in turn reported this to me, adding that he'd instructed them not to recite *yogbani* under any circumstances—not privately, and pointedly, not to me.

We disregarded his admonition.

I faithfully continued to gather more facts. Then I publicized my findings. Because two notable Nepali scholars—poet Parijat and geographer Harka Gurung—supported me wholeheartedly, I felt confident to proceed. Gurung presciently urged me to append the collection of Yogmaya's brilliant verses, *yogbani* (also referred to as *sarvartha yogbani*, or *hazurbani*) to my 2001 book (also retained in this edition, pp. 249-end) and thereby bring them back into circulation. This history would no longer be suppressed. Following Nepal's 1990 revolution when some press freedom was permitted, the issue slowly began to be publicly discussed and eventually, after another two decades, it would be celebrated. (This even though news of the dramatic sacrifices of 68 citizens was impossible to ignore forever.)

As we uncover more details about Yogmaya's campaign and examine *yogbani* more thoroughly, we acquire a deeper appreciation of her acumen and perspicacity. On-going research by established Nepali scholars and writers, augmented by cursory interest from a British professor [10] affirms that she is worthy of serious attention.

Mata Damodara Giri reading the concealed hazurbani text, 1982, later gifted to the author.

Memories of Durga Devi, although she lived until 1973, have not won the same attention—not yet. She conducted her campaign with skill and intelligence. But she has not captured public imagination; nor has she found her way into compilations of notable global women (*Goodnight Stories for Rebel Girls*, [11] a compilation of 100 portraits, does not yet contain any Nepali entry).

Like Yogmaya's campaign, attention to Durga Devi will overturn misconceptions about Nepalis, men as well as women, who spend their lives in those 'remote' corners of the world. Her actions remind us that villagers are far from politically unsophisticated. (Did Nepal's insurgent Maoist movement not take hold and spread across rural Nepal because poorer villagers better understood the need and possibility of reform than did educated urban citizens?)

Durga Devi Karki Ghimire, the villager I highlight in Chapter 3, was a rural Nepali keenly aware of injustices and she was a woman who decided to act. As with Yogmaya, the price she paid was high.

A Village Isn't Just a Village

It may help us to understand these women's achievements when we recognize that 50 years ago and half a century before then, when Yogmaya launched her campaign, rural people were really not as isolated as we imagine. Yogamaya travelled to Kathmandu more than once, and new acolytes from the capital moved to Bhojpur to be near her; she spent many years in India too; Durga Devi and her companion travelled through Nepal to India.

Here again, those of us who grow up with access to international resources believe city residents are better placed to initiate democratic campaigns. This misconception may be corrected as more urban Nepalis venture beyond the confines of Kathmandu Valley and Nepal's southern cities. A young generation raised in cities commonly view their own rural relatives as disadvantaged or somehow limited. If we talk to them, we'd soon learn just how far and wide farmers venture. In 1980, those women at Manakamana spoke to me about Biratnagar, Janakpur and Kathmandu and other distant cities they'd visited. Some had met relatives in Biratnager and crossed to nearby India for pilgrimage, and to places even further from their homes.

If villagers travel by foot and eat from bowls woven from leaves, if they bathe in cold water, if they don't sleep on a mattress, they are not disadvantaged or misinformed. And they may know more than we imagine about conditions beyond their valley or mountain pass.

A colleague whom I know admires my work expressed her wonder over how I 'managed to accomplish your research under the hard conditions of those years'. (She's referring to 1980 there on the east bank of the Arun.) She meant this as a compliment, although initially I was taken aback. True, I had had no mosquito repellent, no foam mat, no hot water shower; I was unable to phone anywhere (not even to Kathmandu); I had no protein power bar to energize me during a walk up the mountainside, no bottled water, certainly no coffee, milk or eggs—the kuti being totally vegan.

When you read my accounts and judge the result, you decide. Would I have done a better job if facilities available today were accessible then, at my age then? Would the women at Manakamana have treated me differently?

With a mature perspective of the ideological and political capacities of our forefathers and foremothers, we can easily imagine that they were receptive to reform. Walking in the hills and limited diet choices were not a problem. The chief obstacle they faced was the supremacy of a centralized, uncompromising power. Durga Devi and Yogmaya are to be admired not for physical conditions of village life but because they dared to challenge entrenched local and state obduracy.

Barriers to these brave leaders were not technical; nor were they geographic; not dependent on formal education either. Calls for justice were simply inconceivable at the time of the Rana regime and under the Shah monarchy. Moreover, to organize political opposition invited harsh retaliation. Blood shed by non-violent protesters in 1990 and long prison terms imposed on vocal opponents are examples of how the government treated dissent.

Yogmaya was one of the few who actually confronted the Rana Prime Minister, albeit gently. She did this through written appeals and in metaphorical verse. She possibly believed the ruler was beneficent. It seems she actually expected to convince him with her repeated appeals. Then things changed. Reality confronted her when troops suddenly arrived in the valley to thwart her plan for mass agni-samadhi—sacrifice by fire. When she saw their show of force, she must have begun to doubt if she and her following would be protected by the proscription regarding Bahun murder.

For threatening to martyr themselves these activists were summarily confined to jail, some for long periods. After the ruler ordered those arrests Yogmaya took her challenge to another level.

(One wonders how those authorities would handle a threat on this scale by a party of Tamang, Dalit or Limbu or other dissidents lacking the protection of high-caste status?)

Our heroes' campaigns may be judged unsuccessful, I admit. Yogmaya, the beloved leader was gone. Men and women had hurled themselves after her into the night waters taking children with them. Inconsolable, terrified survivors fled in all directions. The military purge that

Site of Yogmaya's Jal-samadhi at Majhuwabesi beach, identified by Shanti Nanda at time of her 1982 visit with author and Vishnumaya Dahal.

followed was so severe, how could anyone dare take up Yogmaya's cause? Banishment was complete.

Troops fanned out searching nearby settlements. Since the families who perished were known, investigations of everyone related to them were pursued. Subsequent months and years must have been frightening for them. Everyone fell silent. Years passed and as far as we know no one dared to openly visit Majhuwabesi, the site of that Jal-samadhi on the shores of the Arun. None of the bodies were found, we are told—maybe a rumour started by authorities to stem any further talk of the incident.

Excavated Jal-samadhi stone, 2015, identified and marked by the new Majhuwabesi patrons in the same vicinity as that shown above, (BK, 2019).

Another reason for the ban was to ensure no sympathizers could raise the issue of the ruler's responsibility. Perhaps Yogmaya's aim with her martyrdom was to attach guilt to him, since according to Hindu law, anyone even indirectly responsible for the death of a Brahmin is morally and religiously culpable. Those in power made certain this possibility did not arise.

Rana rule ended in 1951, replaced in 1961 by an equally oppressive monarchy. The Shah kings retained the ban and it was still in effect when I began my research. I did not know this as I plunged ahead with my work. Even when I realized the dynamics of that mass suicide, I still did not raise the question of government responsibility for Yogmaya's death with any official—not to the retired Rana general I interviewed in 1981, not to local Bhojpur or Sankhuwasabha authorities, and not to priests. I don't recall fearing their reaction, but some trepidation must have been operating at some level to quiet my tongue.

As for Durga Devi's end, it passed almost unnoticed as far as I could learn. Her detractors, many who claimed she was mad, were likely glad to see her finally gone. (See postscript to Chapter 3—my brief 2019 visit to Marwa.) There was no one to hail her accomplishments, not even family to tend her burning pyre. (This would not have bothered her.)

Whose Champions?

So ended an extraordinary phase in the political history of Nepal. Apart from Parijat's celebration of Yogmaya soon after she and I met, a generation passed before my work attracted some serious attention. The earlier generation included the ascetics at Manakamana kuti to whom I owe so much. (None of the women who assisted me are alive now, and Parijat too is no more.) The generation following them arrived in a new century where a vigorous discussion could be pursued. They focus exclusively on Yogmaya, although none of this generation knew her or her followers. New research, however confined to secondary accounts, can prove fruitful.

An aspect of these secondary sources I find troubling is how men, both researchers and 'local informants' seem to have taken over the narrative. People questioned by journalists and scholars are mostly local elderly men. A few are grandsons or sons of Yogmaya's followers who offer comments with undisguised confidence, as if they are first-hand witnesses. (This is my impression from the limited cases I've observed.)

I am compelled to ask: Where were you chatty gentlemen during the past decades? Rana rule ended in 1951; by 1990 after unsuccessful attempts with a quasi democracy, the king granted some political liberty. Why did it take a foreigner and her elderly confidantes—a group characterized by you as "old women waiting to die"—tucked away at Manakamana kuti to release this story?

This new generation of informants and enthusiasts seems to be mainly Nepal's highcaste Bahun citizens, rural and urban, most of them originating in East Nepal. A century ago and now too, Yogmaya's revolutionary spirit and Durga Devi's too have failed to enter the political consciousness of Nepal's less fortunate, most vulnerable, and most exploited citizens—now mobilizing as the Janajati Mahasangh.

Reticence among those people most in need of liberation is not uncommon of course. Neither is this unreasonable when economic and cultural forces still bear heavily on our most vulnerable citizens. Except where military uprisings happen, people wait for foreign aid or for liberation by others. In Nepal it came neither from a short-lived socialist administration (led by B.P. Koirala in 1959–1960) nor from a more moderate monarch, but with a leftist militant movement that took hold in rural parts of the country.

In 1996 a nascent Maoist revolution emerged and grew to become a serious opposition to the monarchy and entrenched parties. A people's revolt spread and gathered influence, reportedly over as much as 75% of the country. Maoists' attacks on landlords and police outposts led to sustained military confrontations. Wealthier villagers fled to cities while many poorer farmers joined the movement. (The guerrilla campaign was initiated by mainly educated, urban dissidents.) A civil war followed, with up to 13,000, a modest number by international standards, lost on both sides.

The conflict ended with a ceasefire in 2006, followed by Maoist and Communist Party participation in the 2008 free elections. Those who credit the Maoist uprising and war with ushering in a true democracy view the movement as positive, although many have been disappointed in how, once in power, it has grown as corrupt as any earlier administration.

The nation is certainly enjoying a more vigorous political dialogue. But it is incumbent on us to question to what degree leftist parties, including the Maoist, helped bring a Dharma Raj into being? Involvement of women in the military operations and in ideological Maoist thought are well known. Nepal's current president, Bidhya Devi Bhandari, an activist since her youth, was a Maoist/Communist revolutionary with fellow party activist Madan Bhandari. She is one of many women leaders in the party and the new government. In a 2018 meeting with her, she expressed delight about the resurrection of Yogmaya. "I myself am from a Bhojpur family; I knew nothing of this revolutionary woman during my youth," she commented. Bhandari is credited with facilitating the flow of large amounts of government funds for Yogmaya projects. One must ask: do Ms. Bhandari's Maoist credentials and these projects really reflect her predecessor's "Dharma Raj" ideals?

I'm curious how Yogmaya's work may have impacted on the development of Maoist and Communist ideology in Nepal. It was probably slight. When her critics called her 'communist', it was meant pejoratively. In any case she was active well before Marxism helped define Nepal's new political character.

We should credit Maoist and Communist leaders for their exemplary practice of inter-caste marriage. Colleagues familiar with the personal history of the current generation of leaders believe that in its formative stages the UML (United Marxist Leninist) Party adopted a policy of strategic inter-caste marriage. Thus, among the foremost members in government and media we find an extraordinary number of Bahun men married to Newar or other non-Bahun women. Of course intellectuals anywhere are well known for breaking social barriers. But when a sizable number of political leaders do so, it is noteworthy.

On Yogmaya's philosophy in relation to Marxist/Communist ideology, the dedicated communist, political commentator and writer Ninu Chapagain is one of the few who can contribute to that debate.[12]

Among those attracted to Yogmaya's contributions are literary figures. Beginning with the highly regarded poet and activist Parijat, many Nepalis express admiration for *yogbani*, appreciation which could lead to concrete literary actions. Sankhuwasabha-based scholar, Matrika Timsina, is one serious researcher analysing characteristics of her verses. Several young men who assisted me temporarily took up the challenge of translations. Occasionally, such as in an October 2019 morning radio program, one might hear *yogbani* broadcast over Nepal's airwaves.

Will Yogmaya's unparalleled artistic creations remain simply an inert relic of the past? Let's see if a more creative approach emerges in response to wider dissemination of the *yogbani* collection. For example, modern poets might copy Yogmaya's style and rhythms to pen new *bani*.[13] That is, they might create political barbs with new words while still following *yogbani's* artistic motif—similar to new compositions of 'haiku' in the Japanese poetic tradition, or how musicians across the world are adapting Black American 'hip-hop' to their own culture and politics.

Social Injustices, Past and Present

Finally, in this chapter, I try to address the relevance of Durga Devi and Yogmaya's campaigns in view of specific social challenges presently facing Nepal. Considering how much attention is devoted to women's status and to corruption nowadays, these are obvious issues for us to address. Yogmaya's campaign was directed to both.

We'll start with the latter first since it is the least complex.

Anyone who knows Nepal—those living in the country and expatiates too—agree that corruption, along with nepotism and persistent patriarchy, is an uncontrolled disease underlying most of the nation's woes. Most accept this status as incontestable—a troubling state of affairs because the Maoist/Communist parties leadership is itself deeply infected by this ailment. Graft, payoffs and fraud have become a way of life, a normal component of bureaucratic procedures.

Prof. Matrika Timsina, researcher on Yogmaya history and yogbani; Khandbari, 2019.

Any mention of governance will invariably lead to anecdotes about corruption and extortion. If you need a paper or a stamp, you must pay officials. Few can escape these fees. If you are a would-be migrant needing a passport or a loan, a family seeking medical treatment or transferring children to a new school, bribes are expected: under-the-table payments are necessary to register a business, arrange imports, conduct any inspection, transfer property, and on and on.

Appointments to university posts are often based on party allocations and bribes, not on merits. Assignments to government posts, high and low, are likewise assigned to party cronies depending on deals struck with elected officials. Administrators pass whatever is in their power to party lackeys. A government printing house reportedly publishes the poetry of ambassadors or other political figures, with literary quality a secondary matter. Tax collection is a sorrowful game of what you can pay to evade any levy. To avoid surcharges a citizen must devote energy and time establishing inside connections. The leftist party now in power seems even more corrupt than their opponents were.

Given endemic corruption across Nepal, we should not be surprised that it reportedly infiltrates organizations associated with Yogmaya. Rumours are circulating that government funds—and they are substantial—allocated for Yogmaya memorials are swelling the pockets of individuals. Elected officials in Bhojpur and Sankhuwasabha, keen to secure funds for their districts use party contacts in the ministries to fund Yogmaya projects. Their petitions have been rewarded with as much as 10 crore rupees (around U.S. $1 million) in the past 3–4 years. Allocations to newly registered Yogmaya foundations fund the construction of statues, temples, rest houses, and protective barriers at two locations in Bhojpur: Yogmaya's meditation cave and the site where the jal-samadhi occurred. Majhuwabesi, the consecrated place of her martyrdom—for more than half a century it remained an abandoned, eerie stretch of white sand—now houses temples, guest houses, priests' residences, a furnished park where families gather, along with facilities for volleyball tournaments. Gaudeni cave, a natural hollow in the mountainside, in the words of one critic "has been concretized"—i.e. encased in concrete. Project promoters argue their improvements will draw tourists and devotees here, and indeed, the beautification process is well handled, with new construction affording easier access to the steeply graded site.

I myself received reports about project directors competing for grants accusing each other of misappropriating funds. Whatever the reality, it's troubling to hear such rumours associated with our belatedly recognized champion of justice.

Any taint of corruption flies in the face of the revered woman's noble messages and her hard fought mission. Furthermore, the proliferation of structures represents capitalization of this symbol of asceticism, anti-corruption and sacrifice. (The absence of any photograph of this leader during her lifetime suggests she spurned any representation of herself—not unusual for genuine ascetics. Yet today drawings and statues are commissioned and constructed in her honour.)

These developments are summed up by writer and culture critic Nirvaya Subedi: "Ultimately, selfish crony interests have literally hijacked her philosophy and thus the politics around her iconization."

Gaudeni Cave visited by Manakamana
bhaktini in 1982 with the author.

Babita Katwal, one of many new
worshipers to Gaudeni Cave, (B.K. 2019).

Given criticisms arising from construction at those two sacred
sites, what will be the fate of a proposed university in the name of
Yogmaya? More government funding is in the works for the authorized
Yogmaya Ayurvedic University. This campus' location, though still
under discussion, is generating excitement among local landowners as
well as prospective hosts from other parts of Nepal. Land speculation
in the area is heightened by rumours of the project's generous budget
(several crore rupees, from the central government) assigned, I am
told, just for planning! One April 2019 Yogmaya Facebook page that
posted the university announcement includes group photos where
not a single woman is to be seen among those assembled dignitaries!

"Is anyone planning an institute where people can gather to study
Yogmaya's Dharma Raj, women's history, socially conscious art and

poetry, political activism, and to develop policies to tackle corruption?" asks a university colleague in Nepal.

Turning to changes in the status of women, we may find more encouraging developments. Without a doubt, much progress is underway here. It is hard to connect breakthroughs by modern Nepali women to our daring pioneers from Bhojpur. But let's review the status quo on some points—widow marriage, women's property rights, priests' weight in family matters—issues raised by both Durga Devi and Yogmaya.

Marriage presents a problem for any widow, including widows with children. Remarrying in any caste including Bahun women is not illegal but social sanctions are strong. To resist tradition demands that a woman possesses uncommon confidence and determination. Pressures on women to allow the family to care for her—not always a happy solution, for her—are hard to resist. Any declaration of

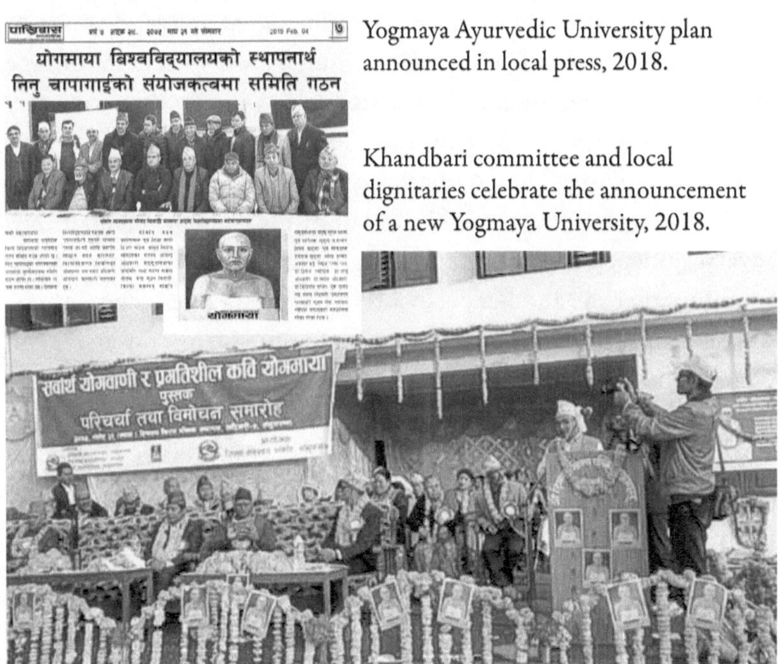

Yogmaya Ayurvedic University plan announced in local press, 2018.

Khandbari committee and local dignitaries celebrate the announcement of a new Yogmaya University, 2018.

independence raises the thorny issue of property. Although legally entitled to her husband's share of family property, if she tries to assert control over it, she'll face opposition. If a widow marries she forfeits that right; if she has a son he can claim his share of the property only after maturity—21. If a young widow stays in the family house she may find herself the most vulnerable among the daughters-in-law, possibly subjected to humiliation and bullying.

These points apply to women across Nepal, in cities as well as in the countryside. A widowed woman of exceptional character may prevail; if so, she could become the matriarch! If she decides to take her fight to the courts she'll face opposition and hostility. She can run away, perhaps marry secretly. But that would mean abandoning all property rights in the first marriage. Bahun widows sometimes leave the family to find work as a cook, Bahun being preferred as cooks in families observing caste prescriptions relating to food.

Joining an ascetic order and moving to a kuti such as the one at Manakamana—or if she is Buddhist, to a nunnery—is also an option. Returning to her natal house, her maitighar, after divorce or widowhood is generally not possible. Durga Devi spent a lot of time in her maitighar because, as I understood, her only brother was sickly and died soon after being betrothed, leaving his wife a child widow (for more on Durga Devi's buhari, see Chapter 3).

Knowing the pressures of joint family life, some women, if they have an independent income, may agree to a betrothal only on the condition that she and her partner set up a separate residence. This is still uncommon however and the pressure is intense for sons to remain with parents after marriage.

Conditions facing widows in Nepal are not good. To what degree social activists are taking up this issue is difficult to say; one sees few programs to assist hapless widows in the Nepali press. Among the many women who run away you'll find beleaguered widows as well as women escaping abusive husbands. That option exposes her to many hazards, among them entrapment by traffickers.

It is exceedingly hard for a widow—for any woman—to assert her legal rights in a court of law. Property rights of women may be protected in the law, but even if she's educated and with resources, exacting her share is not easy. Durga Devi was exceptional. Which is not to say she can't be a model for others. In fact she may be an ideal model—she faced her adversaries, applied her skills, and prevailed. First, like Durga Devi, a woman has to know the law; that in itself is a challenge. Second, she needs advisors or allies. Third, she must be prepared for public criticism, even bullying.

As illustrated in the new global movement known by the moniker #MeToo, confronting deeply patriarchal practices like sexual predation is a challenge for all women. Laws exist to protect abused women and indict their predators. But how many victims are able to speak out, demand compensation, and call for criminal charges? We have learned how even wealthy women, celebrities, and media professionals remain silent for years. They dare not challenge men they work with, fearing humiliation and losing their jobs.

Similar intimidation can operate against women in the family. "We will take care of you", her brothers assure her; "Consider your reputation—our reputation," they plead. A single woman who chooses not to marry is gently coerced by family members not to claim her independent share. If she insists on independence, she will ask herself: Where will I find lawyers to take up my case? How will I pay them? Where will I live meanwhile?

If activists are inspired by Durga Devi's experience, they can search court records for others who pursued their property claims through a court and then study the strategies and arguments in successful cases.

Evidence of successful claims offers powerful encouragement. Favourable publicity of victories can remove negative stigma. Young men can be appealed to reflect on the discriminatory laws their sisters suffer under.

It seems that Durga Devi had a litigious father. Apparently very attached to his precocious eldest daughter, he made an effort to introduce her to the vicissitudes of court procedures. She had another ally, her mother-in-law (Sasu) who among other audacious acts shared the family's deed with Durga Devi.

Let's not exclude Durga Devi's relevance to us today with the argument that she was unique. Unusual, yes. But a model nonetheless.

If we cannot find sociological data on widows' lives, let us begin to gather anecdotal data. All of us know older women—perhaps our own relatives. Invite them to share stories. They are certain to know others who confronted these all-too common property issues. I myself know three women in my modest circle who are personally engaged in or had faced property disputes. (Not all of those claims ended in their favour.) Many of us will have witnessed a perpetual state of anxiety suffered by women who appeal to courts for redress.

Widows face more than the question of whether or not to marry. Did Yogmaya have a solution to offer widows regarding their property? She fiercely advocated widow marriage and she supported women who took that difficult decision. Doing so, they faced banishment from their homes, probably from their village altogether. Cohabitation by remarried Bahun women among Yogmaya's following is probably the basis for accusations that she encouraged prostitution.

At Manakamana in the 1980s, among the ascetics I knew who'd been followers of Yogmaya, some had children not far away who ensured their mother received a portion of their harvest, and perhaps some cash and cloth. A true sanyasi should give up all claims to property of any kind. Even so, their children usually stay in touch with them. Other residents of the kuti said they had no remaining family. (I didn't ask for details about property issues.)

Followers of Yogmaya were of varying marital status. What happened to the property of widows (and men) who joined her compound? How many widows moving to her camp tried to claim her rights to a husband's share? And, in taking the radical decision to join the campaign, did they abandon property rights altogether? Again I did not inquire about those arrangements during my interviews at Manakamana. But we know a few of Yogmaya's followers were already married couples, some with small children. One of Yogmaya's brothers and his wife Ganga Devi were among her most devoted followers.

Durga Devi who would have been a young adult when Yogmaya was at her peak—mid 1930s—would surely have heard of Yogmaya's admonishments and declarations. As a widow suffering a stingy and a mean brother-in-law (dewar), did Durga Devi feel empowered to fight for her land rights because of the senior woman's call for widows' rights? Possibly. Since we know Durga Devi's mother-in-law encouraged her to fight, perhaps it was this older woman who was initially inspired by Yogmaya and thereby urged her daughter-in-law to take legal action to secure her property share.

As for other issues, one wonders to what degree Yogmaya asked followers to observe comprehensive gender equality. Neelam Karki Niharika,[14] in her studiously crafted novel of Yogmaya's life, has the rebel questioning husbands' and wives' discriminatory use of terms of mutual address. For example, women are generally expected to use the formal, respectful pronoun tapai even to a dear partner, while he customarily uses the diminutive ta rather than the more respectful timi to his wife. (This may apply in any caste and any class.) Through

Manakamana 1980; bhaktini dwellings as originally constructed.

her novel, Niharika, a well known author and a person deeply attached to Nepal, raises this issue first to appraise Yogmaya's teachings and next to question gender equality in general. She thereby helps us to more poignantly evaluate Yogmaya's standards of equality. Is she posing a candid question to her readers, namely, do you yourselves, perhaps unconsciously, adopt these disparities?

Niharika's artful inclusion of an imagined dialogue about terms of address among Yogmaya's followers begs the questions: a) how much real equality did Yogmaya advocate; b) how broad was her feminist agenda?

Fictionalized episodes allow the novelist to explore deeper questions of justice, among them inter-caste dining, within a personal context. If Yogmaya's followers included other than (high caste) Bahuns, to what degree was casteless cooking and dining observed? (Although not practiced everywhere, strict Hindu law prohibits a Bahun or other high caste member from taking food and water from anyone considered 'less pure'.) Were there lower caste families among Yogmaya's devotees and to what degree did they disregard caste rules? Did all share food cooked at the same hearth?

"Throw your caste away", Yogmaya urges. In her verses, she explicitly denounces caste distinctions. Do the most enthusiastic of her fans today practice this ideal? Do they debate it? (For a comparison on this challenge, consult the Indian revolt to inter-caste dining led by Sahidaran Ayyappan.[15]

Hindu priests are a primary focus in Yogmaya's calls for change. She charges them of not living according to the Vedas they study. She accuses them of extorting the poor:—ordering costly rituals and seeking material benefits for themselves with disingenuous concern for others' welfare, insisting on strict caste observances.

In a Hindu national state, priests endorse the ruler, endowing him with supreme moral authority. It is they who define purity, who prohibit women's participation in certain rituals, who assert her impurity during the menstrual cycle, who sanction patriarchy in the home and in the palace. Yogmaya's attacks on caste regulations and priests' authority were inseparable.

Late 2018 witnessed a revolutionary act challenging Hindu purity laws when millions—yes, millions—of Indian women, supported by a court ruling, marched on the Sabarimala Hindu temple in Kerala, South India.[16] (Proscriptions vary widely across Hindu communities. Other religions ban women from so-called sacred areas of a temple or monastery for the same reason.)

The obligatory presence of a priest at religious occasions allows them to define procedural rules. For example, a family is expected to pay what a priest demands for officiating; he also orders them what to offer the deities. Funerary expenses are onerous. (Similar to Hindus, Buddhists can also face heavy expenses, but the obligation on indigent members is less severe.)

An increasing number of people, unable to bear costly obligations of their religion —ritual fees and feasts—is opting out by leaving the faith. Conversion was illegal under Nepal's Hindu monarchy; the new republic reversed that prohibition so the country has seen a sharp rise in the number of Christian churches and converts. While some citizens may be disturbed by this, others seek conversion to escape those burdensome costs.

The injunction that only sons may conduct funerary ceremonies for parents is also weakened, a revolutionary step. Durga Devi's insistence on officiating at her mother-in-law's final rites on the shores of the Arun River was highly unconventional. (It may have been a final rebuke to her brothers-in-law.) A similar position today would be hard, but women performing funerary rites in the absence of a son or brother is less rare. While we cannot credit Durga Devi or Yogmaya for these reforms, we can appreciate their insights in calling for changes of this sort years earlier. Nepal's new Maoist/Communist administration and its educated citizens are not the first to realize the injustices embedded in these everyday procedures.

Daily interactions of men and women everywhere and in every class are imbued with inequalities and unchallenged social rules. But women's development programs designed to advance equality may disregard these intimate, less conspicuous social routines we're reviewing. (Injustices are built on such unarticulated habits.) An educated colleague from a wealthy Kathmandu family remembers how, as a daughter she'd been free of kitchen work; "I never scrubbed pots at home; when I married, I moved to my husband's house and my mother-in-law ordered me to do that. I had to; I was a young daughter-in-law; I had to live in her house and follow her orders." Unable to challenge the older woman, she felt humiliated.

Relations between a woman and her daughter-in-law, or a younger woman and her brothers are often ignored or downplayed in discussions of reform. Conjugal relations and earning power become the only idioms around which social progress is defined and measured by media and gender rights agencies. I suggest we need to change how we assess what really underpins women's social and moral rights. Looking back, I ask: How aware was Yogmaya about these dynamics? Did her support for women to break free of patriarchal rules include inequalities they experienced within the household?

As these questions arise, we become more aware of how much mystery remains, of how few hints—except for what we may find in her *yogbani*—are available concerning Yogmaya's ideal of Dharma Raj. Can we enter deeper into her personality and her social circle to speculate on what she might have expected in the realization of her Dharma Raj?

The Leap from Empiricism to Fiction

Pursuing this question we arrive at a novel quandary—discovering Yogmaya's real personality. Durga Devi's character is easier to imagine. Durga was righteous; she was angry; she yelled; she laughed with intimate friends and she inveigled local children to tell her the gossip about family disputes; she exhibited arrogance and pride; she was quick and uninhibited in physically lashing out at whomever she accused of wrongdoing, even high officials. Working alone, she preferred solitude. Yet, she also seemed bent on attracting attention; she made her appeals in the courthouse; marching through town, she invited everyone to see the khukuri, the weapon she carried in her belt. She was self-taught. She was a close companion to her father; she went to extreme lengths to defend her brother. She and her mother-in-law formed a solid partnership. And even though Durga Devi reportedly disapproved of Yogmaya's approach, she showed compassion for survivors of the rebel's campaign who gathered at Manakamana to spend their final years in solitude and prayer.

Compared to Durga Devi, Yogmaya's personality is imprecise. It's further obfuscated by public iconization of the woman, both when she lived and today too, as she becomes more widely known and discussed across Nepal.

No one disputes Yogmaya's extraordinary actions:–she was daring and brave; she was talented and uncompromising. Brilliance leaps out of every line of her *yogbani*. She seemed clearheaded and unapologetic about what she advocated.

Yet, now, reflecting on the time I've devoted to Yogmaya, I find myself unable to feel the ambience—the mood or temperament, apart from the awe—surrounding this peerless woman. I don't question her authenticity. But I wonder, for example, about her and her daughter Nainakala: was she gentle with her child, aloof, demanding, inattentive? Nainakala seems to have been closer to her aunt Ganga Devi. What about Yogmaya's relation to her brother? His role is less clear than that of his wife Ganga Devi, according to stories I gathered. Her two husbands' personalities are totally obscured. One wonders why?

Yogmaya seems to have been impulsively independent. We know she spent months meditating in seclusion. Was she accompanied by any helper, and if so, who?

Yogmaya was certainly defiant in the face of traditional authority. Within her circle, was she similarly uncompromising? How did she handle devotees who could not follow her caste declarations? Did she herself decide on her political tactics? Or did she rely heavily on those close to her—Ganga Devi, Prem Narayan, Bhim Bahadur Basnet?

1981 view of Manakamana prayer hall and bhaktini dwellings shows the earlier course of Arun River.

When I inquired about Yogmaya's teachers or advisors, the women at Manakamana insisted she had no teacher or mentor. "It all came from within her, spontaneously."

Yogmaya could have been a savant—a genius. Parijat believed she was. Many savants lack the ability to interact normally with others. Yes, Yogmaya was able to attract a dedicated following. But was she able to articulate and implement a credible concept of social justice?

Was Yogmaya gentle or testy; was she feisty or contemplative, capricious or calm? Was she easy to laugh? Were her teachings conducted in public lectures? Was she a skilled orator? Or were all her declarations through *yogbani*? Did she inspire confidence and calm, or anxiety and a sense of urgency?

Investigations into Yogmaya's verses, like those being carried out by Matrika Timsina of Khandbari, might help move us toward a more mature understanding of her character. Dipesh Neupane,[17] a scholar devoted to the study of the Yogi's work, particularly her philosophy of resistance, notes: "So complex and advanced are her verses (*bani*), they imply a deep knowledge of Vedas. Even scholars of Vedas find difficulty interpreting them logically. Yogmaya herself declares that her *Sarvartha*

Yogbani is her fifth (Panchau) Veda." He adds, "It is still unclear where she acquired such a deep knowledge of Vedas".

Have we now arrived at the boundary of empiricism on this subject? Without more documents and first-hand witnesses, we move to the realm which Neelam Karki Niharika envisioned and wisely chose to step into:- historical fiction.[18] By means of fiction, one can (and one has to) climb over

Dr. Dipesh Neupane, researcher and author

all the trivia, the glamour, the drama, and government obfuscation. We have to dive into those roiling waters of history to imagine the dynamics of what was underway so long ago on the shores of the Arun. (Durga Devi may require the same from us.)

I would argue that the production of Niharika's eponymous novel about our most celebrated sahasi Nepali is timely and potent. Yogmaya is heavily mythical today, in part because like Durga Devi she was so preposterous and because the feudal system in place at that time seems so alien to contemporary Nepalis. Some creativity on our part may help make these women 'real' and relevant to today.

A fictional narrative can retain the ideals of these women and accommodate new empirical facts as they emerge. We know for example that Niharika consulted written accounts about Yogmaya and made extensive interviews with people involved in that history.

Biographers sometimes admit to fictional leaps they have to make when reconstructing a life story. Historians of still-living people are given a license to speculate or to exaggerate points for the sake of literary effect. Even autobiographies are subject to bias and omissions.

At this point, in anticipation of the next chapter in which I review my experience of arriving and then settling into Manakamana in the 1980s, I want to add something about choices I faced in bringing these histories to the public. For example, even though I'd assembled whatever I learned of Yogmaya's history from several 80–year-old ascetics at Manakamana—most of whom personally knew her and who had engaged in her campaign— I struggled for years to decide on the best narrative form in which to present their accounts.

I had never written a biography. I had to try.

That meant discarding the conventions of anthropology. An experienced ethnographer with well-received publications and

Novelist Neelam Karki Niharika with author in New York City, 2019.

reasonable knowledge of Nepal, I nevertheless realized a new treatment was needed here. Struggling with worthy translations of *yogbani* required more care and a lot of reflection. (That partly accounts for the hiatus of ten years between my research in the 1980s and my first report on my findings at a conference on Tibet and Himalayan Studies in Zurich in 1990, followed by publication in 1993.[19]) In 2001 thanks to CNAS at Tribhuvan University, my reports were published in a single volume that wisely included the original *yogbani*. To set the social and economic context to the two women's campaigns, I created three semi-fictional chapters whose relevance I've already discussed.

Many more investigations, interpretations, and evaluations are possible, and probable. The *yogbani* text remains a rich resource for philosophers, social activists and translators. From interviews completed, we can be confident these women are not myths. The basic message of their campaigns is irrefutable. They spoke and acted against injustices and corruption, for reform, and for equality. This can be laid along the path to Nepal's future.

Community events at Majhuwabesi include volleyball tournaments. (BT, 2019)

I invite you to move to the next chapter with me. In the context of changes in the past two decades, I narrate how I reached the shore of the great Arun and a new frontier of my own life.

Notes

1. In his preface to Dipesh Neupane's 2018 book *Amar Jyoti Yogmaya*, Professor of Philosophy Satya Mohan Jhoshi regards Yogmaya's philosophy as quintessentially Nepali and original in nature.
2. See chapter 5 where translations are included; also consult the appended entire original Nepal-text of *yogbani*.
3. This I elaborate in the concluding sections of Chapter 2.
4. See bibliography of new sources on Yogmaya.
5. See Aziz' bibliography of selected Nepal articles.
6. https://www.khumbule.com/nepal-the-rape-and-murder-of-a-13–year-old-girl-sparks-a-national-outcry-about-elusive-justice/

7   See Aziz: https://www.counterpunch.org/2019/01/16/how-long-can-nepal-blame-others-for-its-woes/, https://www.asia-pacificresearch.com/migrant-labor-a-central-pillar-of-nepals-grim-economy/5628220, https://www.asia-pacificresearch.com/nepals-economy-can-contented-tourists-match-desperate-migrant-laborers/5628213.

8   http://www.globalresearch.ca/Nepalese-women-symbols-of-historical-achievements-and-political-leadership/5569227 in Aziz bibliography.

9   www.nefin.org.np/en

10 Michael Hutt, professor of Nepali literature, University of London, U.K. His 2015 lecture, "The Iconisation of Yogmaya Neupane" was presented at Social Science Baha, Nepal (3 May, 2011).

11 https://www.rebelgirls.co/products/good-night-stories-for-rebel-girls, a popular short history of rebel women across the world.

12 Chapagain, N. 2018, *Sarvartha Yogbani ra Pragatishil Yogmaya*, (*Sarvartha Yogbani and the Progressive Poet Yogmaya*).

13 A poetry competition and literary prize might be created with *yogbani* as the motif. This would seem more appropriate than statues or volleyball tournaments in Yogmaya's name.

14 *Yogmaya*, 2018, Sangrila Books, Kathmandu.

15 https://www.magzter.com/articles/1713/230697/5975945ce250c

16 https://womenintheworld.com/2019/01/02/women-form-385-mile-human-wall-to-protest-exclusion-from-hindu-temple/

17 This he shared in a private conversation; Neupane's 2018 book *Amar Jyoti Yogmaya* investigates Yogmaya's philosophy of resistance. Neupane's and Timsina's publications are included in our general bibliography.

18 https://www.kantipurdaily.com/koseli/2018/10/06/153879427213244251.html – a translation of my August 2018 article "Literature Can Displace Anthropology."

19 See bibliography.

An Evolving Narrative

My research for this book began forty years ago. Since then a generation has passed and across Nepal a new and promising political era succeeded the ancient, absolute monarchy.

I myself am surprised and positively delighted that these four decades find me still somehow involved even marginally in the evolution of the biographies in this book, exploring what the two women featured here mean to this nation. That's largely because of two factors: first, the subject matter itself, thanks to individuals this study introduced me to; second, the need to transcend boundaries set by traditional anthropology so that what I learned in the course of this work shaped the direction of my life which in turn affected what I wrote.

In the 1980s, after uncovering Yogmaya's and Durga Devi's campaigns of the early and mid-20th century, I began rethinking anthropology and politics. This, not only in Nepal but globally as well. Throughout this process I enjoyed a sustained and rewarding association with a number of inspired, engaged Nepali writers and thinkers.

This resulted in my evolution into a political animal. I came to understand how an ideology or a principle can unexpectedly and spontaneously emerge and spread, leading to unimaginable consequences. I now view culture as an inextricable part of politics; I understand how power relations likewise are thoroughly embedded within culture. One cannot comprehend even the most benign custom without considering and acknowledging the political context in which it emerges and thrives, or fades and vanishes.

Witnessing a progression of political awakenings in Nepal, I appreciate how protest sometimes has an immediate, positive outcome; other times, changes arrive only after many years, following a period of despondency, struggle and hardship. If a revolutionary spark cannot find oxygen, its promise of change lies dormant for decades. Then, with favourable conditions, women and men who'd hitherto been fearful, indolent or uninformed, become receptive to a long-buried spirit. There's renewed optimism, then a blooming.

Nepal's transformation today is evident in a growing diversity and energy we see in media, in literature, and in film production. It is manifest in the halting but unstoppable process of assembling a framework for the new democracy. We see it in the imaginative, determined way linguistic and regional communities are redefining their place and their rights within the nation. Individual lives take unexpected turns as new corridors open and old paths clear of detritus.

A blossoming now seems to be underway in the case of one individual, Yogmaya Neupane, the first of the two Bhojpur-born women featured in this book. Public interest in Yogmaya is firmly rooted and will flourish across many spheres. A flame has yet to ignite however around the career of the second rebel woman, Durga Devi Karki Ghimire.

My association with these women's histories continues to deepen. This, thanks to the value which several Nepali activists and scholars give to this book and to the kindness they continue to extend to me. The celebrated and courageous national poet Parijat with whom I initially worked introduced me to several young associates. Among them is Uttam Pant. When we met after a hiatus of many years, a renewed interest in Yogmaya put him in touch with a new generation of committed, energetic Nepali scholars whose combined efforts are making a significant impact in Nepal's intellectual and public spheres, and he introduced me to them.[1]

Since 1993, after Parijat's passing, while I turned my attention and my career to another part of the world, I remained in contact with Sukanya Waiba, Parijat's sister. She kept me abreast of volatile political changes within Nepal. This astute, articulate guide offered me a perspective of the country I could obtain nowhere else as I watched disquietly from afar. Real stability finally arrived after the adoption of a federalist constitution in 2015. However imperfect, I know the young republic is secure and evolving.

In today's more open political and intellectual atmosphere Yogmaya is not only redeemed; she is an established national icon. A postal stamp was issued in her honour; she is the subject of an ambitious novel which in 2019 won the Madan Puraskar, the nation's highest literary award (see below f.n. 17 and f.n. 29). Based on that novel, a new drama was produced and staged in June 2019 in Kathmandu. (Its main character was played by a leading actor and the production, which ran for several weeks, was well received.) Government funds have been assigned to projects related to Yogmaya; under discussion is a Yogmaya university (noted in Chapter 1); an annual national award, now in its 11th year, is presented for outstanding women writers and activists [2]; statues and lodges and other structures have been erected and festivals created around her legacy; women's community groups founded social projects in her honour; a embryonic religious sect claims her as its spiritual ancestor.

Before long, I expect Yogmaya's truly phenomenal career and outstanding character could become the subject of a feature film.

All this is possible because of fundamental changes in the country's political climate beginning in 1990, even before the

President Bidhya Devi Bhandari, originally from Bhojpur, welcoming Niharika, Babita Katwal and the author, (BK, 2018).

Women's committees in Khandbari and Biratnagar invoke Yogmaya in contemporary social programs; Khandbari, (BK, 2018).

arrival of full democracy. Although we still await implementation of social ideals advocated by Yogmaya reviewed in the previous chapter.

Today anyone can debate issues surrounding her courageous, uncompromising campaign for justice. However shocking an event, her martyrdom has become an awe-inspiring occasion for 21st century Nepali citizens. Additionally, we can passionately and proudly recite her verses and wonder at her political sagacity during that oppressive era; we can wonder in admiration at her methods to challenge an uncompromising religious and political authority. Examining Yogmaya's endeavours on behalf of justice, we can more clearly appreciate the suffocating atmosphere of Nepal a hundred years ago. Invoking democratic rights, we can demand government archives be opened to locate and examine more details of what actually happened; we can probe the memories of people to recall when they were only youngsters, what their grandparents may have said about Yogmaya and Durga Devi.

Another Century, Another Era

Open debate was smothered during the years before and after I completed my work in Sankhuwasabha and Bhojpur[3]—the locations of those astonishing events. Only a few people, mainly women who'd been members of Yogmaya's campaign, were still alive in 1980. How privileged I was to find them ready and eager to share their experiences with me.

When I arrived in the Arun River Valley on that first of my many visits democracy was decades away and political dissent in Nepal was outlawed.

In the 1960s regardless of its ban on free speech and political dissent, Nepal became an alluring destination for Europeans and other foreigners in search of the exotic. Politically disinterested visitors could be relied upon to comply with the status quo. Self-indulgent youths smoking in their hippie compounds and trekkers striking out into a mythic, bucolic countryside should not be disturbed by political realities. Naturalists and mountaineers focused on high altitude flora, quaint customs and colourful ceremonies, and on a landscape populated by farmers like Manu (featured in Chapter 6) bent under laden baskets. Beyond cultivated hills lay those irresistible glaciers. A mountaineering expedition may stop to camp on a ridge well away from any settlement before proceeding toward the beckoning peaks. If an occasional anthropologist intruded herself into a village for some months, it was only to record 'unknown' ways of living and speaking.

Those regularly traversing the main route up the Arun River Valley into Sankhuwasabha were villagers—some accompanying the corpse of a deceased relative to offer in at the burning ghat by the river, some conveying offerings to an Arun-dwelling deity, some heading to district headquarters for a document, to register a land transfer, a death or a birth. Women on the path are likely to be young mothers returning to their maitighar to spend leisurely days with sisters and mothers.

By far the most numerous travellers were farmers; they tramped a hardened, dirt path north from Dharan where until the late-1980s the northward road ended. From there all manufactured goods from India and produce from the fertile lowlands arrived at village shops and Saturday market stalls in Nepal's interior on their backs.

That silent, interminable human convoy moved throughout the day and even during dark, early morning hours. Numbering in the thousands, porters passed me on the occasions when I myself took that route northward.

As for us interlopers: an occasional stranger, linguist or anthropologist, arrived unannounced yet was somehow welcomed almost anywhere, in any hamlet or hill town. We set up our household and commenced inquiries, studying things we vaguely conceptualized as culture. Understood was the taboo on investigations into governance. Those days, any critical examination of either national politics or local affairs was out of the question. Visiting researchers readily accepted this. Why not? In Nepal we can find a limitless treasure trove for cultural discoveries in city, village, forest or high pasture. This is a land embracing multitudes of rituals, distinctive stunning architecture, sundry languages, abundant folktales, myths and playful songs, practicing shaman, animist ceremonies, agricultural variation and complex caste distinctions. Nepal's jungles even offer the possibility of encountering a lost tribe or an unrecorded language. These can keep scores of researchers thoroughly occupied, and visa renewals assured.[4]

In 1980, as far as I recall, telephone and electricity across Nepal were limited. Dharan and other cities in the Tarai enjoyed services of all kinds. But civilian communication beyond Dharan would be by foot and by word-of-mouth for another decade. Even staff at Tumlingtar airstrip relied on the military police for notification of changing weather conditions and incoming flights.

A researcher, foreign or Nepali, expects discomforts and isolation. (Offsetting any hardship is the glamour and enchantment that others attribute to our profession.) Physical impediments might be viewed as a test of our resourcefulness. In fact, our profession actually exploits such tough conditions, arguing that a fieldworker so immersed can better grasp the reality of others' lives. Social problems and solutions, fault lines and alliances, frailties and creative energy, resourcefulness and philosophies—ordinary routine life—become grist for our academic deliberations. From our standpoint, it's a great challenge to identify the myriad subtle ways this society is held together.

Our participation observation is elevated to the rank of 'scientific methodology'. Then there is the romance of living alone in the wild (sic)—a theme developed for reality television and a commercialized status for which wealthy tourists pay handsomely. Non-governmental social and medical projects in these remote areas are viewed with excessive respect.

Modern technology actually makes such isolation nearly impossible today. If a visitor travels without a smart phone, any villager will loan theirs to her.

These facilities notwithstanding, I firmly believe anthropologists' strategic isolation from our own culture can still be an asset to our endeavours in 'the field'. As an outsider, Nepali or foreign, we are forced to totally immerse ourselves among the women and men whose culture we enter. This immersion allows uninterrupted, concentrated engagement.

'Participation observation' is its scientific name. It demands ingenuity, an intense curiosity, and good humour. Conditions initially perceived as hardships become manageable; we can proceed with our work.

I had passed lengthy periods in Nepal before I settled in Manakamana.[5] Blessed with a strong constitution and the trust of those around me, I produced well-received articles and books which helped introduce to readers fresh ways of thinking about history, humanity and culture.

I began in 1969 with a year in Solu, northeast Nepal, studying Tibetan and Sherpa social history. Wanting a change of scenery, I next moved to Therathum further east where I chose to live with Limbu people.[6] I made shorter visits to Jomsom and Langtang, and to towns in Kathmandu Valley. As long as I remained healthy, able to consume local brews, adapt to diverse diets, negotiate steep climbs and descents, I could accomplish a lot.[7] My occasional indiscretions—I admit to being guilty of some—were, on the whole, tolerated. No mishap or stressful encounter was great enough to threaten my career as a fieldworker. (The profession has its rewards.)

Significantly, I was always blessed to find a committed assistant, usually a young man, to work with. (I trust that nowadays more women are choosing this career path.) Either I employed a youth to work as fixer/translator/teacher. Or I lodged with some family in the village I chose to stop in, and I hired someone there. A household could always use extra cash; a woman residing alone might welcome my company.

There was really no need to be burdened with porters and servants. My work proceeded smoothly and I enjoyed the companionship and cooperation of enough people to feel comfortable, content and safe.

Jangbu Gharma is the man I invited to accompany me to the Arun River valley. I'd been in Solu during the summer of 1980 wrapping up several years of involvement in an exciting historical project with Tibetans there. By chance Jangbu was available; eager to leave his teaching job in Salleri, he agreed to spend a month with me to travel an eastbound route across the hills to the Arun River Valley.

A taciturn and capable fellow, Jangbu was an astute observer, ready to learn about another part of his country. I welcomed his advice and attentiveness. We hardly talked while traveling together but the intimacy and harmony we achieved during two weeks en route and another two weeks working at Manakamana kuti[8] would make us lifelong friends.

Jangbu and I fell into a pattern that suited both of us. As a party of two, we needed no special equipment and only a limited supply of food. We sought accommodation in a farmhouse when we stopped for the night, bought an egg or two—perhaps some milk too—paid the householder for sharing their firewood and cooking oil and whatever else was available to supplement our modest stock of rice, lentils and sugar. We preferred to bed down in the corn shed to escape the smoke-filled family room with its bothersome bedbugs, chickens, curious children and drunken visitors. (As it was September we didn't need to be near the hearth for warmth.) We stayed no more than a night anywhere. Before retiring each evening with directions toward our destination, we prepared a thermos of tea. By dawn the next day we set out just as the family was beginning to stir.

The First Traces

Upon arriving at the kuti in Manakamana on the shore of the Arun and finding myself among a cluster of women ascetics, a trace of something unexpectedly powerful and enticing overcame me. It was beguiling. After a single night, I decided to stay there with these ladies clothed in cotton wraps, slipping barefoot along paths around their huts and garden patches. Why they decided to share their stories with me, I do not know.

Seeing me settled in Manakamana, Jangbu continued southward alone, as we had agreed. He was eager to make his way to the capital in search of work, joining Sherpa friends who'd already moved there. A

The author in 1980 with Mata and other bhaktini teachers.

few days after his departure I interrupted my inquiries at Manakamana to walk up to Khandbari town to seek confirmation from others about what I'd learned from the aging ascetics. Khandbari is the district headquarters on the ridge above the river and residents there would be familiar with local history. However, their reception to my inquiries about Yogmaya and Durga Devi was chilly.

No matter. I was already infatuated.

The dismissiveness of those townspeople only made me more determined to pursue what traces I'd detected at Manakamana.

One benefit of visiting Khandbari was meeting another young man ready to work with me—Dharma Shrestha, who became an indispensable companion.[9] Dharma was equally smitten as I was and together we pursued clues to the remarkable lives of these two rebel women.

Within a few days the residents of Manakamana were calling Dharma nati (grandson). On his side Dharma was completely comfortable there and keen to learn more. At one point, he confessed, "They remind me of my Phuphu; I never before thought about her life as a widow, in her white sari, bare of jewellery, her head covered". (She was Dharma's paternal aunt who lived with the family in Khandbari.)

Gradually we pieced together what happened more than half a century earlier in the case of Yogmaya Neupane, barely more than a decade earlier for Durga Devi.

Here was I, a stranger with no knowledge of Nepali or Hinduism, accompanied by two young men, neither of whom were Bahun, moving into a community of elderly women, all ascetics and almost all Bahun caste. Considering these differences, that we were proceeding without foreknowledge and unsure where our curiosity might lead us—at this point we had neither written nor outside accounts to verify our findings—we managed to do quite a good job.

Thinking of past associations, I suspect that my experience with Buddhist ascetics—nuns as well as monks—at the monastery in Solu (where I easily communicated in Tibetan) accounts for the ease with which I stepped into the life of these Hindu bhaktini and for their earnest welcome. At one level the distinction between Buddhist and Hindu ascetics is insignificant. Their shared aim and lifestyle are testimony to a fundamental cultural affinity that threads Nepal's diverse peoples into a firm carpet.

How fortunate that I'd jettisoned my plan to proceed further north through the valley. I lost all interest in exploring anywhere else. I settled here by the thundering river as it crashed around boulders, flinging froth into the warm air and settled into layers of mist up the mountainsides. We inhabit the land but the watercourse is our final destination. The ungraspable authority of the Arun's interminable bellowing and its unstoppable onward rush harbours echoes of its terrestrial human partners, with our daily offerings and pleas, our joyful celebrations and the many mysterious events that occur along its path.[10]

The hot night air throbbed with screeching, pulsing insects and birds.

I had a cassette recorder with me. So I was able to document some of my conversations with the women and their recitations of *yogbani*. I ate the same vegan meals and I slept on a straw mat loaned to me by Mata, head of the kuti. Bhattini Aama's hearthside remained my base where I retired at nightfall to listen to her drumming invocations.

My work proceeded at an easy pace. Sometimes I sat patiently through hours and hours of uninspiring mantra-like repetitions of bhajan, which the women recited during their three-times daily assemblies led by an itinerant priest. "Suneko-bela ayo", they half-heartedly declared. I suspected the women found these assemblies as boring as I did. (Was it my imagination that they seemed to stir so passionately only when *yogbani* rolled over their lips?) Although, as their only communal exercise, these bhajan may have been important to them in ways I couldn't appreciate. I know they relished time alone in meditation and tending their plots of vegetables and herbs.

Bhattini Aama 1980.

I had no specific interest in Hindu philosophy or ritual, I confess. I tolerated those gatherings in the kuti prayer hall waiting for the interludes. Then I'd slip away with Mata or another bhaktini. On their doorsteps or wandering together among boulders half buried in the white silt along the shore, I gently pressed them to tell me more of what they remembered.

How keenly they welcomed my curiosity. With so many years of their lives gone and so few remaining, I wonder if in transferring this history to me, they felt some sense of urgency.

Women Working

Before coming here I hadn't consciously planned to gather stories about women. True, I enjoyed my years with Tibetan nuns. I found women the best companions in the course of my pilgrimage excursions to holy places, occasions when I witnessed how, free of their domestic preoccupations, women are chatty, playful companions.

(This compared to their demeanour towards me at their homes when, toiling in field and kitchen, they silently watch from afar while husbands and brothers engage any visitor.)

Anthropologists began to concentrate seriously on women as respectable subjects of research after 1980. By that time, feminist critique of traditional research methods affected how I too approached the study of culture. Women became worthy of our attention—my attention. So anyone in Khandbari who counselled me that those bhaktini had nothing to offer me was too late.

"Stay with these ladies," murmured Tibetan nuns from my past. Ani Chodon[11] and Ani Tsondu were Tibetan nuns—both much older than me—whose companionship I'd cherished. We'd known each other during my stay in a Solu village and at nearby Thupten Choeling Gompa, a Tibetan monastery in Solu. Unhindered by any language barrier we enjoyed genuine fellowship. (Why shouldn't we expect this?) I, like them, was a single, unattached woman; I, like them, could read. And like them I was accustomed to solitude and reflection.

That was in the 1970s. Ani Chodron, another nun with whom I worked, was custodian of the Langkor Nangten relics. Through these treasures she introduced me to the 12th century yogi Pha Dampa Sangyas and that would eventually launch me into a major manuscript project related to his teachings.

Together these women opened to me the world of ascetic, independent-minded and resourceful women. All possessed far wider life experiences than their secular peers. Eventually I would appreciate how important these women were, not as objects of research but as emotional supports. Ani Tsondu became my dearest confidante and mentor those years.[12] Were I to compile a biography of the outstanding woman in my career, it would be hers. Alas, well into her eighties when we were together, she'd passed on two years before I found myself at Manakamana.

To reach Majhuwabesi in 1982, the author and bhaktini used traditional means of crossing the Arun River.

A Banquet of History at The River's Edge

Ten years after that intense experience in Solu, I was walking towards the shore of the great Arun watercourse. I'd never been to this river valley before, and I knew no one here. Neither did Jangbu. Apart from our weariness after many days dealing with swollen rivers and muddy trails, even without knowing what it beheld for us, we gazed with relief at our destination—the grey, silt-laden waters of the Arun. We had detected its roar long before we actually witnessed its icy, silvery waters or came anywhere near the boulders strewn along its shoreline.

What was to be an overnight stop in Manakamana became a month-long stay, with several more visits over the following years. What emerged was unforeseen and unplanned. One can only conclude, as the bhaktini who received me determined, ours was a preternatural encounter. My fortuitous appearance was consistent with the incredible stories I would learn from these women. Just as later, someone asked how I came to know Parijat. My answer: "Yogmaya led me to Parijat".

When I first spoke to them in 1980, some residents in the vicinity of Khandbari, Chainpur, Bhojpur and Dingla did not deny they knew about Yogmaya Neupane and Durga Devi Karki Ghimire. Families in Nepaledanda, Yogmaya's birthplace, could not have forgotten either. But any townspeople I asked were dismissive of these remarkable women; and they disparaged reports of the narrative I was gathering.

It didn't matter to me.

Occupants of the kuti beside Manakamana shrine quietly convinced me of the profoundness of those women. Their enduring love of Yogmaya was evident. Listening carefully and affectionately to them, I committed myself to that history. It was unnecessary to travel further.

Past experience had taught me that I work best when I approach a place without any sociological or theoretical problem to solve. That might limit me. I was not here to dispute or confirm anyone's earlier claims; I had no obligation to a supervising professor or publisher. My general aim was to join pilgrims at tirtha—recognized holy sites where devotees directly connect with deities and other spirits dwelling there.[13] If I myself was engaged in a personal spiritual search, it was unconsciously so.

In recent years, I'd become infatuated with the human compulsion of peregrination while accompanying Hindu and Buddhist pilgrims to renowned tirtha, holy places permeated with boundless divine power.[14] I comprehended how 'place' can embody and make manifest a history. I witnessed how supernatural forces or historical imperatives drive women and men to enter into their history by this route—to 'be a witness'. With that goal, they are prepared to endure real hardships. Everywhere individuals feel compelled at some stage to seek closeness with the divine—to strive towards some 'zero' point. Yogmaya for example declared that her goal was not Nepal's ruler; it was 'zero'.

However few can achieve it, the impulse to transcend sentient existence is irresistible. It is articulated in spiritual terms or in secular idioms. A journey can be metaphysical, requiring no physical relocation. For others, there's a compulsion to engage in a physical endeavour to a distant holy place. There, worshippers can imbibe the blessings emanating from that juncture. Nepal is replete with such places, among them sites along the Arun littoral.

The Arun is one of Nepal's many great rivers. Viewed from the air, it appears as an impromptu filament strewn on the earth's rough surface. Its current glistens as if lying inert in the sun. Up close, its turbulent water swells and unfolds, sending steam upward through the gorge. During the monsoon rains, Himalayan rivers become monstrous forces sucking mercilessly at mountainsides, pulling enormous rocks into its current, pounding noisily onward, night and day.

This waterway holds dual significance for me. My colleague, noted geographer Harka Gurung, while reviewing a draft of my 2001 edition, directed my attention to a map highlighting the Nepal-Tibet border. There, with his finger, he traced the Arun's route upstream through concealed icy passages around Mt. Makalu and beyond into Tibet. Following the thinning blue line over the Tibetan plateau, he pointed out where the river, before it reaches Nepal, is a barely perceptible watercourse emerging as a slow-moving stream from further west, gathering runnels as it proceeds eastward. At its most westerly point, it originates on the windswept, rainless plain of Dingri. Locally known as Phung Chu, it's created from the runoff of Chomolungma's (Mt. Everest) north-facing glaciers.

Most of what's not captured by Tibetan farmers to irrigate their meagre fields soaks into the earth creating wide stretches of peat bog. (On my visits to Dingri, I'd walked across that plain and experienced the difficulty of navigating its soggy terrain.) How fortuitous that I'd composed a history of this arid and treeless Tibetan plateau[15] and a decade later find myself working at the tropical shores of the Arun many miles and a high Himalayan range downstream. Dr. Gurung and I were both struck by the coincidence.

Within Tibet, waterways do not hold great significance. They do not harbour powerful spirits who need to be mollified and worshipped. Not places for bathing and frolicking like in India and Nepal; here, a good death is consigned to the water, and all waters here, even rivers that may become exceedingly polluted, are held sacred.

The confluences of rivers, springs gushing from mountain rocks, and glacier-fed lakes seem to be the favoured dwellings of deities and other intense powers. That's where worshippers travel to purify themselves and honour the deities. Manakamana on the east shore of the Arun is one such place.

Reaching the ridge below Bhojpur, Jangbu and I gazed at the grey ribbon of water far below. Although it's further than I expected, we had no choice but to proceed in its direction before stopping for the night. Slowly, we descended the mountainside, sometimes losing sight of the river altogether. At last we stepped onto the suspended iron bridge.

It was late afternoon. We'd been walking since dawn and had looked forward to stopping for the day soon after crossing the river. We saw only a few porters who'd halted to rest on the grassy flat stretch called Tumlingtar. Developed as an airstrip, planes landed there twice weekly in those years, often less often, and not at all during monsoon months.

If there was a place to sleep nearby, it wasn't at Tumlingtar. The sole structure on the Tar in 1980 was a small cement building that served as the office and warehouse of Royal Nepal Airlines; and it was locked that afternoon. Chainpur and Khandbari towns were another two hours' walk—all uphill. A farmer passing us pointed to a trail that led down through a thicket of bushes. "That way will take you directly to Manakamana on the riverside," he offered. "No, not a village; Lord Arun (shrine) is there; a kuti sits just beside it. At festival time many hundreds assemble there in summertime. Nowadays, no one; you can find a sleeping place where bhaktini stay."

This was our casual introduction to Manakamana, an obscured location sheltered among young banana trees, a home to ascetic custodians of a profound history, quietly waiting to serve up a virtual banquet of treasures.

We followed a barely perceptible path through the jungle for perhaps an hour. The air became noticeably cooler as we neared the water. We stepped through a patch of squat banana trees. As the land levelled off, I saw that small garden plots lined the path.

Between us and the river ahead lay a clearing, in the middle of which stood a latticed wood-sided hall. It was deserted but clearly not abandoned. Rows of straw cushions were set out on the cement floor; colour prints of Shiva, one of King Birendra and Queen Aishwarya along with some fading photos were pinned to the wooden columns. We waited.

Two elderly women, heads covered, and clad in thin, discoloured robes emerged from the foliage. "This is our home; we are bhaktini"; and "Yes, you may stay the night." Learning that we'd arrived from beyond Dingla on the far side of the river, they urged us to rest. No one said anything about a meal, but thirty minutes later, we would be brought freshly prepared rice and vegetables. I walked to the sandy shoreline and stood in the ice-cold water; cool air floating above the torrent embraced me and within minutes I was completely refreshed.

While we ate more women stepped into the hall and looked on in silence. They seemed impressed when Jangbu explained the route we'd taken from Solu.

Sounds of the jungle rose as night fell. One of the bhaktini handed my companion a mat and directed him to a cool cement platform beyond the prayer hall. I meanwhile was shown to one of the huts sheltered among nearby trees. My host was Bhattini Aama. She pointed to the straw mat on the dry earth and I lay down beside her hearth.

The austerity of this kuti was a delight. Sparse and swept clean; no dogs; no children standing around eyeing my every move; only the Arun's roar mixing with a cacophony of screeching insects and birdcalls.

That very night Bhattini Aama initiated me to *yogbani* utterances of Yogmaya. So unsettled was I by the sight of this woman as she sang and the power I imbibed from those words, I hardly slept. In the morning, we were invited to take a tumbler of light, sugarless tea. Damodara Giri introduced herself; she was the Mata. Younger than most of the others, wrapped in a peach-coloured robe, a folded cap covering her shaven head, from her very appearance I recognized she had a special status. I asked: "Who is the Guru whose words Bhattini Aama sang to me last night?" Mata did not reply directly (a characteristic of hers, I would learn). She quietly explained how this kuti was a retreat for her and her companions—all of them women.

Eventually I would meet all thirty-two residents here; each occupied a one-room hut she'd either built for herself or bought from an earlier occupant. Most of the women were elderly; several like Bhattini Aama had reached eighty. Some had been child widows; others married and then renounced family life to follow the ascetic tradition of contemplation, prayer and devotion to Lord Shiva.

It did not take me long after hearing the name Yogmaya Neupane, the source of *yogbani*, to realize these women represented a vital treasure. Despite an image of being negligible in anything of significance to the nation, they'd actually been witnesses and participants in an historic political and social phenomenon. Perhaps my experience working with similarly inconspicuous but engaged and astute Buddhist nuns informed me that these Hindu bhaktini were not docile old ladies mumbling mantras while waiting to exhale their final breath. Their association with Yogmaya remained a vital part of their character. As I would soon learn, they were ready to share their hidden history with me.

Without knowing how things would unfold, I felt compelled to follow traces I'd detected in the earliest hours of my arrival. These women and I entered into an unspoken contract (chronicled in the following chapters). So, however incomplete or sketchy the revelations might be, I made a commitment to gather what I could learn from them. They too decided to trust me.

To their narrations and the recitations of *yogbani* they recalled for me and I recorded, they would add an essential document. This is the written collection of *yogbani*—know as *sarvartha yogbani* or *hazurbani*—utterances of their revered master. This remarkable text would convince anyone who dared question the women's narratives.

Capable investigators are correcting and augmenting items from my initial report in 1993,[16] with critical details and new perspectives. I nevertheless urge anyone engaged in Yogmaya's story and others inspired by what's been assembled thus far to allow for the possibility that somewhere another set of *yogbani* exists. We have nothing to lose and have everything to gain by making inquires in that direction. (The compilation in hand, published in 1940 in Kalimpong, is what Mata handed to me at the end of my second visit (in 1981); the original Nepali collection was included in my 2001 book and we retain it in this edition so readers can peruse the verses at leisure, study them and compare them with other examples that may be uncovered.) How exciting if more *yogbani*—perhaps verses composed or compiled at a different stage in our rebel Yogi's career—come to light.

Meanwhile, as already noted we have a body of new materials produced by various Nepali thinkers, men and women who together demonstrate a remarkable commitment to Yogmaya. Their combined investigations provide more details about her verses, her following, her philosophy and her campaign. Research on Yogmaya is destined to continue and to expand in many directions, perhaps along semi-fictional lines such as the novel *Yogmaya*[17] and from questions and controversies still to be articulated. We invite you to pore over *yogbani* now available. For your perusal, along with the complete Nepali collection of *yogbani* in this volume, Chapter 5 includes English translations of some of these remarkable quatrains while we await more translations, which will help attract an international readership of poets, folklorists and literary critics.

I feel little regret about being unable to participate in future research. The fellowship of this new generation of activists and writers is deeply satisfying. Together they're well equipped to pursue new avenues of inquiry. More women would be welcome in this effort too. Indeed Yogmaya is a phenomenon demanding many minds and points of view—young and old, women and men.

Allow me to use this opportunity to note three promising areas for further research, if they're not already underway.

First is the possibility, noted above, that somewhere, other materials—specifically *yogbani* quatrains composed by Yogmaya, but not yet uncovered—are extant. Why assume that all her utterances, written or oral, are now in hand?

Second, court records that may have been banned or sealed in the aftermath of Yogmaya's martyrdom may lay in a government office somewhere, forgotten or hidden. We need to locate and examine any and all documents relating to her military detention and her martyrdom.

Third, we need to know more about Yogmaya during the years she lived in northeast India; who and what was she exposed to there that influenced her political growth and her evolving ideology?

To underscore the second point: in 1981 when I and Parijat's associate Murari Aryal interviewed retired General Mahadev Shumsher Rana, we pointedly asked him about military or other documents relating to Yogmaya's imprisonment and martyrdom. The alert old man did not deny their existence; indeed, he said he'd look

Retired General Mahadev Shumsher Rana who ordered the arrest of Yogmaya and her followers in 1939, (1981 photo).

into the matter. Days later, he informed us "the files have regrettably been destroyed in some fire". We did not pursue the issue. Was he telling us the truth? Or had we breached a taboo and, realizing this he reversed his decision to help us? If nothing is extant in a government archive in the capital, something useful may exist in a courthouse in the district offices of Sankhuwasabha, Bhojpur or Dhankuta.

Durga Devi Karki Ghimire Redux

Now to Durga Devi Karki Ghimire. My remarks up to now centre on Yogmaya Neupane. It is time to expand the discussion to include her peer, Durga Devi.

Durga Devi is a second remarkable leader who emerged in the 20th century in this same region of Eastern Nepal. Picking up comments in the previous chapter, here are some further remarks offered as an addendum to my chapter devoted to her.

Once again, I learned about this woman serendipitously. During a casual chat near the great boulders where we frequently gathered at twilight, I asked one of my bhaktini companions—"Who owns the land here where your kuti stands?"

"Durga Devi", came the swift reply.

"Was she a devotee of Yogmaya like you are?"

My companions found this question amusing. "Oh no! She didn't like Yogmaya's ways. Speak to Mihili Didi;[18] she will tell you everything."

I did just that.

What I learned from her is recorded in Chapter 3. This history, however incomplete, is unquestionably equally instructive and inspiring as Yogmaya's. It is certainly more tangible.

Why, I continue to ponder, is Karki Ghimire overlooked in the current flurry over her contemporary? Can we not imagine how in the same century, the hills around Bhojpur could actually produce *two* remarkable leaders—both feminists and both striving for justice? Yes, their careers differed markedly, and Durga Devi Karki Ghimire, who began her work after Yogmaya's campaign reached its height, purportedly had little use for the Yogi's strategy to win justice. Still, their missions can be viewed as having much in common.

Durga Devi championed women and fought for the rights of widows and of mistreated women and children. As a child widow, she overcame the hardships and ostracism women like her endure. Durga Devi was brilliant, bold and self-educated.[19] Durga Devi was determined to challenge the status quo; she did so initially to win her property rights as a widow, and later to protect herself. She applied her sense of justice to assist others. Why then has she not yet inspired the same admiration and attention as Yogmaya has?[20]

Everyone in the country is aware of the nation's widespread social problems[21]—hardships that so many girls and women, young and old, experience. Those adversities and injustices differ only slightly from what women endure across the globe. Whether in a village or the city, young brides toil silently in a household of strangers where they are often subject to privations and loneliness. We have heard the woes of hapless women beaten by drunken husbands and fathers, or cast aside when their husbands take a second wife. A childless woman or a child widow is often shunted aside too. When I spot a withdrawn figure in the shadow of a home I am visiting, I suspect that she could be the childless widow of the family's long dead son.

Remember, almost no social welfare programs existed half a century ago. Who was there to defend a young woman who'd been violated, to offer succour to someone banished from her home? Durga Devi's campaign addressed women's plight with sensible, immediate solutions. In my chapter devoted to Durga Devi, you will read about the violated girl she took into her home and how she arranged for the care of her new-born child. In my chapter about young Laxmi, we again return to the issue of raped children.

Who besides Durga Devi would come to the aid of those hapless young women?

I assembled all I learned about Karki Ghimire in that single chapter. I know her story is far from complete; it is waiting for others to pursue, to elaborate, and to celebrate.[22]

It is not too late to begin. Born around 1918, Durga Devi passed away in 1973 (or 1972). A search through court records from the period when she was most active would surely be worthwhile. With details of cases in which Durga Devi was involved, we can fill out our picture of her.

Vishnumaya Dahal, Durga Devi's long-time cook and companion moved to the kuti at Manakamana after her passing. She was one of the younger bhaktini there, around 50 years old at the time that we met. We called her Mihili Didi.

How Mihili Didi loved Durga Devi. I was fortunate to be welcomed by such a cheerful, gentle woman; how she delighted in recalling stories about her former patron. (From her, I had the impression that Karki Ghimire rather enjoyed her exploits.) Mihili Didi could have written an engaging biography herself. Under the circumstances it was left to me, working with her, to assemble at least a sketch of Durga Devi. Mihili's accounts were affirmed by fellow bhaktini sitting with us during our talks; they too had known Durga Devi and they were aware it was she who funded the settlement at Manakamana. (Karki Ghimire also may have left funds for its future maintenance and to support any bhaktini needing assistance.)

My enquiries about Durga Devi among villagers were another matter. Most laughed or sneered when I mentioned her name: "Hah; that one? Mad! A troublemaker!", they remarked. A troublesome woman indeed! (Their dismissiveness was not unlike responses regarding Yogmaya.) The consensus was: "Durga Devi was a menace; she isn't worth your attention".

I recall that someone did point out that her mother-in-law's house was at Marwa, not far from Khandbari. What a mistake not pursuing that clue! Relatives may have been approached. However much her brothers-in-law had despised her, their children or grandchildren may have been willing to talk to me about her. (See postscript below on my brief visit to Marwa in November 2019.) Also still living in this area at that time was the young woman and her baby (or perhaps only the now-grown child) whom Durga Devi took care of. Other beneficiaries of Durga Devi's generosity might also have proffered details of their experience with her.

Despite her reputation as a cantankerous character, from what I learned about Durga Devi, she wasn't an embittered or unhappy soul, although she unarguably courted confrontation. According to Mihili Didi, she passed evenings poring over legal documents, planning her next pursuit, reviewing gossip she'd gathered.

The drama and breadth of Yogmaya's career and her martyrdom eclipse Durga Devi's accomplishments. I first shared these stories with poet Parijat and scholar Harka Gurung in Kathmandu after arriving there from my second visit to Sankhuwasabha. The yogi-poet whose career ended so dramatically proved more compelling for them, more worthy of immediate attention, and I was swayed by their responses.

Yogmaya Neupane was unquestionably a true revolutionary—a Bahun woman who defied Brahmanical law and who boldly attacked priests' abuse of their religious position to accumulate wealth, to suppress any unorthodox thinking, to divide communities, and to admonish people even for minor infractions of caste rules.

Here was a woman rebuking and defying priests! Unheard of.

Then, there were her *yogbani*. A sizable collection is available in an authenticated text. The literary quality of these verses offers indisputable evidence of Yogmaya's philosophy, her brilliance and her mission. How could such a character and events surrounding her escape historians and literary critics? (See how my narration of Durga Devi is diverted by mention of our rebel Yogi!)

Durga Devi wasn't a revolutionary. She was an extraordinary self-styled reformer though. She couldn't compose verses; but she analysed legal documents. She did not attack priests' injunctions; but she flouted a firm religious custom by performing her mother-in-law's funerary rite. She studied how to use the law to her advantage and she learned how to present cases in court. In the political and social climate of the time, this demanded skill, innovation and, most of all, fearlessness. From my understanding of Durga Devi, she seemed as brazen as Parijat was. She faced danger and ostracism like Parijat and her comrades did. Like Parijat, Durga too was driven by compassion combined with a powerful sense of justice. Like Durga Devi, Parijat undertook projects on behalf of unfortunates.

Yogmaya identified oppression in the context of Brahmanical abuse, despotic authority and corruption; Parijat's commitment to Marxist revolution defined her actions on behalf of those exploited by elites in partnership with a corrupt, uncaring administration. By comparison, Durga Devi's struggle for justice was narrowly defined. Yet, wouldn't you agree, she's someone you'd want on your side?

Durga Devi voluntarily chose to live alone with only her cook Mahili Didi. She did so even though this isolation made her vulnerable to an assault.

An outsider, Durga Devi attracted no following. However, she enjoyed the unfailing support of an unconventional mother-in-law. That bond was essential to her success. It was an extraordinary alliance.

Durga Devi's career is deserving for another reason. In contemporary Nepal where women's education and equal rights remain such pressing concerns, it seems to me that Karki Ghimire's activist model, compared to Yogmaya Neupane's, holds more potential.

Even educated women feel emotionally constrained to challenge sons, brothers, or husbands—today as in the past. We are too easily intimidated. Thus, we need to know how to effectively use law and to learn court procedures.[23] To assert our rights beyond basic education, allies are a prerequisite too. We need successful models like Durga Devi Karki Ghimire.

In Durga Devi's time, although the law was imperfect—where is it not? —it could nevertheless offer some respite and retribution. But it only worked for someone as skilled as Durga Devi. She could negotiate her way through court proceedings, something few laypeople anywhere can manage; she called men out; she refused to be subject to patriarchal norms at home. She won her rightful share of property; then she augmented that with compensation won from men who'd assaulted her. In alliance with the woman who customarily is a bride's nemesis—her mother-in-law—Durga Devi secured her rightful share.

Women with a determination and confidence similar to Durga Devi's can be mobilized to launch campaigns against prejudiced and illegal practices. Solid alliances, including backing from members of a woman's own family, are essential. With that kind of support women unable to check the abuse of sons, brothers or husbands[24] need not run away to a city or abroad (where others wait to pounce on them). Women would not have to be subject to a son's legal signature to assure her rights. Widows could marry without censure. Hapless wives could check the abuse of drunk and irresponsible husbands and more confidently demand a divorce and their share of property.

As I write this today, recalling what I learned many decades ago, Durga Devi re-excites my imagination. I can picture her simmering in anger in that inhospitable atmosphere of her husband's house. I can see this solitary girl striding confidently from Khandbari, hurrying over the bridge to her maitighar in Palikot. There her father, recognizing her precocious character, takes her under his wing—another uncommon partnership. Moving through the district with him, Durga Devi discovers a world of discord and ambition, bold arguments and whispered concessions, bargains struck and awards declared. (I cannot imagine her halting the ruler's carriage to shout a plea for her father; but she did exactly that! See amendment in Chapter 3 Postscript)

As corrupt as the justice system may have been, she somehow understood how to legally exact reprisals. She becomes educated not by memorizing holy texts but by learning logic and poring over legal briefs. Did her father decide on this training or did she spontaneously move in this direction? We do not know. And where did her profound sense of social justice come from?

Durga Devi wasn't contemplative like Yogmaya. There was nothing mystical about her, from what I understand. Perhaps we could consider her a secular counterpart to Yogmaya, sharing a legacy of women's struggle for justice in the last century.

Had Parijat lived longer, she would certainly have gone to Manakamana to converse directly with Mihili Didi and others to learn more about both women. I suspect she'd have become so smitten with Durga Devi's character that she'd have embraced her legacy too. Alas, because of Parijat's early passing, that was not to be. Meanwhile Nepali women and men keen to know more about their antecedents are ready to take on that responsibility and augment the historical record.

Poetry Challenges Anthropology

Yogmaya led me to Parijat.[25] Yes. This is the simple, genuine answer to the question often put to me: "How did you meet Parijat?" It is natural for people to be curious about our association. I was not involved in her lifelong political struggle; nor was I a poet. Parijat was already known in India as well as across Nepal, and although I'd been working in Nepal for more than a decade, I'd never heard of this celebrated— some would say notorious—activist and literary giant. (Foreign visitors would be wary of any Marxist activist, especially a fierce, relentless critic of the monarchy and the injustice it represented.)

My initial ignorance of Parijat and her work isn't a personal shortcoming. It's a testament of the limited spectrum of anthropology. It's an illustration of the conservative nature of this profession from its inception. Whether we indulge ourselves in Micronesian islands, in Amazon forests, on the plains of the American West, or through Nepal's terraced hills, we are wary of dissidents; we stay far away from protesters. We are neutral. This is what we claim.

Anthropology continues to enjoy an unchallenged reputation as a cutting edge science. The public preserves a romanticized view of us as discoverers of lost tribes. We win accolades for championing 'primitive' cultures, defending threatened populations and extolling arcane lifestyles. In fact, in general we remain a politically naïve profession. This stems from the nature of anthropology itself. After all, the science was fostered to serve imperialist interests, just as geology and geography across the globe are cultivated by foreign companies to identify mineral resources for later extraction.

Anthropological work may be more diversified today but its traditional role vis-à-vis government has hardly changed, notwithstanding decolonization. The status quo is in place even after Edward Said's highly regarded critiques on culture and imperialism,[26] despite profound feminist-driven reforms in social science methodology and theory, and even with the emergence of 'reflexive critique' in anthropology.[27]

How can we, students of culture, shake off these hoary traditions? Hearing about Yogmaya's historical challenge to the Rana despots who ruled Nepal from 1846–1951 did not in itself awaken me to political realities in Nepal. I needed to escape the bonds of ethnography, a discipline that's suspended in history; I needed to know what contemporary Nepali dissidents faced in pursuit of freedom while I was naively wandering through their land. With that new curiosity, I was open to my encounter with Parijat.

What an impact she made on me. I'd never given a thought to what she and fellow agitators encountered in their struggle for justice. In the 1970s, while I was assembling genealogies in highland villages, these citizens risked their lives to challenge an absolute ruler in the capital. King Mahendra's Shah Dynasty (1951–2008) that succeeded Nepal's line of Rana prime ministers was hardly more tolerant of dissent than the previous regime. Critics like Parijat and her comrades faced imprisonment, and worse.

Parijat and I were an unlikely partnership. While I was unaware of her literary accomplishments and her uncompromising lifelong fight against tyranny, on her side she was contemptuous of the opportunism and political prejudice in anthropology. She criticized naïve scholars like me arriving to prowl through her country.

Well that changed, didn't it? At least at the personal level, for me.

Parijat did not revise her view of anthropologists. It was I who became rehabilitated. Mentoring me in her gentle, practical way, introducing me to her comrades and young devotees—one of whom, as he himself recently reminded me, is Education Minister Giriraj Mani Pokharel—she opened up a new world to me. I began to rethink my professional indulgences and my mission. I needed years of deliberation to articulate my political stance, acquire new tools and define new goals. There's also the hard work of shedding antiquated academic language and allowing oneself to enter into the narrative, recognizing we do so with our cultural baggage and our vulnerabilities.

I think that that effort and the years I needed to grow have proved worthwhile. In journalism I've found an ideal fit for combining my politics, my international experience, my Arab heritage and my research skills. I remain embedded here. It's a career that removed me from Nepal for a long time while I concentrated my work in the homelands of my own Arab people—a rewarding and productive three-decade long pursuit.[28]

The Legacy and the Lineage of Women in this History

Parijat's entry into this chronicle kindles a point on a continuum, a line of Nepali women woven into the legacy of Yogamaya and Durga Devi. I find myself also, somehow, solidly implanted within this Nepali story—Yogmaya Neupane and Durga Devi Karki Ghimire were sustained by Bhattini Aama, Mata Damodara Giri, Vishnumaya Dahal and fearless ManaMaya who could recite *bani* for hours; then came Parijat and Sukanya Waiba; most recently Neelam Karki Niharika asserted her place here. Others like the founders of the Yogmaya Memorial Foundation in Biratnagar are poised, ready to assume their role in the tradition. An opening is awaiting celebrants of Durga Devi's when they arrive.

At the risk of appearing to deny the essential work of a number of dedicated and productive scholars which has drawn public attention to Yogmaya in the past decade, and acknowledging the invaluable contributions of Dharma Shrestha and Jangbu Sherpa, the men who assisted me at Manakamana, I feel compelled to reclaim and emphasize women's contributions here. Without women's initiatives, we would not have reached this point in our exhilarating, still evolving chronicle.

Yogmaya Neupane stands at the apex. Following her, Durga Devi Karki Ghimire arrived determined to upend the status quo, assert her rights as a woman, and support women survivors gathered at Manakamana. I came upon that secluded, humble settlement and found myself in the home of Bhattini Aama. (Building on our women's alliances—let's remember that sharing Bhattini Aama's home was only available to a woman visitor. No man had this license and thus couldn't be at her hearth that night when she uttered those verses.) Aroused by her vigorous and spontaneous recall of *yogbani*, smitten by those haunting lines, I started my inquiries. Bhattini Aama earns a place in this line along with Vishnumaya Dahal, chronicler of Durga Devi.

I could not have stayed in the kuti with the freedom to speak with its residents without the support of Damodara Giri, Mata of the hermitage. Her commitment to me was as a woman. On my departure at the end of my second visit it was Mata who gifted me her single copy of the book of treasures, the compilation of *yogbani*, only some of which I'd earlier recorded from oral recitations (not knowing at that time about the existence of this text). In Kathmandu I located the right person with whom to share these. This was Parijat, Nepal's most celebrated poet and dissident.

Parijat unhesitatingly embraced the stories I recounted. She recognized the brilliance and audacity of Yogmaya. She affirmed the verses' political impact and their inimitable poetic quality. Together we studied them and with her young associates, she set about translating selected quatrains to help me grasp their full significance. Not long after, Parijat curated an exhibition of women authors' books in which she included the collected *yogbani*. Although intending to do more, she wrote a single essay on the subject of Yogmaya.

In addition to a number of ambitious community projects initiated largely by men in Majhuwabesi and Gaudeni Cave, I've recently learned about a program in Biratnagar. In a city with solid historical ties to Bhojpur district and to Yogmaya, women have founded a social service organization to honour their early Nepali feminist and to implement her humanistic principles.

Picking up the line of women in this history, we arrive at Neelam Karki Niharika, the brilliant, committed U.S.-based Nepali novelist. Inspired by efforts underway, reading what others had assembled, she moved from place to place in East Nepal, imbibing the environment, interviewing local residents. This resulted in her 2018 historical novel, *Yogmaya*.[29] Niharika's work together with the award of Nepal's highest literary prize raises the stakes considerably. Because of this woman's youth and talent, building on her established literary reputation, willing to let her imagination go beyond the confines of more scientific approaches, she is awakening many more citizens. Her novel is bound to widen the dialogue about Yogmaya.

A generation of modern Nepali women who had remained outside the orbit of Yogmaya now stands at the threshold. Together with what they will discover about Durga Devi we can expect to hear much more from them through various media and civic and social programs they will certainly create.

Notes

[1]   A number of their publications are referenced in our bibliography.

[2]   Yogmaya Rastriya Nari Srashta Samman, founded by Pawan Aalok, director of Nepal Srashta Samaj, Kathmandu.

[3]   Sankhuwasabha district borders the Arun's east shore, Bhojpur lies opposite, on Arun's western flank.

[4]   I understand that anthropological studies in Nepal today are less focused on cultural particulars and more on new ethnic identity related to the Janajati movement and contemporary politics. Migration and inter-ethnic relations are of growing interest to all social scientists working in Nepal.

5   To be distinguished from the more popular and more famous site by the same name near Ghorka not far from Kathmandu. Manakamana on the Arun has wide appeal for local residents who also gather for annual festivals at Ekadesi.

6   See a 2018 digital publication of one report from my work with Limbu women in www.GlobalResearch.ca, a series of 3 articles "Nepal Hill Art and Women's Traditions", first published in 1978.

7   *Tibetan Frontier Families* (2011, new edition) and the co-edited volume *Soundings in Tibetan Civilization* (2012, reprint) published by Vajra Books, Kathmandu. Earlier writings appeared in Tibet and Nepal specialist journals.

8   A modest retreat for ascetics sometimes referred to as ashram.

9   After a thirty-year gap, Dharma and I reunited five years ago on a chance occasion when we were both in Kathmandu. He and his family had moved to the USA long before and since reuniting we've remained in close touch.

10   My companion Dhamodara Giri told me that even after Yogmaya's jal-samadhi, women sometimes enter the river to join their master, and are seen no more.

11   In 1976 I published a brief biography of her—"Ani Chodon: Portrait of a Buddhist Nun".

12   Ani Tsondu is featured in my "Buddhist Nuns", in *Natural History*, Magazine of The American Museum of Natural History, March 1989.

13   See my "Sacred Encounters at Amarnath Cave", *Natural History*, 1983

14   See also Aziz: "Personal Dimensions of The Sacred Journey" in *Journal of Religious Studies*, 23, xcii,1989.

15   Dingri history and society are the subjects of my *Tibetan Frontier Families* republished with a new introduction in 2011 by Vajra Books, Kathmandu.

16   "Shakti Yogamaya: A Tradition of Dissent in Nepal", first presented at a 1990 conference in Kathmandu, published in the 1993 collection, *Anthropology of Tibet and The Himalayas,* C. Ramble and M. Brauen (eds.). Recent research has determined Yogmaya was not, as I had believed, a child widow, and that her birthdate is1867. Otherwise, up to now, all the facts included in that essay are undisputed.

17   By Neelam Karki Niharika; see f.n. 29.

18   Mihili Didi, Vishnumaya Dahal, is referred to in the 2001 text as Mahadidi.

19   There was one suggestion that she may have attended a school in Dingla established by the revered teacher Shadanada Guru but that was a Sanskrit school and only for boys. Recently I learned what I suspected was the case—Durga Devi's father taught her.

20   Rereading my account of the early exploits of Sher Bahadur Karki, Durga
      Devi's father (Chapter 3), it occurs to me that this man's suspect reputation
      may have sullied that of the entire family, and thereby eclipses Durga Devi
      accomplishments. The daughter, however noble her work, may have been
      tainted by the father's misdeeds.

21   Nepali memoirs such as the 2010 collection of essays *Telling A Tale* edited
      by Archana Thapa, includes testimonies by contemporary women about the
      discrimination they experience within their families.

22   Neelam Niharika, in a private conversation, reports an emerging interest
      in Durga Devi's history by several parties in Bhojpur/Sankhuwasabha.
      We both hope this will materialize in concrete research efforts and
      publication. A February, 2020 Nepali news item out of Khandbari reports
      an unprecedented community initiative regarding Durga Devi; http://
      thahakhabar.com/news/90386

23   Nepal's constitution, promulgated five years ago, enshrined women's
      equality. Yet critics maintain the government is slow to see those provisions
      implemented.

24   Here we refer less to physical abuse and more to economic and psychological
      exploitation.

25   Before my departure from Manakamana on my second visit there in 1981,
      I casually asked Dharma Shrestha about other women in the country who
      compose political verses. Yes, he replied—"The poet Parijat; her songs are
      sung by young people moving through the countryside; you will find her in
      Kathmandu." I sought out the nationally acclaimed poet a few weeks later
      and include a passage about my arrival at her home in this book's epilogue.

26   Edward Said's many critiques of cultural history, political history and
      literature include most notably *Orientalism*, 1979, and *Culture and
      Imperialism*, 1993.

27   "Reflectivity" is a theory that grew out of critiques of text and context
      in critical literary discourse. Advocates argue that social sciences such as
      anthropology are subjective, thus researchers need to take their own role,
      status and feelings into account in their reports.

28   WBAI Radio 99.5 f.m. in New York and www.RadioTahrir.org carried
      much of my journalism output, audio and print; since 2014 www.
      counterpunch.org publishes my articles. See also www.barbaranimri.com.

29   *Yogmaya*, published by Sangrila, Kathmandu. In 2018 author Niharika was
      awarded the prestigious Madan Puraskar literary prize for this book.

Durga Devi Karki Ghimire

"Jethi Devi" – dissenter, advocate and benefactor

History plays games with its human actors. Why do I say this? I personally have seen enough years pass to observe how an event can be enthralling, profound and impacting on the people and places of its time; that same incident can also become buried from view, from memory, and from the record altogether.

Feminist research across the globe and women's fiction and poetry over the past 60 years reveal just how widely and thoroughly women were hidden from history. Our ancestors—this includes my own very capable mother—had been barred or discouraged from reading and writing. In addition, whatever our economic class, we are subject to patriarchal dominance. Our voices and our accomplishments are rendered silent. This suppression is applied to entire populations, not only to women. Everywhere, even today this persists. In our attempts to raise our voices to fight for our own rights and the rights of others, women are by one means or another struck silent. It is up to us to ensure the erasure is not permanent. We must excavate any traces, however faint and recover and reinstate them in our culture.

By chance, by determination, and by awakened descendants, women once hidden to us either purposely or by neglect are found, and reclaimed. The restoration we undertake can rekindle their messages and bring them into the present to serve our own enlightenment and then that of others, men as well as women. It is never too late to sing these women's praises, to share their heroism and their message, and to follow their example.

Durga Devi Karki Ghimire's sense of justice and her matchless dare to confront authority was first apparent on her visit to Kathmandu with her mother and her uncle. It was 1928; she was a child barely 12 years old and probably on her first venture outside Palikot village in Bhojpur. At the time, Nepal was a dictatorship where no challenges to the status quo were tolerated. (See our revision of this story in the postscript at the end of this chapter based on my 2019 visit to Marwa.)

The Karki family's arrival in the capital was likely directly related to Durga Devi's father and brother being imprisoned there. Few details are remembered except an unarguably bold action that would become a hallmark of this young dissident. It occurred in the thoroughfare of the capital where those days, one wouldn't encounter much traffic at any time, even less when the ruler was moving through the city.

Reportedly, this little girl somehow realizing the imperial carriage was approaching lunged at the horses pulling the coach. She managed to halt the vehicle, shouting at its exalted and doubtless astonished passenger: "My brother, my father; set them free."

As scant as this account is, the story signals the career Durga Devi Karki would carve out for herself in coming decades. It unequivocally identifies her audacious character. She might not emerge as a revolutionary leader or reformer, but her life would be one that unfailingly challenges wrongs and fights for civil rights. Her claims would be won, if necessary, through confrontation and guile as well as legal acumen.

These lifelong actions stemmed from a determination to secure what she was rightfully entitled to and, as is often the case with civil rights advocates, to win justice for those in distress and unable to defend themselves. In this chapter we review many incidents of this woman's audacious and unyielding character.

These revelations about Durga Devi emerged as I settled in among the congregation of ascetics living together in a quiet jungle retreat in Sankhuwasabha. I had been absorbed with Yogmaya's history but in the course of my intimate talks with inhabitants of the kuti, I learned about this very different character. She was almost a contemporary of the Yogi rebel and her life was also intertwined with these ascetics—although in a very different way.

Barely seven years had elapsed since she passed away. Not only did these women vividly remember Durga Devi; their personal comfort and their security had been guaranteed by this champion's purchase of this stretch of land on the shore of the Arun River where they were now passing their final years.

Around 1960 a handful of these women (and others who had passed on before our meeting here in 1980), each for her own reason, had moved from her family village to Manakamana's sacred dwelling on the eastern bank of the great Arun River. They constructed their huts and together they led an untroubled life of contemplation and prayer thanks to the patronage of Durga Devi.

But she did not live among them; she would move to Manakamana only in 1973—and then, only *very* temporarily. By that I mean she arrived at the nearby burning ghat to take her last breath, having herself already arranged her final rites.

What follows is a portrait I assembled about her career in the decades preceding that moment, an occasion which fittingly reflects the trajectory of her breathing years.

Durga Devi was an activist whose style was akin to that of contemporary social reformers, a political agitator in the modern sense. Her idiom, in contrast to Yogmaya, was secular.

No one was less like Yogmaya than Durga Devi. A flamboyant and cantankerous woman, Durga Devi was no poet and even less of a visionary. Compared to the unworldly Yogi with her piercing, artful verses, this rebel was a graceless peasant who shouted her way into history. Passive resistance was not her style. Durga Devi was a woman of immediacy.

Durga Devi was religiously conservative however. By caste she was Karki Chhetri, ranked below Bahun in Nepal's Hindu hierarchy. She did not challenge caste protocols as Yogmaya did. She followed Brahmanic rules regarding marriage and from childhood she accepted permanent widowhood. She hired a Bahun cook to maintain her house's ritual purity. So Durga Devi did not seek to end laws imposed by priests and the caste system.

Durga Devi's fight was directed elsewhere. Hers was a campaign to see that the law as it existed—for example, rules covering land rights, dowry, rape and other physical abuse, trickery and extortion—be respected and implemented. She found ample reasons to concentrate on injustices around those laws; corruption, graft, bureaucratic laxity and incompetence, and abuse of caste privileges were common in 1960.

Although the despotic Rana regime ended in 1951 and for a few years a limited democracy was in effect, that earlier regime was soon replaced by a new dictatorship—that led by Shah kings. Now it was their turn at despotism and corruption.

By the time Durga Devi began her campaign in earnest, bureaucratic abuse by an extended civil administration was flourishing across the land: officials worked according to the size of a bribe; the courts continued to rule in favour of the rich; women were abandoned without land if they objected to their husband's behaviour; men violated young girls while police turned a blind eye.

To counter abuse and exploitation she saw around her, Durga Devi's goal seemed straightforward—government officials must observe the law; police must apply the law; courts must be fair. She began her search for justice with a personal appeal for her rights as a widow. Through the court she would claim her entitlement to her husband's share of family property after he, still a child himself, died leaving her a teenage widow.

She would apply her personal successes to help distressed, exploited villagers, daring to name the culprits and demand the police do their duty. She came to the defence of a violated girl child; she helped women abused by husbands or mothers-in-law; she badgered government clerks for essential papers until they complied.

How did she manage this?

She brought to this social mission her profound knowledge of law and legal procedures, a skill she learned primarily as a child while accompanying her father to the courts.

Yogmaya sought to dismantle the Nepali legal code and priestly enforcement of social rules, while Durga Devi found and implemented protections in existing law that might limit abuse and theft. The basic problem in her view was corruption. According to her, if the Muluki Ain were faithfully applied, it could offer people justice.

Durga Devi conducted her campaign in street confrontations, by filing complaints against whomever attacked her, by harassing clerks and by fighting in the courtrooms of the district headquarters of East Nepal. She did this almost single-handedly.

While pursuing my inquiries about Yogmaya at Manakamana kuti, I was fortunate to be introduced to Durga Devi's lifelong friend Mahili Didi (Vishnumaya Dahal)[1]. After her patron's demise, she joined the bhaktini at the hermitage. She herself was a Bahun widow and a former devotee of the Yogi. After Yogmaya's death and before taking up residence at Manakamana, she was Durga Devi's cook and confidante, an association lasting a quarter century (ending when Durga Devi expired). They lived together, first in Malta, Mahili Didi's village, during the 1940s and 50s. Malta is within a half day's walk from Tumlingtar, and not far from Chainpur, district headquarters at the time, where a court was located and where Durga Devi fought her earliest legal battles.

The two women often travelled beyond Sankhuwasabha—they went to Banaras, Haridwar and Assam, and to Darjeeling and other places in India. At home, Mahili Didi witnessed many of the public encounters her friend provoked. Mahili Didi herself was not a social activist. She was a loyal confidant who, fortunately for us, freely shared many details of her patron's activities with me.

Vishnumaya Dahal was cook and companion to Durga Devi.

During scores of extended conversations, whenever I visited Manakamana between 1980 and 1985, I met Mahili Didi to learn more about her departed companion. Mahili Didi had no personal agenda in this chronicle, and the accounts were not ideologically framed. She was not trying to eulogize or champion her friend. Her candour and her welcoming personality made the history of this heroine all the more convincing. I found her reports highly reliable. She spoke dispassionately but with pride—with some hilarity too. Her forthright manner was a great advantage in helping me piece together a biographical sketch of this extraordinary woman.

"Who owns this land where you have built your houses?" I innocently asked Mata one morning while we sat on the hillside overlooking the beach leading towards the icy cold waters of the Arun.

"Durga Devi bought it for us—80 ropani in all," she replied. Mata's response to my question was simple and rather matter-of-fact. From where we sat on the hillside above the hermitage, we could see most of the fields and jungle belonging to this kuti. The place where the women lived stretched along the bank of the Arun for a quarter of half kilometer. At its southernmost frontier, the property started at the pebbled sati-ghat where corpses are brought for burning. It included the open sandbar and extended upriver to a cut in the forested hillside where the path leaves the water's edge and turns uphill.

Agile riverside dwellers, the Kaumal fishermen might walk onto the beach and leap from rock to rock across the current. But that's not the customary route. Most visitors trek downhill through the jungle towards the river and conduct their rituals at the water's edge. Funerary parties heading to the burning ghat pass above Manakamana to avoid disturbing the women and proceed to the beach to construct a pyre. Worshipers sacrifice at the shrine of Goddess Manakamana nearby and others make their supplications to Lord Arun in the current just beyond the kuti. (Some members of a party will occasionally approach the kuti to ask Mata for firewood.)

An ideal location for a retreat, the kuti is isolated but still accessible to worshippers and family members of the women ascetics. An extended thicket of banana and guava trees planted here belongs to the hermitage. A prayer hall sits on a clearing in the middle of the property. Around it scattered among the grove of lemon and lime trees are the thirty-two straw-roofed huts, one for each kuti member.

"Until 1960, this area was uninhabited," explains my companion.

"Tell me more about your patron."

"She was a wealthy lady; she always helped women. She gave this place to us." Mata's reply is casual, as if the arrangement was nothing unusual.

I thought of the Buddhist culture of Sherpas and Tibetans with whom I had studied in Nepal's Solu-Khumbu region a few years before. There, when a rich Sherpa or Tibetan woman takes up a life of contemplation, she often donates her personal wealth to a nearby nunnery or monastery. Or she founds and supports a new nunnery.

"Was your benefactor like those Buddhist patrons?"

"A sanyasi? Oh no", replies my host. She chuckles. "Durga Devi was no bhaktini. Twenty years ago she bought some land here; the place was dense with trees. She hired workers to construct the path through the jungle to the river. In 1963 she bought more space for us, a piece bordering her original gift. You can see everything we have here," as she stretches her arm is a sweep outward. "Mahili Didi knows all about her; she will tell you more." Mata smiles, amused by the idea their benefactor could be a holy lady.

> Mahili Didi was expecting us when I and Dharma Shrestha, the young man who worked with me, arrived at her hut. Already familiar with our inquiries about Yogmaya, she appeared delighted by our expanded mission. She poured each of us a cup of milk-less tea with mint leaves floating on it and plunged directly into anecdotes of Durga Devi's career in the courts.
>
> "We call her Jethi Devi, victorious Devi," explains Mahili Didi—"because she always won.
>
> "She was a widow; so was I.
>
> "Those days," Mahili Didi continues, "our courthouse was in Chainpur. Durga Devi was already involved in the case against the Ghimire family, her brothers-in-law.[2] She could not stay in their house, her rightful residence, because of animosity between them. She could not remain anywhere in Marwa village where the disputed land was. She needed to be close to Chainpur to be ready to pursue her cases at the courthouse, so she came to my village, Malta. She built a house and she asked me to work as her cook. We stayed together for 25 years, until near the end, after she became ill and we moved here to Manakamana."

Such a contract between two widows was rare since widows are normally destitute and rely on the forbearance of their husbands' families. Except for wandering ascetics, mostly men, few people live alone in Nepal. I expect neighbours would not have been thrilled to have Durga Devi and Mahili Didi in their midst.

Only after she had become known for her cantankerous ways and her successes in court, some villagers from around the region sought out this place to ask Durga Devi for help. But she was never welcomed inside Malta houses. Locals considered Durga Devi meddlesome.

She was also unpopular with officials. Durga Devi refused to overlook blatant corruption by government workers. Extortion and bribery were common.

"You visited Khandbari," Mahili Didi reminds me. "You saw clerks drinking tea, playing cards and gossiping outside their offices. They are there all day. You know how our elected Pradhan Pancha dynamites the river to gather fish for himself and his fellows. You know his friends buy up land when he tells them where the hospital will be built. What do they care about the porter who comes to them for help, holding a paper from the landlord that he can't read? 'Go to that office;' 'We are closing;' 'Come next week;' 'Go to Bhojpur; this is not registered in our district;' 'We didn't receive any police report; go; ask them for it,' and so on. That's what they tell the fellow who has lost a day's work and has walked four hours from his house to their office.

"She was smart. To learn about local mischief, our Durga waylaid children; or she met them in the fields when they were idly watching their cattle. She inveigled them with candy to tell her their family gossip. She asked them: 'Who's beating whom? Who had been cheated or insulted? Which auntie was sent away? Which little girl is unfed? Being an outsider in Malta village Durga Devi had neither sisters nor aunts to tell her these things. You know how, in any village even minor disagreements—in the family, between neighbours—become public; our children know as much as adults about people's squabbles and indiscretions".

Durga Devi must have lived an isolated life if she needed to cajole children for information. One would not be surprised if officials and others warned villagers to stay clear of this woman. Gossip would be plentiful.

But I did not tap that side of Durga's work; I was more interested in her legal pursuits.

To lodge complaints in the court, a plaintiff would have to be literate, educated in law too. When Durga Devi was a child, there were hardly any village schools and few girls attended class, even up to grade five. Nepal's national education plan was introduced only in 1971 and Palikot village where Durga Devi was born could not have had a school before 1970.[3] (By then Durga Devi was already 50.)

Where and how was this child educated? Where did this woman study law? My curiosity grew by the day.

"Sher Bahadur Karki, her father, taught her," came the answer.

Some children were schooled by family members. In this case, the leap from basic literacy to a legal career was immense.

I pressed Mahili Didi for details. "Was Sher Bahadur a lawyer? Perhaps a distinguished judge?" My naiveté about Durga Devi's father amused Mahili Didi.

The man was not an unknown character in the valley, but he was far, far from being a respected judge! Mahili Didi hesitates to elaborate more about this man. She would not actually say he was somewhat of a rogue who took advantage of others. But it was apparent she did not care for him. (He was described to me in 2019 by Marwa inhabitants as a 'tax-collector'.)

In fact, reflecting on this much later, I realized that no one had uttered a word of admiration for Durga Devi's father.

"He was a man of the courts', Mahili Didi tactfully explains. "Always in court gathering more and more land." He probably loaned money to farmers. Some may have fallen into debt, and although land is not supposed to be transferred, this man could have known how to obtain their deeds. He travelled on his horse from one town to the next, perhaps filing foreclosures wherever the fields of besieged farmers were registered:– Dingla, Bhojpur, Dhankuta, even Kathmandu. Knowing litigation procedures, Sher could file his papers himself and make his case directly to a judge. He may have paid the judges as well! Ordinary farmers could not read or write. And there were no lawyers to defend the poor. So Sher Bahadur Karki collected one field after another, working through courts on that side to courts on this side (of the Arun River).

"Durga went everywhere with him. She was just a girl. She had her own horse, one she chose herself; it stood taller than her father's mount.

"He entrusted his legal papers to this little companion and she carried those in her saddle bag. She kept them with her in the courtroom. At a nod from her father, Durga opened the bag and fetched the relevant document.

"I never met Sher Bahadur. Only, I heard that people feared him," adds Mahili Didi. This reminds her about the abduction of the woman who would become his wife (and Durga Devi's mother). "He was traveling by horse on the trail between Palikot, his village, and Dingla. Over there, on the ridge," she says, pointing across the river from where we sat. "He saw her walking with her servant. He knew she was married, but he was determined to have her for himself. So he ambushed them in the jungle and he captured her, telling the servant to go home and inform his master he would pay for the woman. Later, he sent the jari (fine for divorce) to the woman's old husband. That was all."

The abduction was settled according to procedures for elopement— not an uncommon event in Nepal those days.

Sher Bahadur became a wealthy man. From Mahili Didi's account, however, he did not appear to be an entirely noble fellow. He and his brother Bir Bahadur may not have been above bribing others to obtain what they wanted.

If Durga Devi learned to read and write from her father, she likely learned court procedures from him too. Neither Sher Bahadur nor Durga Devi was a lawyer. Understanding legal formalities and being fearless, she learned to defend herself and to win her rights. Eventually she would apply those skills very differently than her father had. From the time of her childhood, she showed a righteous bent and a deep concern for others, especially fellow women.

Durga Devi's first known appeal was a dramatic, heroic (and defiant) act carried out on behalf of her own brother. The boy could not have been much older than 15, but somehow, he (and his father) had found themselves in legal trouble. Both were imprisoned in Kathmandu at one point. According to Mahili Didi, they had slain a Rai man who'd first attacked them.

This incident occurred around 1928. Durga Devi was hardly 10 years old herself when she accompanied her mother and uncle to Kathmandu. This was still the era of the Ranas when the same dictator, Juddha Shumsher, whom Yogmaya had challenged, ruled. Durga Devi later told Mahili Didi what happened and Mahili Didi retold the story to us. "The family was walking in the main road in the city, when the coach of Juddha Shumsher appeared in the road, drawn by four great horses. When people saw this carriage they knew the ruler was inside and hurriedly moved well away, turning their eyes downward. Durga Devi however did not step back when she saw the ruler's vehicle approaching. Instead she ran into the animals' path and grasped the bridle of one horse, somehow bringing the team to a halt. 'My brother, my father,' she shouted towards where the ruler was seated—as if she could see him from where she stood. 'My brother, my father, let them free, they are innocent. Oh Sarkar, I ask you to release them.'" That was all Durga Devi uttered, according to Mahihi Didi. She'd reported that she actually saw the ruler gazing down at her. And when she let go of the harness, his carriage rushed on as the police surrounded Durga Devi along with her mother and uncle.

"They could have taken all of them to jail, maybe shot them.

"Others saw this; you can ask in Kathmandu. They will remember."

According to Durga Devi's account to Mahili Didi, the police questioned her uncle but they did not arrest any of them. (Again see my postscript based on information from Marwa residents whom I interviewed in 2019.)

"When they left the capital, Durga Devi did not know what the outcome would be. The family only learned of her victory on their return to the Arun Valley. Soon after they

Marwa residents and relatives of Durga Devi recall her exploits and display their collected genealogy (which does not list women), 2019.

arrived in Palikot, the man and his son were back home. They'd been freed from prison! According to Mahili Didi, Durga Devi's bold demand direct to the ruler had made that possible.

"Thereafter, Durga Devi was never far from Sher Bahadur's side, mounted on her own horse, riding with him and with her uncle, Bir Bahadur." They always moved by horse while conducting their business affairs. Apart from high ranking officials who tour remote villages on horseback, only this trio travelled by horse.

Mahili Didi surmised that whenever this family passed through the area they wanted to be certain everyone took note of them.

Durga Devi's young brother was not among this team however. It seems he was a sickly child who would not live long.

"Durga Devi accompanied the men right into the courtroom too. She carried his satchel holding his legal files. She closely followed everything her father and uncle did."

Probably Durga Devi acquired her legal knowledge largely from studying the documents her father discussed with her and by following his example in court. They were a formidable team, it seems. They shared many more victories in land disputes. Durga Devi's sense of invulnerability or her arrogance and righteousness must have been born from those successes.

Despite his adventures in law, Sher Bahadur Karki was socially a traditional father. Even though he arranged for his daughter's education, he still betrothed her according to custom when she was barely 7 years old to the Ghimire family in Marwa. (Sher betrothed his son when that lad was just a child too.) Durga Devi's husband Bir Bahadur Ghimire was a 9 year-old boy she'd never seen and who died soon after betrothal was completed.

"Durga Devi became a widow before she even took up residence in the Marwa marriage house. Her brother too, Sher's only son, died before he received his young wife, so this girl also became a child widow (about whom we shall hear more). Following custom, Sher insisted neither girl should marry; neither would bear children either. With their dowries paid, the marriages were legal and the girls should eventually move to the homes of their husbands, houses of strangers. Durga Devi's little sister-in-law would come to the Palikot house, and Durga Devi would go to Marwa village, birthplace of her husband.

Sher Bahadur belonged to Karki Chhetri caste, yet he followed the strict Brahmin practice that prohibited a widow to marry. Without a husband to support her it was not unlikely that Durga Devi would be mistreated. And if she were unable to somehow protect herself she could become one of countless cases of injustice perpetuated against young women.

Since Sher Bahadur survived his son, he should have anticipated problems arising over inheritance around his daughter's status. He could have searched for a solution, even if this involved rejecting social rules. It seems he did not. As for Durga, even as she matured and faced difficulties in her husband's house at Marwa, she never challenged her father's arrangement for her marriage. Ending child marriage and widowhood were critical to Yogmaya's struggle. Not Durga Devi's. She neither fought to overturn her fate as a child widow, nor did she campaign against the practice in general.

"Durga Devi knew she would eventually have to leave her maitighar and move to the Ghimire house in Marwa. But she was able to spend much her childhood in Palikot with her father and mother. Only when her father died did she move to Marwa. That was about 1933 when she was 14 or 15."[4]

Durga Devi, according to her friend, was happy at her home in Marwa, initially. Her husband's brothers were still adolescents themselves and their wives had not yet moved there. That early cheerfulness was probably due to her affection for her sasu (mother-in-law) and the proximity of her sister Chitra Rikka whom I learned only in 2019 was married to another Ghimire in Marwa.

> "Sasu welcomed this girl from Palikot and a magical union sprung up between them; the older woman became devoted to the young widow.
>
> "That bond endured until the moment the older woman, with Durga at her side, took her last breath and was consumed in fire at the ghat near Manakamana." (Confirmed by Durga Devi's younger sister's son, Surendra Ghimire whom I spoke to in Marwa in November, 2019)

A remarkable partnership would emerge and become Durga Devi's redemption, as we shall see.

This kind of bond between a woman and her daughter-in-law was uncommon. If a woman has several sons, she receives the wife of each into her house dispensing her affection to those who bear her grandchildren, especially grandsons. Her eldest daughter-in-law wins favoured status if she's the first to give birth to a boy.

Women like Durga Devi, destined to remain childless, find themselves marginalized and are often badly treated. Without a husband to protect her or a male child to assure the line, widows are subject to cruel treatment by their mothers-in-law and by sisters-in-law too. They exist on the margin of a household. Some young widows run away. If lucky enough to have a brother willing to take her in and give her work, a widow might return to her maitighar. But this option is only possible if her brother's wife agrees; even then, a widow is not always kindly treated there.

My translator Dharma sat nearby following my discussion with Mata about difficulties of these child widows. Mata knew Dharma's family and noting his thoughtful mood as we talked, not unkindly reminded him about his phuphu, Dharma's father's elder sister.

"She'd been living with you since before you were born, Dharma. I know."

Mata guessed that Dharma and his brothers and sister hadn't thought much about that loving but sad woman among them.

"Your phuphu was a child widow. She did not want to fight for her land so she left her house empty-handed and returned to your father's house (her maitighar). Your mother finally agreed to this. But had Phuphu not accepted to work as the family cook, you may never have known your sweet auntie."

Dharma was deeply moved by this information. He thought about what our friend had told him and began to recall the on-going tension between his parents concerning his father's sister.

"True, I was a child but I remember how my auntie once ran away after an argument with Aama. My older brothers went in search of her and they brought her back to the house. 'She has no money, no jewellery, no land,' Father explained. Aama and Auntie hardly spoke to one another; I didn't understand. For years I'd thought our phuphu was a poor relative who father was helping. I thought she wanted to stay with us because she loved me and my brothers and sister.

"Now I understand that she must have had her own fields somewhere, land she lost because she hadn't demanded her rightful share."

Dharma, with tears in his eyes, promised he would go home in a few days to talk to his auntie. He had a new awareness of her and he wanted to learn more about her feelings and her past.

As Durga Devi's campaign demonstrates, legal redress for women is available. Even if widowed and childless, a wife retains some rights in her husband's family property. And those rights are guaranteed in the national social code, Muluki Ain. Few women feel able to assert this right however, just as they will not legally challenge a husband if he brings a new wife to the house.

"Durga Devi was different from most women. She decided she would not forfeit her land. She was 25 and had been living in Marwa for ten years, working her fields, caring for the animals, repairing the house, enjoying the confidence of her sasu. She was not about to let her dewar (husband's brothers, the Ghimires) and their families steal the produce of *her* fields.

> "But what man will voluntarily give up his dead brother's portion." To insist on her share Durga Devi needed the court's sanction; she would have to fight for that. A public dispute of this kind was certain to bring the scorn of the whole village onto any woman who attempted this.
>
> "What do you think? Was Durga Devi prepared for that?
>
> "All three brothers-in-law joined forces; they were determined to keep Durga Devi's share under their control. First they tried to win their mother's support. A woman will usually side with her sons, but not in this case. Sasu refused.
>
> "This was crucial. Sasu's support for Durga Devi was essential; as the senior woman of a household, the land deeds were in her possession, not her sons'."

Although women may be subject to many constraints, and even though they will not ordinarily overrule a son, as head of the house they can determine how shares are distributed.

> "All three Ghimire sons found their own mother standing firmly with Durga Devi. 'You must give Durga Devi her share,' Sasu insisted. Then the men asked their wives to help assuage Durga Devi. 'Promise her anything,' they pleaded.

Durga Devi would not be mollified.

"Finally the men decided on a strategy to get rid of this adversary. They would marry Durga Devi off to someone from a distant place.

"A new groom might be of lower caste and thus bring shame on the family; but they calculated that would pass. If Durga Devi were sent far away, they expected she'd soon be forgotten.

"The men began to search for a new partner for their troublesome sister-in-law. They even agreed to offer a small dowry to help lure someone. It was worth some financial sacrifice to rid them of her ill temper and constant demands".

Mahili Didi herself was not a witness to that confrontation and only learned about the plot from Durga herself years later. With glee and pride, she recounted the episode to us.

Dharma and I felt like spectators at a sports match.

"Everything was arranged. The expectant groom was a man from far away, down in Madhes. At the time they'd fixed, he was on his way here to fetch his bride. An old, old man, according to Durga Devi."

Mahili Didi explains, grimacing as she pulled her spread fingers down her cheeks, evoking the image of a withered old fellow. Her large eyes open wide with mock amazement.

"Durga Devi knew nothing about the scheme. The Madhesi fellow was due that day, already near Marwa, and about to claim his wife! Hah.

"He brought musicians with his party who began to play their horns and drums as they came near the house. You can be sure the brothers and their wives grinned with delight. Their saucy sister-in-law would soon be gone.

"They miscalculated. Sasu knew of her sons' plan and she did not like it. Up to this point she had remained silent. But something made her change on the day when the old man arrived to claim her daughter-in-law. You will never believe what she did, that sasu? Against her own sons!

"Against her own sons!" she exclaims. Listening to this account Mahili Didi's enthusiasm for Durga Devi's mother-in-law infected us with affection for the elder woman. This sasu was the kind of mother-in-law every Nepali woman might dream of. "Against her own sons," she repeats.

Dharma and I were not the only ones enjoying this tale. Another bhaktini at the hermitage had been listening from nearby, seated against a shade tree. She smiles as she steps into our circle to listen with us, crouched between me and Mahili Didi. She knows the story, but she wants to hear it again, leaning forward to catch the best part of the tale. Her thin wrap is pulled over her close-cropped head reminding me that she too had probably been a child widow, perhaps a desolate daughter-in-law too. How much of a model are Durga Devi and Sasu for this woman? I wonder, watching her sparkling eyes. Or is this just a wild and humorous story? We wait for Mahili Didi to continue.

This is a cherished moment for an anthropologist. A field researcher often finds herself groping blindly in the early stages of her inquiries. In my work in the Arun River Valley, I began without a map, not knowing where I would end, unaware of how few people would or could verify this history. In retrospect, I feel I was blessed, first with my naiveté and second with these women's tolerance of me. Like my innocent questions about the poems, or the ownership of the land where the women lived, my uncharacteristic innocence had led me here, and then kept me here. Having stayed on, finding that these women's lives were so charged with passion and so full of controversy, I felt compelled to make a pact with them.

We anthropologists are mere visitors here. We usually can't see beyond the colourful and curious customs of our hosts; we are entranced by the deviant and the daring. We don't usually seek out the abnormal since norms are difficult enough for us to make sense of. We concentrate on learning people's habitual ways because custom tells us how a society is held together; that's what we want to know. We seek endless examples of caste norms, of inbuilt or 'inherent' exploitation, of inequities, of backwardness, of the endurance of traditions, of family values, of people living unchanged century after century. We become so enchanted and overwhelmed with those norms—after all we are only visitors and we do not have to abide by these rules ourselves—that we can't accommodate anything out of the norm into our conclusions. This is the case especially in Asia, in the Arab lands and across Africa—possibly everywhere. We concentrate on others' traditions—not because social life in India or Myanmar or Bangladesh is inherently inflexible, but because of our own limited vision.

Most anthropologists develop a narrow view of what is possible for example in Asian societies. We come here to understand these norms and the power of the rules operating in these cultures, so we have a vested interest in what's commonplace. We accept a picture of social rigidity because many of the people we speak to are clear about what they can and cannot do. We encourage them to tell us what is normal and we record that. We hear so many stories about forlorn and abused widows that those experiences seem unassailable. If we become too emotional about their problems, we won't stay long. If we feel nothing can be done, we write about the tenacity of Asian traditions.

Mahili Didi's account of Durga Devi cut through all that. This was more than a story. It was these women's history, these people's history, and as such it became a record of their potential.

It was during those early weeks hearing such accounts that my aims as a chronicler changed. I found my skepticism fading. My British professors had stressed how scepticism helped us better evaluate truth. I decided to continue this pursuit without the usual tools of verification— news articles, chronicles written by my predecessors, or some statistical information. I had to measure these reports qualitatively, perhaps using my emotions!

I learned there are occasions when facts cease being paramount. Facts can be useful, but their selection can be highly subjective too. And facts have their limits. The personality and the character of events become far more significant, more real. They could lead me to a different truth.

I abandoned my scepticism. I allowed myself to enter this history and I did something a scientist should never do—I was cheering for Durga Devi, cursing her dewar, as I sensed an approaching victory. She would never let that toothless old dog take her, never let her brothers-in-law dump her. I also felt a growing confidence that Sasu would not betray Durga Devi.

I was no longer a detached observer. I felt destined to be here with Mahili Didi and the other bhaktini. I resolved to write Durga Devi's story even without 'traditional' empirical facts. Durga Devi became a heroine for me.

> Sasu had to help her daughter-in-law, and she did, crossing a sacred line to openly ally herself with Durga Devi, rushing to warn her of the old Madhesi's imminent arrival.

There was still time for Durga Devi to escape.

> "But Durga Devi did not run away" our narrator interjects. "Not Jethi Devi. No. What she did was devise a plan to scare off the foolish intruder. In what was to become her style, she positioned herself for an assault, running into the path and single-handedly confronting him and his party. Mahili Didi paused to laugh before the punch line. "She attacked the poor chap, physically. He turned in the opposite direction and fled, back to Madhes, we suppose; never heard from again."

And Durga Devi?

> "She was screaming, cursing both the old man and her dewar. The whole village watched this so the men must have been chagrined. What a blunder. They had not only lost their dowry. They had aroused Durga Devi's wrath." Their failed scheme made Durga Devi more determined to take what she was owed, and more. She was confident Sasu would always be

a trusted accomplice. Soon after that episode, Sasu indeed handed over the land deed to her favourite daughter-in-law—a kind of reward. They had taken the first step together.

But a woman cannot just walk away with a deed. There would have to be a court hearing. Moreover, Durga Devi's share was not one coterminous piece of land on a hillside. One plot was many hundred meters below Marwa near the river surrounded by fields allocated to her brothers-in-law. Another piece bordered the path to town; a third was in the meadow on the shade side of the mountain; a forth was east of the village. Until now the family easily ploughed and seeded and harvested their combined fields together. Who would want to purchase those disparate plots if Durga Devi took them over?

First Durga Devi would have to go to the court to force a sale at fair compensation and second, somehow exchange plots so hers would be coterminous allowing her to cultivate them independent of her hostile relatives. That would take time.

> "Durga Devi's struggle for possession of her land involved a series of court cases lasting a whole eight years. During this period, Durga Devi moved to Malta and lived with me while she supported herself from the produce of her Marwa fields. Sasu watched over her land, but Durga Devi regularly returned there to plough, sow, hoe, and harvest. The two women tended Durga Devi's fields together. At harvest time, Sasu sent her daughter-in-law's share of the harvest to Malta, and Durga Devi sold whatever surplus she enjoyed, saving her profits in the bank."

Court battles continued.

> "The fight became ugly at times, with Durga Devi and her three opponents shouting insults at one another in the street, first in Chainpur, where it is said she actually kicked a judge, and later in Khandbari, after the district court was moved there (not to escape Durga Devi but because of a district re-zoning).

"These towns are the domain of men, mostly government officials. Idle hangers-on and rich merchants who befriend officials sniff for news about government contracts. The town square is their clubhouse and their business centre. To the last person, from Bhojpur south to Dhankuta, these men knew Durga Devi's character; they were perpetually watchful. They never welcomed her. No; they feared her and hid themselves."

Here was a woman, a widow with no formal education intent on applying government regulations—not with bribes but with threats to invoke the law to secure her rights. Not surprisingly the community's sympathy lay with the Ghimire men in their drawn out dispute with this upstart widow.

On my early visits to Chainpur and Khandbari soon after I first learned about Durga Devi, I sought residents' opinions about her. Those who volunteered a comment were dismissive of the woman, warning me that she was not worth my time. They offered no details about her work, only repeated how, "She was a troublemaker; she was always making trouble." This was their simple, singular characterization of Durga Devi. They had made up their minds long ago; to some she was a pest; to others she was simply mad. Everyone spoke in the same sulking tone, as if personally offended by her.

My inquiries about Yogmaya had already jeopardized my chance of befriending these gentlemen. They insisted that Yogmaya was a communist whore. Here was another strange woman to deal with and they used equally derisive language to spurn my inquiries. I was undeterred; and at the same time I found their reactions instructive. Hostility to Durga Devi was founded in men's solidarity with her brothers-in-law. Not a few of these men had widowed sisters-in-law staying in their own homes, women whose shares they felt entitled to. They must have asked themselves: "What if she decides to follow that troublemaker's example and take her share of our fields?"

(Fortunately these men were not hostile towards me. I was a visitor in their country and they could have me shipped out, or they might have pressured the women at Manakamana to end their association with me.)

In any case, those dismissals and rejections made me more curious about this woman. The men, from police and clerks to farmers and merchants, hated the Palikot woman's abrasive style. Her confrontational manner was unacceptable in this culture. Her behaviour is akin to the ambitious and aggressive American or European women today labelled as militant, abrasive—"unhelpful".

"Durga Devi felt extraordinary pity for women and men who simply needed the help of a clerk. 'Even a high-school educated fellow can dissolve a plaintiff's fears with a few kind words.' That's what she pleaded. 'It takes a few moments to tell them what's needed. But those officials refuse to work; they will not help villagers submit their forms. Sitting with the bosses makes them feel important; they are bored with their job; in full view of petitioners, they sit together playing cards. They have the simplest work, those office sitters—filing reports, directing papers from one office to another, explaining government regulations to citizens. What do they do? They send these poor people away and take bribes to help the rich get more."

Our Durga Devi would not be dismissed so easily.

"Every week Durga Devi marched into town with one complaint or another. She openly accused police of taking bribes, the land office of extortion, the bank clerk of corruption, the school superintendent of fraud. They would claim to have misplaced her files, demand that she submit more forms, and otherwise harass her at every turn. When she was spotted heading into town, word spread through the offices, and whoever could manage, shut their doors and disappeared for the day.

"Durga always won, and they didn't like that. 'Our people are poor. They cannot write. Who will help them?' she asked.

"One day a man brings to Durga Devi a sample from a sack of corn he bought at the market explaining how the grain is laced with pebbles. He knows who the responsible merchant is but he's unable to confront the man alone. Would Durga Devi help him?

"A woman came to us seeking protection from a husband who beat her; 'He'll toss me out if I don't accept his new wife', she told us. Would Durga Devi file a report for her with the police?

"Another woman arrives to report that her husband died last month owing 800 rupees and the landowner says that to cancel the debt, her son must work for him until the monsoons—nine more months. She has no way of knowing if the debt is real. She fears the landlord. How can she find out about her husband's debt? What is she to do?"

Mahili Didi was the only witness to those private moments at their house in Malta where Durga Devi met the hapless villagers, men as well as women, seeking her help. Only this loyal cook witnessed how kindly Durga Devi received them.

"'Who will help them? Who will stop this cheating?'" she pleaded.

"Sometimes she wept. She became angry and she wanted these peasants to be angry too."

Mahili Didi mimics Durga Devi, flinging her arms about, recalling her patron's indignations:

"'What! They can't do that; tell him the law does not permit a second wife; you can divorce him and take your share; your son does not have to work for the guy; demand to see the debt paper with your husband's signature. Tell him Nepal has a law protecting you and your son; tell him.'"

Mahili Didi sighs as she recalls those moments for us.

"They could not do that alone. They were afraid."

Durga Devi was a person of action. One example of this was how she exposed falsified grain measures. Grain merchants were well known for using measuring pots with false bottoms. The police were supposed to check the vessels but for a small bribe they'll find other things to occupy themselves.

More than once, our self-appointed prosecutor Durga Devi periodically took matters into her own hands. This would happen on market day when crowds gathered in the town, a scene cheerfully recounted for us by our chronicler.

> "Hiding in a nearby shop, she watched merchants measuring grain, and at the opportune moment she'd rush at them and grab the vessel, then smash it on the ground exposing its false base. Oh, how other merchants quivered as they watched from behind closed doors. People in the street stopped, amazed. Everyone seemed to disappear. So Durga Devi would call a child and gave him a few sweets to run and fetch the constable. Meanwhile she stood over the evidence and shouted accusations at the humiliated shopkeeper."

In the short term, these ambushes might be seen as victories for her. Long-term benefits were another matter. Young people, like my assistant Dharma, never overcame his early image of Durga Devi as a wild and disagreeable person.

> "I remember my father talking about her with others as we sat in front of our shop. I was nine years old when I actually saw Durga Devi for myself. She was screaming, running through the square, shouting 'police, police!' She had her kukuri in her hand, and blood was streaming from her head. I admit, we children laughed and called, "bahula, bahula—a crazy woman."

Mahili Didi listened to him patiently for a moment. She knew about the incident.

> "Listen to me Dharma; it all started at the Chainpur court when Durga was going there every week trying to get her land back. After one visit there, she and a brother-in-law were screaming at each other in the middle of the street. She always carried a pole as well as her knife and that time she swung her stick at the man and when he hit her back, she was cut in the head and she bled a lot. I know, I took care of her.

Learning details about Durga Devi's history from Mahili Didi, he began to appreciate her a little more.

> "You didn't understand Durga Devi, sweet Dharma. Since she was bleeding from that fight she decided to run through the street shouting for the police. Why? Because she wanted everyone to witness the evidence of the assault; she shouted to onlookers: 'You are my witness.' She insisted the police take note of her wounds and write their report. Before she left the town that day, she filed a charge for assault against that brother-in-law. Again they went to court. And you know Dharma: he had to pay her compensation for what he did.
>
> "See why we came to call her Jethi Devi!"

With each victory Durga Devi's grew rich and began to give away some of the wealth she'd accumulated, beginning with a project at the riverside site of Manakamana. The summer after Durga Devi returned to Tumlingtar from Banaras, following the death of her only ally, her beloved Sasu, a flood swept away the river bank around Manakamana. The sacred Manakamana stone that lay in the shadow of a rock on the beach had been accessible to worshipers up to then. After the flood, it was buried deep in the mud and villagers could no longer reach it. Who but Durga Devi came help them?

"She did not believe in the power of Goddess Manakamana. She said, 'Only ignorant hill people pray to that spirit. That is not our religion,' she argued. 'They cut pigeons and goats to please those gods. They eat meat. We do not.'

"Nevertheless Durga Devi so pitied those peasants that when they asked for help, she couldn't refuse them. She paid to have a new shrine for Manakamana built on the hillside and the stone placed safely there. It was a solid building—you can see—brick and wood. And the guard who lives there? Durga Devi put aside money to pay him to stay at this place and care for the shrine. He is still here."

Durga bought 80 ropani, a big piece of the land, around Manakamana. This would be the site of our kuti, a place for women who leave their families and want to become sanyasi. After she purchased the land, she arranged the construction of the hall—where we gather for our bhajan.

"That was not the end of her generosity. To help protect the kuti and its residents she hired workers to build a levee fifty meters from the beach to hold back the Arun waters during monsoon months. She put aside funds to help needy women build huts for themselves and then she ordered hundreds of fruit plants imported from Madhes, and she labored side by side with bhaktini to make a garden of trees all across the hillside. Even today the women harvest

Manakamana bhaktini tend their gardens on land donated by Durga Devi.

the fruit of these trees which they can sell so they have some cash to buy clothing or utensils."

Was her attention to Manakamana and the ascetics a sign of Durga Devi's growing piety? Was she making amends with the divine after reflecting on her early misdeeds? Was she finally abandoning her political mission?

Mahili Didi laughed at my questions, assuring me Durga Devi was a fighter until her last breath.

"Ahh, you still do not understand. Durga Devi never cared about dharma. When she saw people in need, she could not ignore them. She gave food to beggars. She took pity on any poor man and woman she saw. That was her character."

Durga Devi had one more notable adventure in court—a final battle.

"After the passing of Sher Bahadur Karki and her mother she would fight for her own brother's land in Palikot, for property rightly belonging to the buhari (daughter-in-law, Durga Devi's sister-in-law). This buhari too was a widow from childhood and thus childless. Since Durga Devi had but one

Excavated sacred relic stone has become a focus of worship for visitors at Manakamana, (BK, 2019).

brother, this woman found herself the sole heir to Sher Bahadur's lands, a full half of what he and Bir Bahadur had accumulated throughout their careers. It was considerable and it did not seem right to the sons of Bir Bahadur that this lone woman should take all Sher Bahadur's property. Why should this widow without children own all that while we seven brothers and our families must share the other half? They resolved to somehow take over their uncle Sher's lands."

Mahili Didi knew all the details of this episode too. With the land deeds in her possession Buhari had been firm about not relinquishing them.

"Her cousins tried to convince her that she should let them take care of the land for her. They explained what every family tells a widow—'You cannot look after the field yourself. Stay here with us and we will take care of you.' She would not agree. When they threatened her that the land was theirs by law and they would take her to court, she still refused.

"Those men were determined. But they needed the papers. They decided to secure the documents by force and they made a plan to lay siege to her house and rob her. It would be simple, they expected.

"Knowing Durga Devi was the only one who might help in this crisis, Buhari called her sister-in-law who came straightaway to Palikot. The next day they registered Buhari's petition with the Bhojpur court to separate her fields and arrange to sell them."

"Durga Devi expected the men might try to attack them, so she stayed with Buhari in her Palikot house that night. No, they would not run away. No, no; the two women waited for the men. They had a plan to defend themselves, first by locking themselves in the house. See how my Durga would outwit those chaps.

"When the brothers found the women barring their entry, they began to push on the door to break it in. Durga Devi and her sister-in-law were ready." According to Mahili Didi, just before the men smashed the door down, Buhari tossed the roll of documents to Durga Devi who was waiting secretly in the corn bin loft above. Without the attackers knowing, Durga Devi then slipped out through a window and escaped into the night.

"Breaking down the door the intruders found Buhari alone, acting terrified but unprotesting; the men ransacked the house searching for the papers. Meanwhile Durga Devi was on her way to the police post. She walked to Bhojpur that very night, and went directly to the police and reported how burglars had broken into her sister-in-law's house and were now in pursuit of her. Next morning she filed charges against all seven men for assault, for breaking into the house and for attempted burglary. She sued her own uncle's sons.

The legal proceedings that followed took months and during that time Durga Devi remained in Palikot. "She stayed until the case was concluded. She won Buhari's right to keep all her property and dispose of her lands as she wished. Those men paid heavily."

Another fantastic story. Dharma and I listened to all these accounts in disbelief. Mahili Didi was not one to exaggerate, we knew. Eventually the court documents can be retrieved from Bhojpur court and Durga Devi's brilliance and audacity will be irrefutable.

Our final story of Durga's brave and bold character remains for us to document here. This case never reached the courts but it engaged Durga Devi in a no-holds-barred pursuit of a criminal. It concerned the rape of a child.

I can't recall how I first learned about this violated girl. Perhaps it was when we were discussing rumours about a teacher in Khandbari who had molested a student. This case was more grievous; the predator was not a high school teacher but a local policeman and he'd assaulted a child who was deaf and unable to speak.

Dharma, after listening to Mahili Didi recount this story, admitted that he had heard something about the incident years earlier. "I was young but I knew it was bad, shameful." Again Mahili Didi was able to provide details.

"We have children who are homeless, even here in the hills. Little ones—usually girls, but sometimes boys too. The child whom Durga Devi rescued was named Dom Kumari. People called her Lato because she was deaf. She came from somewhere across the Milke Danda ridge. Maybe because she was handicapped, her family felt they could not look after her and simply sent her away. Maybe she ran away and they did not care enough to look for her. We did not know.

"The girl arrived in Khandbari alone and was taken in by a sympathetic Sherpa woman who managed a drinking place there. This Sherpa fed the child too. Young Dom Kumari was so helpless and simple that no one expected she might be in danger. She lived in the Sherpa house for four years; then the woman figured out Dom Kumari had become pregnant. She'd noticed a change in the girl, how the child cried constantly, how she'd become nervous, hiding when any man entered the shop. Learning about the girl's condition and not knowing what to do, the Sherpa sent a message to Durga Devi who ordered her to bring the girl to her place at Tumlingtar.

"Oh, what a scene! Of course it was evident the child had been raped; Durga Devi was determined to find the perpetrator.

"Only Durga Devi could take on a problem like this. 'Who did this to you? Who did this?' she demanded, shaking the child, before remembering the girl was unable to hear or to speak. What could be done?

"Durga decided it was useless to go to the police or the district officer. Even the elected Pradhan Pancha would be incapable of handling this. We had no clues and our appeals for help were spurned.

"Durga Devi went to the town and called women together; even the few who agreed to meet us explained that they could do nothing. Perhaps they feared the molester was someone in their own family."

But what about Dom Kumari?

"Durga Devi admitted her plan would be painful for the girl but she decided it had to be tried. She took the child by the hand and marched her in front of every man in the town, even boys, everyone over the age of 15. Durga Devi instructed the girl to look at each man and shake her head yes or no. They did this in front of the school principal, in front of each teacher, before each government officer, each shopkeeper. Every time the child shook her head, Durga Devi pulled her away and marched on to the next fellow. The men protested; when some turned their face away Durga Devi threatened them. They had to let the little girl inspect them.

"When Durga Devi eventually went to the police station to seek out any suspect there, the town was shocked. What is she doing? they protested.

"But yes, there on the veranda of the police post, the child began to scream and cry. 'Is he the man?' asked the older woman, pointing jabbing her fist towards him. He wore glasses, one of the few people in the village wearing glasses. Dom Kumari showed no hesitation in nodding her agreement.

"Durga Devi walked from the police post directly to the government office to buttonhole chief officer Pradhan Pancha, obliging him to accompany her to the head of the Khandbari police where she forthwith filed charges against the culprit. Rape: by a policeman! This shocked everyone. You could not find a man in the street that day."

Durga Devi stayed in town that night to ensure necessary papers were expedited by early morning. Then she headed to the courthouse, only to find she had been tricked.

"A clerk from the police office arrived at the court with a note: the man in question, the suspect, has been posted out of town, it said. He left during the night, ordered to report somewhere in far West Nepal. It was urgent and he was obliged to leave before morning."

"Had she been younger Durga Devi might have rushed away in pursuit of the scoundrel. All she could do now was file a charge, knowing little would happen. Papers lay in the court, unprocessed. No one spoke about the incident while Durga was alive, not after she passed either," concludes Mahili Didi dolefully.

I inquired about Dom Kumari during my visit to town some months later, but I did not try to meet her. Among those I questioned about the episode was Dharma's mother. She nodded yes, and then, like others, she turned silent.

Durga Devi would still find a way to somehow compensate the wronged child. At least she could arrange care for and the young mother and her infant. Again Mahili Didi knew the details:

"She opened a bank account for Dom Kumari to be managed by the Sherpa woman who continued to offer a home for the violated child and her baby, a girl, when it was born a few months later. Durga Devi left them enough money for years to come. They were comfortable; the child eventually went to school."

By the time I learned this history in 1984, that baby was twelve years old. She and her mother had remained in the town although. Dom Kumari was rarely seen outside the Sherpa woman's house, the girl—she was not deaf—passed through town on her way to and from school.

Dharma, even though he would never view Durga Devi as a heroine was more willing than his mother to discuss that story. I was sorry Durga Devi never won his appreciation. Although when we learned how she managed Sasu's funeral, Dharma showed some sympathy for this sahasi from Palikot.

(By comparison Yogmaya had deeply touched Dharma and his admiration for her was unwavering. He understood the style and the mission of Yogmaya far better than I did, even though he was born long after Yogmaya passed away and he knew little about her before this sojourn at Manakamana. Captivated by that history during the weeks we spent there with the gentle bhaktini, he overcame whatever initial doubts he had about Yogmaya.)

Finally there was Sasu. The remarkable bond between Durga Devi and her mother-in-law, continued to the end of the older woman's life, literally. When Sasu was near her last breath, Mahili Didi was at Durga Devi's side and so could recount every detail of what transpired.

"When we came back from our visit to Darjeeling we learned Sasu had fallen ill. She called for her daughter-in-law and I went with my sad friend to the house at Marwa. At the frail woman's side were her sons with their wives and all of their children too. Sasu insisted her first daughter-in-law must be present. The end was near, she told them; all must accept their mother's final decision. Then she announced that Durga Devi, not her sons, must perform her saradhaya.

"This was Sasu's order." It was a supreme, final, symbolic act of solidarity between the two women.

Saradhaya is the Hindu commemorative ritual for the departed performed by the eldest son for either parent, an obligatory rite in which women customarily take no part. If no son is available, another male relative steps in.

The other women at Manakamana, some of whom were present at Sasu's saradhaya, admitted to me that they could never abandon this tradition. Here again Durga Devi would challenge a deeply held social convention. She hadn't performed the ritual for her father; yet she accepted this duty for her mother-in-law.

Any Nepali will affirm the importance men attach to this obligation. One young man recalled his experience for me. "My father left home, renouncing his worldly obligations when he went off to India to live out the remainder of his life as a sanyasi. We did not perform saradhaya as some do, since entry into sanyasi is a kind of social death. Every son considers saradhaya for his mother and father an indissoluble duty. For us it is an honour, an honour which, if we cannot discharge, we feel unfulfilled. When my father reached Banaras, his fellow sanyasi undertook his saradhaya. I was not there. As his eldest son, I am forever pained that I was denied my right."

Mata explained that when she decided to leave her family and take up residence at this hermitage as a sanyasi, she could not deny her children their wish to perform saradhaya for her. "Even when I first joined the kuti, my children would not agree to my plan to be sanyasi," she explained. "They cried. They said I could not leave; they begged me to stay with them. Only after they saw I was unwavering, they relented.

"And my saradhaya? That was the biggest problem. The older boys understood but Kancha, my youngest, wept and pleaded with me. I could not cause him such pain for the rest of his life so I allowed him to accompany me to Banaras, and there he completed his duty as my son. He is a sweet child." She adds, "I was not as strong as Durga Devi's sasu."

Yes. Sasu was indeed an extraordinary woman. Mahili Didi reported Sasu's family actually accepted her wish, knowing they must not overturn her decision.

> "When the old woman expired, all of them were beside her. But only Durga Devi washed the body of her beloved mother-in-law.
>
> "She bound Sasu's body in white cloth, then wrapped it in an orange shroud. She prepared the old woman's bier as well. The men stood back as Durga Devi lifted the lifeless body of dear Sasu on her own back, carrying her from Marwa all the way to the riverside, to the ghat there on the river's edge. The rest of the family followed—silently, obediently."

Mahili Didi returned to that day as if it were yesterday, then she continued the story.

> "I saw my friend weep. She prepared the pyre. She tended the fire while the body was consumed. Then she searched through the ashes to locate a piece of the skull. She turned back to me: 'We will go to Banaras straightaway. Prepare our things.' She paid the Brahman priest for his service. Then we left."

"How did her sons allow this?" Dharma, listening in astonishment, pressed Mahili Didi for an explanation:

> "Every son respects his mother and cannot refuse her final decision, especially at the moment when she is about to leave this world. Sasu ordered them to comply. Her sons knew how Sasu unfailingly supported and protected Durga Devi throughout her struggles. They could not deny her this final wish."

Later, when Durga Devi's time to leave the world was near, in the last hours of her life, her companions at the hermitage carried out her funeral rite. (Some of the family from Marwa were present too.) After weeks of illness and four days without food, when it was clear Durga

Devi had not long to remain in this world, the indefatigable warrior called her family to her bedside. Her three Ghimire dewar and Buhari from Palikot attended. Durga Devi's faithful companion Mahili Didi was present along with a priest to administer the sanyasi mantra.

A clerk from the land office had arrived to record her final orders regarding deposition of her properties. He wrote down Durga Devi's orders: most of her wealth was to go to Manakamana shrine and hermitage, to be administered by Buhari; the remainder would revert to her husband's house but she stipulated how it was to be used. Ten per cent of her crops were assigned for the support of Dom Kumari, ten per cent should be used to upgrade the trails around Manakamana.

The document was signed by Durga Devi, her brothers-in-law and other witnesses. Then Durga Devi dismissed everyone except Mahili Didi and some bhaktini from Manakamana kuti. They stayed to light her pyre by the Arun River when she left this world nine hours later.

So ended the remarkable career of Jethi Devi.

Postscript following my November 2019 visit to Marwa

In November 2019, after a brief trip to Yogmaya's holy places on the west shore of the Arun River, my colleagues Babita Katwal and Rajendra Thapa suggested a visit to Marwa. What a wonderful idea.

This is the village to which Durga Devi was betrothed, and where she had so many unhappy experiences and hostile relatives. Because of that association in my mind, I had had no earlier interest in visiting there. My mistake became apparent as soon as we arrived in Marwa. Unknown to me, Thapa had made initial inquiries and arranged some meetings. Very soon after our arrival, I found myself seated around a table in a quiet café talking with four Marwa villagers about their 'troublesome' relative of more than half a century ago.

The men did not speak about Durga Devi as enthusiastically as Vishnumaya Dahal had, yet they were ready to share stories and answer a few or our questions. Most revealing is news of the survival of

Arun waters swirl around the base of the magnificent boulder at Manakamana, 1980s.

The altered course of the Arun is evident in this 2019 photo of the now embellished boulder, a major feature on Manakamana beach (BK).

Durga Devi's sister, Chitra Rikka, the mother of Surendra Bahadur Ghimire, one of the men speaking with us. (I hadn't known anything about her.) She is almost 98 now, born in 1921, two years after her sister. Because the men reported that she is very frail and unable to speak, we did not try to meet her—another mistake on my part. I hope however that someone will visit her very soon and learn directly from Chitra Rikka more about the Karki family and the remarkable Ghimire Sasu. (The men we spoke to could not tell us Sasu's name but promised to find out.)

The other men seated with us were not direct descendants of Durga Devi, but grandsons of her brothers-in-law: Joya Bahadur, grandson of Gyan Bahadur, and Saligram Ghimire, grandson of Bir

Bahadur (?). They know many of the stories I report in this chapter and are unarguably an important resource for followup research.

Two points seem worth noting here. First, we have Surendra Ghimire's confirmation of Durga Devi's alliance with her beloved Sasu, and her performance of Sasu's saradhaya (as I reported above). "My mother told me about this," he affirmed with some pride.

The other issue is a correction regarding Durga Devi's confrontation with the Rana leader. These men knew about it: "That happened not in Kathmandu but in Bhojpur town on the occasion of Juddha Shumsher's visit there," Saligram explained, and then elaborated on the event. "Bhojpur was where Durga Devi's father and uncle were being held. The horse in question was her father's "Fury" (or "Fire"). She mounted it and sped from Palikot to Bhojpur where she confronted the ruler, pleading for Sher and Bir Bahadur. Apparently she succeeded in securing their release soon after."

Another elderly gentleman we met said, "Yes, of course we remember Durga Devi; we loved her." Then he added: "Everyone feared her." Why? "She hit them. She beat the police and she even beat the chief district officer when they were indolent and irresponsible."

Surendra Ghimire of Marwa remembers Durga Devi, his aunt, 2019.

Our visit was brief but enjoyable and encouraging. At least we knew this was a place where much more information could be gleaned. We learned enough to open the path for further research, which would, as I've always maintained, have to include the perusal of court documents.

If these men and others in Marwa prove as receptive in future interviews as we found them that afternoon, a reliable full biography of Durga Devi can be properly prepared and made available to any interested parties. Care should be taken to include private interviews with women in the Ghimire family.

(My thanks to Rajendra Thapa and Babita Katwal for this belated Marwa adventure.)

Notes

1   *Mahili*, second daughter.

2   Durga Devi would have been about 19 years old when she began this eight-year long court battle for her land. It would have occurred around 1940.

3   As noted in the preceding chapter, she could have attended Shadanada Guru's school in Dingla; this was discounted by Marwa residents I spoke to in 2019 who insist that this centre was for Sanskrit studies for boys.

4   Sher Bahadur and Bir Bahadur Karki reportedly met a tragic end. A police report, I was informed, indicated they'd drowned after a landslide swept them into a river. Durga Devi maintained they were murdered by men who ambushed them and stole their legal papers.

Here was death.
That ragged cart-puller
crushed on the road.
The shiny car
of a drunk city guy
in slick white suit, speeds off,
fleeing in the night...

from 'Mreetyu', by Parijat

A Child Named Laxmi—Nepal 1980

"Laxmi must work," the woman says impatiently to the child's father. "We need help in the fields. What harm can come to her there? The field is safer than the house where, remember, she has twice spilled boiling milk. She's not this much use," mother argues, poking the tip of her smallest finger with her thumbnail.

The weary woman reaches out to haul a tub of bubbling rice from the hearth. Still crouching, she pulls another heavy vessel onto the iron grill over the fire. In it is a stew for the milk cow—potato peelings, onion skins, rice husk and other bits of kitchen waste.

She rises and thrusts her hand into a basket hanging from the scorched wall beyond, pulling out a fistful of salt and splashes that into the steaming mixture. She stirs the gruel, stops and sighs deeply, wearily. Setting her plaits behind her neck with one hand, the woman bends toward the coals in the fire, her face brushing the hot pot. She pokes sticks into the ashes, then blows on their coals to reignite the fire. When small flames leap out she reaches for the ladle, and stirring the brew resumes her complaints about her oldest girl seated nearby.

"Laxmi is fourteen. This girl has been idle too long. We keep our daughters with us so they can work, to be some use before they marry. Then they are gone." Laxmi seems unmoved by her mother's grunts and moans.

From the time of this child's birth, the girl had exhausted her. Every mother needs the help of daughters, especially after she has a son to care for. A normal girl, even by the age of six, can coddle and feed a baby brother, rock him to sleep, clean him. By the time she's nine, a daughter can easily support a baby strapped onto her back, leaving her hands free to assist Aama in the kitchen, with the animals, even in the fields. Girl and baby follow mother from place to place, so when the child cries, she can hand the infant to mother who interrupts her work to suckle him for a few moments. Anywhere, night and day, a girl child is a great help.

"Thuli, see your brother, pick him up, hold him, sing to him, pat him." "Thuli, stand here so I can bind him to you." "Thuli, light the fire"; then "Thuli, rock your brother. Carry him to Grandmother. Thuli. Where are you Thuli? Bring him here."

"Thuli, the milk!" "Thuli, more fuel under the pot. Thuli, heat water."

But how can Laxmi do any of these things?

She is blind!

Somehow Aama finds a way to overcome any obstacle posed by her daughter's blindness. She straps the baby to Laxmi, then ties a rope to the girl, anchoring her to the main pillar inside the house. Thus Laxmi can keep moving, walking in a circle to comfort her young ward. "Keep him calm. Rock from side to side as you move forward; you must keep him calm."

The little girl has grown remarkably competent and can manoeuvre herself through the house and creep across the courtyard too. She taught herself to recognize every patch of the stone yard. Should she step beyond these stones, she knows she might topple onto the terrace below. The courtyard ends with a drop of three meters, father warned her; if she were carrying baby, they would both die. If that happened, he adds, Laxmi's spirit will be lost and the family will forever be visited by demons. So Laxmi ventures outside only when roped to someone or lashed to a spike fixed into the ground.

Laxmi once walked behind her mother all the way to the town and she hadn't fallen, though she stumbled occasionally. Pleased by her success, she tells her father: "Baba, I walked to the market. Baba, next time, I shall be able to fetch little brother from school." The father laughs at his girl, but Aama has no patience. "Silly girl, you are blind; who will accompany you? Silly blind girl; how can you lead your brother?"

Before schools came to the hills, by the time he reaches seven every boy is put to work. With other lads in the neighbourhood he leads one or two cows along the path to search for sprigs of grass that have been overlooked by goats or by foraging women. During the day a young lad can watch a few cows and in the evening he can help bed the animals. He might also bind whatever grass he collects in his basket. During planting and harvest time, boys work side by side with older brothers and sisters in the paddy fields. Girls too are expected to wield a scythe to collect grass, then shoulder a bari loaded with fodder. They might not go far from the house but they can guard animals fettered in the courtyard and chase birds from sheets of drying grain. Indoors, even young girls help prepare food while still holding smaller children on their hips or their backs.

After schools were introduced in the countryside, somebody had to take over whatever work boys did so that sons might join the classes. So sisters were assigned work beyond the courtyard. Girls welcomed this initially because they could flee their mothers' incessant orders and reprimands. In the fields they find new companions—other girls taking over animals' care for the same reason. They teach each other songs as they play above the riverbank while their animals graze nearby. For a few hours they escape the confines of the house; they become children.

Laxmi wishes she could be near other children, whether working or playing. She hears them passing above the house. She dreams of running along paths in pursuit of wayward goats, singing jingles with playmates as they juggle stones in the air. Oh, if only she could see.

Thulo Aama, Laxmi's grandmother lives with Aama and Baba. Thulo Aama is tender with Laxmi, but she still expects the child to work; so she trained her blind granddaughter to do simple chores. For example, after spreading corn kernals on a mat to dry she brought the child to the courtyard and set her on the edge of the straw mat with a thin bamboo pole in her hand. "Laxmi, here is the lathi to shake at the birds; this way you can help me guard the corn." Laxmi finds herself in the sun alone with only those troublesome birds as companions. She raises her switch in the air yelling "wha, wha, heee ya!" to the hens and ravens she hears fluttering nearby. Laxmi first finds this fun, but after two days of waving her rod in her darkness, she grows weary. Why has she to chase away her only companions?

The birds do not take long to learn that this solitary sentry can't see them. Losing all caution they lunge onto the blanket of seeds, unhurriedly help themselves, then fly off. Laxmi flails her rod and shouts "jau, jau", but she is too late.

"If she were deaf and not blind, she could be more useful to us," her mother grumbles. (That may have been better for the child as she wouldn't hear Aama's curses and complaints.) "She doesn't need ears to work in the field, gathering corn or cutting rice paddy. She could thresh too; she could even pound the rice."

But Laxmi is not deaf. She can hear her mother's endless remonstrations. She can also notice the sounds of passing children as they skip on the path above the house. She can hear her brothers reading their lessons and father's applauding "Shabash, shabash! Bravo, bravo!"

Eventually Laxmi's mother convinces her father that the child may be of some use in the terrace below the house, and he arranges to take her to a nearby plot. He leads the girl across the courtyard and guides her down two steep ledges to a small paddy field. He ties a rope to her, anchoring it to a peg in the ground just as he does with a cow. He puts a scythe in her hand and instructs Laxmi to cut everything around her, explaining where the field is bordered by a mud parapet. "Don't step outside here," father warns, "You'll topple over like an old cow."

Even though these terraces are not large, being blind, Laxmi needs many hours to clear the field.

One morning soon after she'd again been left alone there, Prabhu the teacher sees the girl groping across the earth. The young man knows Laxmi. (Who in the entire Arun Valley would not know a blind child?) Unnoticed, he'd watched the girl's uncle depart. Now, he steps off the path and down to the terrace where the girl sits in her tender, dark cage. "Laxmi?" he whispers, cautiously stepping towards her.

Laxmi knows this voice. Prabhu visited their house, she remembers. He is to marry Ram Bahadur's daughter. Aama mentioned his name, impressed that a teacher had stopped at her house. He's being posted to the city, to Biratnagar, so his family wants to marry him before he departs. That news allayed villagers' anxieties about their daughters attending school since there were rumours of romance between young teachers and school girls. Already villagers had suspicions about one case and took their concern to the chief officer. Their fears proved well founded but when they expressed their dissatisfaction that the court only levied a fine of five hundred rupees against the man, the official's answer was: "This is all we can do; the best solution is to take your girls out of our school."

Schools were new in villages those years and families worried for the safety of girls spending hours away from home. Girls could not proceed to high school anyway, argued parents; high schools were only in towns requiring village pupils to lodge away from their homes. Too many problems faced village girls in those circumstances so families who'd initially enrolled daughters in a local school saw no reason for them to continue.

The government was embarrassed by this exodus but building an elementary school for each cluster of villages was costly. How could His Majesty's government be expected to arrange special schools for the convenience and safety of girls?

One temporary solution was to hire only married men as teachers. This would surely avoid trouble arising around girl pupils.

Laxmi had heard her father and mother talk about these things, but she could not comprehend the actual problem; she couldn't imagine any connection between this issue and her own life. All she remembered was that Prabhu was a teacher betrothed to Karma who was the daughter of a wealthy cloth merchant. The wedding was soon, before Prabhu departed to take up his post in the city. Laxmi thought any teacher must be a trustworthy person.

Weddings are grand affairs in a village where the daily news typically dwells on debts, on accidents in the jungle, on lost goats and abnormal births. Weddings offer a change from routine. Whether or not neighbours know the boy and girl, everyone debates the match, speculates on the dowry, and evaluates the skill of go-betweens who help finalize the union. Women comment for days about how beautiful the bride is, how light her skin is, the weight of her jewellery, the texture of her hair, how industrious she is, how modestly she walks, if she is shy or weepy, talkative or sullen, bossy or demure.

Laxmi heard all this gossip. Even though no one spoke about her marrying one day, the child found herself entertained by endless talk about other girls' wedding plans. She laughed when the others laughed, and she silently agreed that Prabhu was a fine and a handsome young man.

Prabhu and Karma's marriage became more than gossip for Laxmi when before the wedding the boy and his father actually arrived at her Baba's door. "Prabhu, come. Drink." Laxmi's father insisted while also boasting of his wife's fine brew. The room soon filled with neighbours offering felicitations for the coming celebration so they could later boast how they personally knew the groom. The betrothed teacher and his father joined in as if they all were old friends. After the guests had left, some neighbours stayed on drinking and gossiping about Prabhu's good character.

Laxmi's parents felt privileged and could now report authoritatively on details of the betrothal, the negotiations, and so on. Such talk was not only entertainment; it cemented relations among families.

"Waa! Laxmi, daughter of Rajendra", the man calls softly from somewhere above her. Laxmi knows Prabhu's voice from that visit so she's unafraid when he utters her name. She does not know how long he'd watched her, how he'd glanced up and down the terraces to ensure no one saw him stop here. The child hears only a kind voice. "Laxmi", he repeats softly, suddenly very near her. "You are working too hard. Here; I have a cigarette for you," he offers as he steps down to where she is anchored.

She feels safe. "Rest and I will help you," he says, and he lifts the scythe out of her fingers and holds her hand, easing her close to him. Although weary from sitting in the mountain sun, his presence makes her feel some kind of excitement. She should like this man; after all he's a teacher.

When she reaches out to grasp the cigarette as he puts it to her lips her fingers touch his hand. She lets him hold the cigarette there. She eases herself, trusting, against the earth wall of the hillside behind her, unaware of how it hides both of them from anyone passing on the path above.

She shudders, dropping the cigarette as she feels a hand grip her skinny thigh. Fingers press hard around her flesh. Prabhu's hand yanks at her skirt and lifts its thin folds up and against her chest and face. The man's chest is over her, covering her young body.

She's confused. What does he want? Being blind, she welcomes the soft touch of another person, a hand finding hers in her darkness. But there's no tenderness here; she is unsure if this is good. This is new for Laxmi.

The man leaning hard against her is snickering. Why?" she asks herself: "Prabhu, why are you laughing?" she shyly demands.

She struggles to rise and push him away. This makes him laugh again, more quietly. Her skirt is pulled completely free of her legs. He grabs her close to him. His voice softens; "I'll take care of you. Don't you want me to take care of you? I will take you to the schoolroom and teach you to read." His laugh is very weak now. He'd liked her since the night he saw her in her father's house, he says, grabbing her more firmly.

He continues laughing quietly even as he presses harder against her and pushes her arms from his chest. He pulls her blouse above her barely formed breasts. She likes the sensation of being so close to another warm body. Yet something's not right. She's more confused as he pushes her more securely, secluding them both against the hillside. Feeling the mud on her back, she moves into him. She doesn't know that sheltered there they're invisible to anyone above or below the terrace.

The man grabs at Laxmi's thighs pulling her legs around him. He is completely covering her, pressing harder. She feels pain, but doesn't know where it actually comes from. Has she done something wrong? "Be still; be quiet," he hisses. He's smothering her with his weight, pushing himself again and again against her. Then, he abruptly stops. His body falls heavily against her. Her legs feel wet. Dizzily, she thinks, "Oh, oh, I've hurt him." She waits, afraid. He pulls away from her gasping. Finally he speaks: "Be silent. Here I will help you", and he pulls her blouse down, pinching her nipples as he steps back. Her body hurts and she begins to cry. Prabhu's voice turns soft and he pats her skirt and strokes her small feet. He becomes gentle. "I'll come again. I'll teach you many things, but only if you tell no one how I'm helping you."

"He is a teacher, an educated man; he will visit me and finally I'll learn to read." Despite the pain between her thighs and the unpleasant memory of his weight on her, she doesn't feel angry.

Weeks passed. Prabhu never returned. Laxmi feels sad and confused but what can she say; whom can she ask? After silently waiting and hoping the nice teacher could find her, she decides he may be waiting in the terrace and she tells her father she wants to resume her work in the fields. "The paddy is harvested!" Aama snaps. "Did you think we can wait for you to clear the field? What a silly girl!"

The summer ended and two months passed when Laxmi did not have her menses. She did not know the meaning of this and pushed it far from her mind.

One day she hears Prabhu's name. "Perhaps he's coming back," she wonders. But no, the family is reporting his forthcoming wedding and they will go with neighbours to town to watch the arrival of the groom. However modest or grand any wedding is a spectacle for children and an occasion for people to gather and drink. Everyone reports how beautiful the bride looks. Karma is the prettiest of Ram Bahadur's three daughters, they agree.

Ram Bahadur had insisted his daughters would not marry a simple village boy. Prabhu's family had paid 1,500 rupees—a reasonable sum—to Bahadur, and supplied food and liquor for all the wedding guests. It was not chicken curry—only the wealthiest merchants in Khandbari could offer meat at a wedding feast—but Prabhu's family made sure there was plenty of food: plates of flattened rice, dishes of curried potatoes and chutney for everyone, with ample leftovers for curious children who came to watch. Government officers, shopkeepers, high school boarders, policemen with their wives and children joined school teachers at their assigned seats in the front row.

Because the groom would arrive after the banquet ended and night had fallen some guests lingered in the square to await him. A groom's appearance, a hero marching in to take his prize, is a climax of the event. Perhaps today's parade of a groom strutting into a village on a white horse is a symbolic re-enactment of past practices where a young bride is taken forcefully, or carried away by the winner of a contest.

Any appearance of a horse in hill towns attracts attention and creates excitement. Horses are not common even in rural areas, neither for ploughing nor for transport. They have a ceremonial purpose only—to convey a visiting official from the airstrip, for example, or to carry a groom to his bride's house.

So here was Prabhu arriving to fetch his new wife. Accompanying him were cousins and neighbors from his town. Attendants walk on either side of the horse holding the reigns and the saddle. The all-male party is led by boys banging drums and tin pots and playing flutes. The lads prance back and forth in front of Ram Bahadur's shop on the town's main street.

Karma, the bride, is secluded in a room at the back of the shop surrounded by sisters and friends. Outfitted in layers of red decorated with golden threads, garlanded with flowers and jewellery, she waits among the whispering women and giggling girls. Her head is wrapped in a scarf so her face is barely visible. She seems at ease, although she acts diffident and bashful, as a girl must on this occasion.

When Karma's mother hears the girls snickering, she scolds her daughter playfully. "What is this? Why do you smile, girl? You must weep. You are going to leave us and live with strangers far from home. Shameful girl. What kind of daughter will they think I have? Weep; weep."

In the street beyond, the drumming intensifies. Boys surge towards the edge of the square. From the dark path below, shouts and clanging rise into the clear night. Onlookers see the light of a lamp, swaying from its pole. Prabhu's entourage makes its way slowly up the hillside. The petromax lamp hisses in the night air. The white horse, hardy a noble-looking steed, is prodded forward and finally comes into view. "The groom; the groom is arriving!" Cries erupt from a crowd of mainly boys and men in the square. Boys clap and dance in front of the horse. More cheers rise from children as they prance around the mounted hero. All eyes are on the bridegroom.

Even though the horse is so docile, Prabhu seems to sit on it tentatively. It must take some effort to appear dignified in his oversize suit, mounted on a horse for the very first time.

A canopy with gold and red trimmings is raised above him and his mount, held upright by poles gripped by his aides. Prabhu shifts nervously in the saddle waiting for his helpers to direct the horse forward. Men shout, "The groom. Clear the way for the groom!" Children join in, chanting: "Clear the way! The groom, the groom!"

Horse, rider and his attendants proceed slowly down the street amidst clanging and shouting. Finally reaching Bahadur's shop Prabhu is lifted off the horse. He quickly disappears into the dwelling, and the petromax lamp is extinguished.

The horse and the crowd are left in darkness. Boys disperse to their homes to tell their parents about the arrival of Prabhu the conqueror. The square falls silent.

Next day, almost unnoticed, bride and groom walk out of town and down the mountainside to Prabhu's family's house. Karma's sisters and their mother weep openly watching them depart. Neighbours report that Karma smiled as she walked beside her new husband, accompanied by her two brothers carrying the dowry of utensils, bedding, suits of clothes and a carpet. (It's more than Bahadur's other daughters would see at their weddings.)

On the third day, according to custom, Karma returns to visit her parents at the maitighar. Returning here even for a short visit is usually a happy day for a girl. But this young woman's smile is gone. Since the shameful news has now reached every household, no one is surprised by her sulking appearance and her father's grim face. The disturbing news was not allowed to disrupt Prabhu and Karma's union but now the rumor is confirmed. Yes, this teacher is the father of a baby carried by another girl. Still more shameful: the mother-to-be is Laxmi.

A village has no secrets; neither has a hill town. Details spread from house to house about how, just days before the wedding, Laxmi's mother had became suspicious about her blind child's condition. Thulo Aama took Laxmi to a woman who did something that frightened her causing the girl to yell "Prabhu! Where is Prabhu?" When they calmed her, she told them about his visiting her in the field.

Laxmi's father reportedly went straightaway to the boy's house and confronted Bahadur. With the marriage two days away and all plans for the wedding finalized, Prabhu's father shouted denials and ordered the accuser out. Laxmi's father waited; then in the presence of Karma following her wedding, he dragged his hapless little girl along with him to confront the family.

Poor Laxmi. She wept and cowed but her father gripped her firmly, shouting "Stop stupid child! I have my right". Karma began to scream, pulling her hair and turning in circles as if she had gone mad. Prabhu was sent for and after feeble denials, broke down and admitted his guilt; then he fled his father-in-law's house. The older men fell silent, surveying the disaster.

Not long after, the senior men of the town gathered to address the calamity. They summoned Prabhu's father and Laxmi's father to their council. All were distressed and angry with Prabhu, publicly condemning his actions and declaring they must move swiftly to resolve the matter. No one would be happy with the final agreement but the council was gratified they could reach a unanimous decision. The self-appointed commission prevailed on Laxmi's father to accept the fine they levied against Bahadur. Next day the two men met in public to drink together and to laugh once more as friends.

Karma stayed with her mother for some days, weeping ceaselessly. Then she left for Bahadur's house; from there she would eventually join her husband in Biratnagar where nothing of his past crimes would be known.

The town's residents shared opinions about the episode for many months. The men seemed more involved than their wives about how this had happened, who was to blame and what more could have been done. Several men who'd help resolve the problem were town notables who'd been involved in the original betrothal, and then the wedding ceremony. They had to redeem their self-respect. Madev, the go-between for the union had to protect his reputation as a match-maker. Attendants who led Prabhu on the horse and celebrated his manhood in the public square would defend him, asserting the emotional needs of an educated man. They discussed the custom of child betrothals for girls. Perhaps they should wed daughters at eight or nine, as their fathers had. They argued the monetary settlement between the fathers: how much was fair? What terms should be attached to the fine? Some even argued that Laxmi's family should have said nothing and instead found a way to quietly end the child's pregnancy. A few men argued that Prabhu was a coward for breaking down and admitting his crime.

What happened to Laxmi and her baby, no one was sure.

It happened on a mountain bridge:
A cradle on her back, crossing to barter beans for salt.
Unsteady from hunger, she stumbles.
Ahh! The cradle slips.
The baby topples, crying ahhh—
into Kali's greedy waves.
That was death.

From "Mreetyu"
by Parijat

The vicinity around Majhuwabesi (Yogmaya Shakti) on the shore of
the Arun River, north of Katike Bridge.
Longitude 27.393 N; latitude 87.142 E. Courtesy Google Maps

Yogmaya
poet, teacher, insurgent

<table>
<tr><td>

तेरा काखको मै नानी,
मेरा काखको तै नानी ।
दोस्रो त अर्को होइनन्,
तेरै आँखा भित्र देख् पानी ॥

</td><td>

I am the child in your lap.
You are the babe in mine;
There is nothing between us, nothing at all.
Your eyes have tears, just like my own.[1]

</td></tr>
</table>

"Yogmaya had a two-pronged agenda, not only one," explained ManaMaya after she quoted these lines. Proud to be able to offer us details and comments on the history we were gathering, this member of the kuti became one of our most forthright helpers. ManaMaya spoke as a clearly unrepentant acolyte of the Bhojpur Yogi.

"Hazur's first target was our Brahmanic system propagated by priests assigning privileges to some and overseeing the lives of Hindu citizens to keep them bound and compliant. Among the most restricted lives are those of our Brahmin women, women of all castes.

"Yogmaya's second object was our ruler, the Prime Minister.[2] With his generals he ignored corruption and sanctioned widespread inequality. Our master Shakti Yogmaya showed us how these two evils are intertwined. She feared neither priests nor the ruler." With this summary, ManaMaya, who had memorized many *bani* and could recite them, one after another for more than an hour, uttered one of Yogmaya's compelling verses.

ब्राह्मण् भई सर्व चिज्को विक्रि गरेको,
मालिक् भई दु:खिहरूको वृत्ति हरेको ।
अहिले गर्छौ भलादमिहो आफ्नो खुशइले,
भित्रृ जरा हालि सक्यो लोभि घुसुइले ॥

Nowadays Brahmins, live as you wish,
Like lords, you plunder the poor.
How corrupted, you sell your trust.
How deep, the roots of your greed.

In these two quatrains lie the essential teachings of a woman who launched a brilliant and a daring political campaign from her base in the hills of East Nepal. This took place during the first part of the 20th century and ended in 1940 with her martyrdom, along with sixty-eight of her followers who one by one followed her into the thundering current of the Arun River. After leading a campaign for reform and justice, Yogmaya finally confronted the ruler with an ultimatum: "If you do not grant us justice, we will die," she declared.

Juddha Shumsher responded to the rebel's initial threat by sending his army to round up the protesters.

The tragedy that resulted—the sacrifice of the leader and her many followers—remains a stain on the government, even to this day. Nepali authorities covered up the episode and banned all mention of the leader. Her campaign was thoroughly expunged from the nation's historical record and almost lost to the nation's political consciousness. However, the powerful verses composed by Yogmaya—*hazurbani*—survived. And they embody the story.

I am the child in your lap/ You are the babe in mine.

On the surface these lines may appear politically innocent.

They are not. They denote the very principle of equality and the anti-Brahmanic message central to Yogmaya's teachings. They call for parity and mutual respect. Embraced within the metaphor of a child protected by equal partners, Yogmaya's words appeal to the humble, common origins of each of us.

There is nothing between us, nothing at all.

In a society in which people are strictly and irrevocably distinguished at birth according to the caste membership of their parents, this invocation is heresy to those demanding caste observance.

Her ideal of intermingling would be possible only if caste differences are abandoned. Yogmaya called for her people to engage in unfettered reciprocity, through nurturing, through marriage, and through other social exchange.

Your eyes have tears just like mine.

Her words are a tender reminder of the universality of compassion. "We have common needs, joys and suffering," she declares. Perhaps those tears Yogmaya speaks of are the laments of men and women bound against their will by society's caste rules. Those laws destine some to be a lower, second class, also poorer and thereby subject to more deprivations.

Caste is a system of defining the social world of humans in terms of a hierarchical spiritual scheme, with the high-born Brahmin representing the head of Lord Brahma while everyone else (not born Brahmin) is ranked below. Considered to be "pure" by virtue of their caste status, Brahmins are segregated by social rules which especially bear on the lives of Brahmin women. These women may only marry Brahmin men and they cannot remarry, even if the boy they are betrothed to dies before they take up residence together. Caste rules were laid out in the Hindu scriptures long ago. The system continues into modern times and defies all attempts to end it. In India it seems as firmly entrenched as ever. During the past century in Nepal, caste practices have spread with the growing influence of Brahmin priests. They have penetrated almost every corner of the country, converting Buddhist and shamanic believers and incorporating them into the caste hierarchy. Newar and many Gurung, Tamang, Magar and other tribal groups have adopted the Hindu system of segregation. Since caste ideology bestows privileges and moral authority on those deemed higher in the social hierarchy, people accept the ideology hoping to win a high status and the privileges that go with it. Most converts find themselves in the lower ranks. Their efforts to challenge the system are opposed by the priests and the government. Yogmaya not only rejected her caste status. She attacked the priests.

अठार पुराण नौ व्याकर्ण,	*Eighteen puranas, nine vyakarnas;*
यही सचेत जिव्को सबै चाकर	*He who knows these is well served.*
ब्राम्हणको छोरो बेद् पढ्छ,	*Sons of Brahmins, go read your vedas.*
म थाड़्ने लाई भेद गर्छ ॥	*For us ragged ones, they're of no benefit.*

Yogmaya accused priests of hypocrisy. Their teachings, she said, served only to gain privileges for themselves. The power of Brahmin religious authorities was intertwined with the ruler's, so Yogmaya's attacks extended to the reigning Prime Minister (referred by his subjects as Teen Sarkar) equally boldly as her assaults on the clergy.

धन्य हो राजा तिन् सकरि,	*Teen Sarkar, you are so great;*
सलामि दिन्छू बारम्बार ।	*Again and again I praise you.*
माकुरो कपास्को कमाइ नलाग्ने,	*Like a spider who neither ploughs nor sows,*
धागै धागाको र उहि घर भर्ने ॥	*Yet swells, growing rich, and richer still.*

She called for the end of the traditional alliance between religion and state. Religious practices cannot absolve the corrupt, she asserted. She wouldn't allow religious protocol to shield anyone from her attacks.

हरिका तिर्थ हुन् महिमा गर्नलाई,	*Visiting tirtha to cleanse their sins,*
जान लागे सब वाहि मर्नलाई ॥	*Tyrants and cheaters rush there to die.*
अघि त निर्धाको सम्पती हरे,	*Plundering the poor and stealing their food,*
क्षत्रमा बसेर खर्च त्यै गरे ॥	*With that loot, paying their fare.*

Yogmaya warned those seeking redemption through religious rites to beware. Theoretically speaking, should a worshiper die during pilgrimage they are assured a more favourable rebirth. Thus, as a rich person approaches old age, he or she attempts to improve their chances of high rebirth with abundant ritual observance, including visiting tirtha—holy places. "You can't win redemption by paying with what you've stolen from others," said Yogmaya. "Instead of winning rewards in the next life, you'll be punished for your crimes."

The four verses cited above summarize the Yogi's basic message. They are formidable for the era in which she taught them, and daring in today's political climate too.

In 1980–81 when I first heard these verses, they were recited without textual reference by women like Bhattini Aama and ManaMaya. Although I could sense the political implications from the women's delivery, I needed time to grasp the full implications of such creations. I was after all illiterate in Nepali language and unaware of their simple but metaphorical message, being also ignorant of the political history of the region. I was a mere transient, intending to stop only for a night at the hermitage in Manakamana which initially appeared to be a sleepy retreat inhabited by feeble women who had come here to escape their personal problems or the ailments of their society and government, and pray together.

हेर्न केटा तमसुक्मा येति बडेको
अनतरयामि पभु देख्छन् धर्म छोडेको ।
लोभर अन्यायका अक्षर लेखौ,
आफु सत्य भगवान्ले रछ, देखेको ॥

Any child knows an inflated bond.
So our Lord is witness to fraud.
Some play blind to greed and injustice
But never, our Lord.

Enchanted, then smitten, then compelled to pursue what lay behind verses I heard that first night, I stayed on, and then returned year after year to work with those women. ManaMaya would be assigned as my teacher by Damodara Giri—Mata, head of this hermitage. She welcomed Jangbu and me straightaway after we walked out of the hot afternoon sun into the shade of the prayer hall. We bathed in the icy river, then ate, and rested. That night, my companion slept in the nearby shelter where male visitors are bedded.

I was taken to the hut of one of the sanyasi (Bhattini Aama). Before I slept, I heard her singing the verses. I was stirred by their force. These were not the normal praises to the divine—neither Hindu nor Buddhist that I had heard when I worked with Tibetan nuns and monks or when I visited Hindu ashrams in the course of my travels through India and Nepal. They were unlike the cheery folk songs all Nepali enjoy.

These verses possessed elegance; their rhythm was completely unfamiliar to me. My host seated in the dark next to me uttered the words with such energy; they lifted her out of her humble asceticism and erased her frail 80 year-old body. Sensing that her song embodied a vital message, I sat up and gazed directly into her face across the hearth from me, imbibing a testimonial which was still mysterious at this point.

For a long time I could not sleep; the rhythm and some insistent quality propelled through the songs engulfed me, and I was aroused forever by them. Outside the jungle air throbbed with the calls of night insects and the Arun River flowed with a rumbling chalung, chalung.

धिरेधिरे यो कलिका स्वभाव टानेछन्,
माहा राज्का पल्टन् सबै सपेत पार्ने छन् ।
जान्न त म जान्ने हुइन यति भने लौ,
अहिले हत्पत् गर्नु छैन पछि बुझ्ने छौ ॥

An evil man's rule cannot last.
His army is certain to crumble.
Powerless though I am, I'll say
Your reign will end.

Early next morning I went directly to Mata and asked: "What are those songs I heard in the night?"

She replied quietly, "These are the teachings of our guru." She leaned her head back against the trestle fence. "Hazur[3] is our leader," she sighed.

This was the morning after my arrival and I knew nothing about Mata, the women with her and these verses. But in that first brief conversation, I felt she was unburdening herself of a long held secret.

The head of the kuti had already decided that my arrival here was by divine provenance. My attraction to and curiosity in *hazurbani* now convinced her of this, and she received me as if it were her duty to help me. In the coming days, and on my subsequent visits, she saw to it that I had every assistance from her companions at the hermitage, women who proved to be the most reliable source on Yogmaya. I would find they were also the only people willing to risk teaching me.

Mata, like other inhabitants of Manakamana kuti, spoke about Yogmaya as if she were still among them. I saw no outward sign of Hazur Yogmaya, no photograph on the wall below an image of Lord Vishnu or next to a colour poster of the monarch or the portrait of a local notable. There was no distinguished dwelling, no sign of a monument. "Where is your guru now?" I asked.

"Hazur went to heaven. In the year Vikram Samvat 1997."[4] I said nothing, and Mata added: "The gates of heaven opened for her."

This guru was not a man but a woman they called Shakti Yogmaya. Being a revered yogi and poet still did not explain the aura of mystery that surrounded this woman. "And the *hazurbani*?" I asked.

"These words are the teachings of our master." Mata did not refer to them as prayers. Before you came, no visitor asked about *hazurbani*," she said with a warm smile. "We are glad you are here; we will help you." Then she asked a puzzling question: "Are you not afraid?"

यसै लोभले गर्दा अन्याय परेको,
मालिकहरूले आशा राखेनौ भरेको ॥
प्रभु देख्न लागें त्यो निर्धो मरेको,
मालिकहरू हो यो के काम गरेको ॥

All this greed makes more injustice.
Oh Master, you promised us hope.
God, we watch the helpless die.
Oh Master, what is it you do?

Mata's head was shaven and only a thin covering of her white hair was visible at the edge of the orange cap she wore. She was clad in a light cloth sari, the dress of a Hindu ascetic,[5] a sanyasi. Mata was 68 at the time. A few years before, she had taken complete vows of asceticism and she lived at the shrine tending a small garden patch beside her hut. Her family lived elsewhere and she kept in touch with her sons through letters. She ate only once a day, and never touched meat, milk or eggs. She managed the hermitage but still spent most of her hours alone in prayer. Occasionally her sons and grandchildren visited her, she told me. Fellow ascetics, local farmers who came to make offerings at the shrine of Manakamana god or to Lord Arun, and other visitors to the

Mata Damodara Giri, 1982, who facilitated the author's research at Manakamana.

hermitage all showed great respect for Mata. Despite this status, and even though she was gentle and generous, Mata seemed to me to lack real calmness and inner peace. (Later I concluded she regretted she had not accompanied her master through the gates of heaven more than 40 years before. Becoming a sanyasi did not seem to reconcile that decision). Now, with my arrival, was she seeking to somehow redeem herself by trusting me with a long-held secret?

Mata did not undertake to teach me herself. But she knew precisely who among the others living here would be most helpful for my research. "Come," she said, standing and extending her hand to me. "You will meet ManaMaya and Bhattini Aama. They will teach you about Hazur."

ManaMaya was a treasure: she had an energetic voice and was known for her ability to recite *hazurbani* uninterrupted for many hours. She sang verses for me during those first days; with Jangbu's help, I recorded many of them on my cassette recorder. Without careful translations and a political appreciation of Nepali history, I was unaware of their

ManaMaya, devotee of Yogmaya spoke freely
about her departed Guru Aama, 1982.

full meaning at that stage. Nevertheless, I was convinced these verses were very precious. I noted how, when either ManaMaya or Bhattini Aama sang them for me, they did so in the privacy of their small dwellings, and at night. Why did they not sing these beautiful words in public?

The night before I was to depart after my second visit, Mata called me to her hut, and as if to seal our bond, she handed me a gift. From under her sleeping mat, she lifted a small bundle bound in cloth. Reverentially she slowly removed the wrapping to reveal a sepia brown booklet. Lifting it from its protective wrap, cradling it in her palms, she extended it to me: "Take this, along with the recordings you have made."

I turned the book in my hands. It was a printed text, not a manuscript; still it felt precious. Mata said, "In here you will find Hazur's teachings." I leafed through the book; it began with a few pages of prose, then sixty pages of verse, all quatrains, each numbered. All were in Nepali language. On the back cover was stamped the name of the press. It was not published in Nepal but in Kalimpong, northeast India.

Those few days and a handful of verses began a long inquiry, where, verse by verse, episode by episode, I began to piece together an ephemeral, fragmented history. I learned it only slowly and haltingly.

At the beginning, these women spoke mainly about Yogmaya's spiritual powers. In the first verses I examined, its author appeared to extol a state of bliss. Her followers referred to her "fearlessness of nature" and they praised her "meditations in the icy river."

"Hazur accepted no authority but that of the divine," they explained. "She worked for Dharma Raj," they told me. Dharma Raj? Dharma: religion; raj: ruler. Was this rule by religion? Was she advocating a theocracy—government by priests? If so, how could she be anti-Brahmanic?

ManaMaya, who was a frequent resident at the shrine, became my chief guide. She did this primarily by reciting *hazurbani* for me, because, she said, these embodied the teachings of Yogmaya.

<table>
<tr><td>

यक् वर्ष दिन्का दुई भाग् लगाई,
गर्ने विधि आफ्नु रितू जनाई ।
गर्मि भए मा पनि अग्नि तापनु,
ठण्डि भए मा जल भित्र पस्नू ।

</td><td>

Parting the year in two,
Accordingly I perform my rites.
In summer, favour a scorching fire;
In winter, delight an icy river.

</td></tr>
</table>

Praise of nature. Also love of land, or homeland.

<table>
<tr><td>

पर्वत् माहाँ मुख्य भनेर, भन्छन्,
हिमालययै देखि नदी बहन्छिन् ।
नाउँ अरूण् हो सँगमा बरूण छन्
इन्दा वती फेरि च्याहि मिसिन्छिन् ॥

</td><td>

Supreme among peaks, this our Himalaya
From where waters flow, Arun merges
And with Barun, flows on
To mingle with Irkhuwa.

</td></tr>
</table>

Here begin clues to her vision of equality. ManaMaya explained how Yogmaya, though her long meditations in caves and on the banks of the great Arun, overcame extreme physical conditions but social distinctions too.

From my earlier studies of Tibetan and Indian ascetics, Milarepa and Pha Dampa Sangyas, I'd learned about women and men who renounced social life with its burdens of attachments—material and emotional ties that entangle us all—and escaped to mountain caves, removing themselves from temptations and obligations. They invented techniques to achieve and test their detachment. Yogmaya's verses, by contrast, seemed to be about creating attachments. She invoked images of her jungle surroundings. But viewed from the perspective of an ideal of equality, the verses become transformed. *"As the rivers Arun and Barun mingle,"* Yogmaya declares. Surely she is saying that people must merge into a society of equals. We can grasp her political goal here:-- to move towards equality.

She and her followers needed supreme confidence to face the power structure they would challenge in pursuit of this dream. Public rebuke, threats by priests, and arrest by government troops would inexorably follow.

लोभले गर्दा धर्मको नष्ट पारी,
नियाँ त्यसको थियो लियो घुस हकारी ॥
दोहोरो त्यो दण्ड त्यसैमा लगायो,
थियो जित्ने मुद्दा त्यो मुद्दा हरायो ॥

Virtue, stained by greed.
Justice, undone by bribes.
'Though innocent, we lost.
Thus, we're twice punished.

Eventually, Yogmaya's teachings became a comprehensive utopian ideal, linked with a non-violent political strategy she devised to bring it about. It began four decades before the United Nations sponsored an international convention on women, long before the current generation of American and European feminists was born, and even before Mahatma Gandhi's non-violent 'Quit India' movement, a campaign to rid India of British occupation, was underway. But Yogmaya's movement went further because it included a call to end injustices against women and girls.

ManaMaya was a superb choice as my teacher, and Mata, who had instructed her to assist me, was gratified with our progress. On my second visit and during my stays between 1983 and 1986, ManaMaya was there to take me step by step back into history. This time Jangbu was not with me, but I was lucky to have another assistant, Dharma Shrestha from Khandbari town. He came to stay with us in the hermitage and worked as my interpreter on each of my successive visits there. He himself unexpectedly became attracted to Yogmaya and asked the women to teach him *hazurbani* too. In turn, they treated him like a grandson. I respected how this contemporary young man who was not a Brahmin but Newar Hindu was completely at home with the lady hermits. Dharma was a faithful translator, but I think his overriding value to our project came from his growing love of Yogmaya as day by day we learned more about her campaign.

During daytime hours we worked with ManaMaya gathering the disparate fragments of this mysterious, brilliant woman. At night I retired to Bhattini Aama's room, and after the flames of the hearth faded to a glow, still reclining under her cotton cover, in the dark, she resumed reciting the beloved *hazurbani*. We would rekindle the fire, and I would watch her face glow, transformed as her voice rose into the pulsing atmosphere of the star-filled Arun night. Her eyes were moist and her body was lithe. Watching her I easily imagined this 82–year-old woman as a young militant fifty years earlier, energetic and inspired by the remarkable guru whose verses she jubilantly now invoked.

घेटिया काम् नभै दोलथ् जम्दैन,	*Wealth cannot multiply without fraud.*
होइन भन्नता कोहि पाउदैन ।	*No one says this isn't so.*
सम्पति हुनेको तिर्थमा छ फिल्	*The rich make pilgrimage to garner benefits*
दुखिले गर्दछौ आत्मा चिन्ने बल् ॥	*While we poor go in search of our souls.*

Bhattini Aama stirred the air with her hands, her fingers flicking, her voice escalating. She had been one of hundreds of couples who took their brothers and young children and travelled upriver to sit near their master. There, they were able to name the villains, and to declare their equality with others.

बिन्ति गर्दछु, सकरि मान्नु होस्,	*When greed and malice fade,*
अब ता धर्मको स्थिति बान्नु होस् ।	*The earth will tremble, the corrupt will fall.*
लोभि लुब्ध चाल् सकल ट्ट्नेछ,	*Teen Sarkar, hear my verse.*
उल्का लोकमा ज्यादा उड्ने छ ।	*It's time for justice.*

While Bhattini Aama recited Yogmaya's verses in private, I continued to rely on ManaMaya to explain the rationale of Yogmaya's teachings and her ambitious campaign. ManaMaya was a feisty and frank woman without restraint when speaking about the past or the present. She had not yet taken her sanyasi vows and so did not shave her head, eschew her jewellery or don the simple peach coloured, cotton robe that sanyasi wear. But because she planned to renounce her family attachment Mata gave her permission to build a hut at the hermitage and live there intermittently.

"What can I do? I must go home to hoe and plant my fields," ManaMaya explains. It was not easy. A year earlier, she tells me, forty years after they had wed, her husband decided to take a second wife. "Why? Because I had birthed only girl children. When he brought his new wife home, I'd reached almost sixty. I did not agree; I refused to be silent. I insulted him; I told all the family how he disrespected me; in public, I cursed him.

"I must divorce him and take my land. I cannot live in my own house with his new woman. He expects me to help her. Phuh. My children cry, my grown daughters and their husbands are ashamed of their father. Yet what chance do I have in these courts where the Brahmin priests tell our judges how to rule. Phuh. Where shall I go? Shall I become a servant cook? No. So I am here, with the permission and kindness of our Mata. I spend winter here. In summer I must go home to tend the paddy and harvest the rice. If I stay here all year, I cannot trust anyone to collect my share of the grain and carry it to me here in Manakamana. If I can harvest it myself, I will take the real share due me. I have enough surplus to sell, and I can deposit my earnings in a bank."

Unless she obtains a divorce—and that would be difficult—ManaMaya has no control over her family's fields. She cannot dispose of even a square meter of it. If she remains in the farmhouse, she may use the produce of the fields, but she must also cultivate them for others' use. Most women do not challenge ill treatment from their husband or his family. If abused, they tend to submit, fearing they will be turned out and find themselves completely homeless and penniless. Because of this fear most women tolerate the indignity of receiving their husband's second wife.

ManaMaya had loving daughters, but staying with them was not an option for her. Each girl lives in a distant village with her husband and her mother-in-law. "My girls come to see me at Manakamana. Sahili here is my favourite daughter."

Sahili, seated with us, wears a flowered print skirt; like her mother, she decorates her hair with a blossom plucked each morning from the jungle. She has brought her little girl with her. "This is my first grandchild. How sweet", says the grandmother pulling the child closer. "Yet even now, Sahili worries that if she bears no son, her marriage might end as her mother's did."

ManaMaya was not a woman to grumble; she talked little about herself. Around me, she wanted always to speak about her guru. She became animated—like Bhattini Aama did—and was happy to allow *bani* to elevate her to another realm and time, and she led me there with her.

How eagerly she spoke about her experiences with Yogmaya. "Even though I was newly married I was still determined to go to hear Shakti Yogmaya. Each time we travelled upriver to Majhuwabesi more boys and girls from our villages joined us. My husband would not come; never mind, I took my sister with me. Bhattini Aama was joined by her husband and her daughter. Mata's husband was another who refused to accompany us. He even tried to stop his wife. Do you know: Mata went despite his objections; her brother and his wife and their children too. Shanti Nanda joined us as well. See how feeble Shanti Nanda is today; she has more than four score years.

"Those days, she was young, strong-minded like the rest of us."

ManaMaya remembered her companions as if they were together on this adventure just a few years before.

"Bharat Dhoj with his new wife escorted his uncle and aunt. All went together to be with Hazur."

ManaMaya spoke of those gatherings at Majhuwabesi as if they were political rallies. Which in fact, they were. These men and women were Nepal's 1930s equivalent of contemporary European, Asian or American protesters enthusiastically gathering for a teach-in. This grandmother talks about those assemblies similarly to how elderly Americans who took part in anti-Vietnam war rallies recall that era and the Black civil rights movement which preceded it.

Again, ManaMaya's voice fills with pride: "We were discovering truth. We convinced our friends and cousins to join us, certain that Yogmaya's words would change them too. As our numbers grew we became more fearless, not holding back even when our master began to direct her demands to the ruler himself."

Doubtless the young rebels were emboldened by their growing numbers and the addition into their ranks of men and women from well-known families. As ManaMaya explained: "After some of our people heard Yogmaya teach at Pashupatinath in Kathmandu they left their own houses (this was around 1935) to follow her to Majhuwabesi and they joined us. Often we remained at Majhuwabesi through the night, singing with our master."

छापा यिनका जाहाँ लाग्यो ताहाँ लाग्यो चीनु,	*Your seal is sovereign; clear any path.*
हुकुम भइ गो त्यसलाई रस्ता खुला गराइ दिनु ।	*Your order is supreme; name any wish.*
मस्तक्बाट निस्केको जिव् प्रप्ति हुन्छ, वाहि,	*Unopposed, you decide, you rule.*
छैन त्यसको देह रहँदैन कही ॥	*Now you command, decree. But not forever.*

Dharma asks: "What drew you to Shakti Yogmaya when you were so young?"

ManaMaya replies unhesitantly. "I was fifteen, newly married—an arranged marriage like everybody. So many women are forced into these unions. Old men take young girls. Why? Because a man must have a Brahmin virgin. Oh, how we endured those unhappy ways; '*Ke garna sakchha?*—what can one do? It is our life:' we consoled each other. Who dared shout this is unjust. Then see; we destine our daughters to the same fate, marrying them when they're still children. If a boy dies, he leaves his widow a mere child. What should be done

ManaMaya, the most learned woman in yogbani, proudly recorded them for the author.

with her, poor thing? We let the priests answer, and they say she must not marry again; it's forbidden, they insist. Imagine; even though they had not lain together and she remains a virgin, to join with another man would bring disgrace on the family, on the whole caste. If a man of lower caste touches her, this is a disgrace too. So we keep her home or send her to India to work as a cook, because some think only a 'pure' Brahmin may prepare their food. Serving as a cook is all she can do; that's what they say.

"Some of our girl children kill themselves because they cannot bear the loneliness, the abuse they find in an unkind home, the ordeal of serving others all their life. Even today, we know women who step into the waters of the Arun to join Hazur. Do you know?

"The basic problem lies with the priests. We allow priests to dictate who is right and who is wrong, who is pure and who is not, who is strong and who is weak. They work with the ruler to make laws; then they use those laws for their own gain. Whoever ruled, this was the way. So Master Hazur's aim was not to oust a boss man. We know that another guy, maybe worse, would replace him. She showed us injustice was not a mere man who ordered the army to imprison us. Yogmaya's object was to throw out the political system and Brahmanic laws and the priests. The whole system had to be undone. That's what she taught us."

Through her verses, Yogmaya was able to imbue her followers with extraordinary courage. Some even dared to abandon their caste. ManaMaya told me how the Yogi applauded a widow who defied caste law and remarried. She said, "Let Brahmin and Limbu unite. Let the babe in your lap be mine."

"Shakti Hazur did not give speeches. We did not have to be taught. We felt her guidance through *hazurbani*. All Yogmaya's teachings are in *hazurbani*."

Those teachings and the assemblies around the Yogi at Majhuwabesi between 1930 and 1940 mark the later stages of Yogmaya's work.[6] Before she became recognized as a savant, she endured years of difficulties, starting with her banishment from her village, Nepaledanda. In the early part of the 20th century, when still a girl, she had to run away because of her liaison with a man. She went to India. She returned home only after she was more than thirty years old. Afterwards, she wandered alone through the jungle in the hills above the Arun River and she passed long periods of isolation in caves.

Her campaign may be compared with other political protests. But Yogmaya's strategy was unique, although it clearly belongs to Asia in its religious idiom. "She was deep in meditation night and day," said ManaMaya. "We (her followers) sat nearby, above the bank of the river, and waited for her to emerge from her meditation, because that was when she uttered her *hazurbani*. Sanu Hazur ("little master," Yogmaya's daughter Nainakala) was at her mother's side and it was she who wrote out Hazur's utterances, line by line.

"We did not have to be taught. We heard her words, and the spirit arose from within us."

Visualization by artist N. Wohlstadter, Laitpur mural, (NS, 2013).

दौल थिया हुनु भयो त्यहि निर्धा बाटै,	*How riches grow by trickery.*
आसामिले कर्जा तिन्यो तमसुकट ठाडै ।	*You say the debt still stands!*
तोरो थियो बालख बाबु मरेछ,	*I know the dead man paid his due—*
लोभ साहु माग्न गयो तिन्नु परेछ ॥	*Yet to his boy, you say 'give more.'*

Yogmaya's repeated reference to corruption and trickery were directed at the Brahmin class and families who used their high-caste positions to intimidate hapless peasants. Meanwhile they themselves escaped the law because of their alliance with the government.

In the distant past, the lives of most inhabitants of the eastern hills—Rai, Limbu and Magar peoples, for example—were subject to the powers of earth and water spirits mediated by local spirit-experts known as shaman. Some villagers still use shaman to communicate with those spirits. They are viewed as intermediary agents who can appease divine forces with the blood of goats and pigeons, or by fire; they call on the earth and water and mountain gods to remove afflictions, to bring them sons and to repel hail.

In the Arun Valley, villagers offer goats to Manakamana goddess to win a boy child; they come with gifts to the riverbank to ask Lord Arun to help women conceive boys, to ensure children pass their examinations; they ask that their loved ones be restored to health. Brahmins and other high caste people frown on these practices. Hindu influences are spreading into these areas through the arrival of priests who convince beleaguered villagers to accept their guidance for redemption and protection. Even tribal peoples now seek help from the Brahmin priests who claim to possess real solutions for their afflictions. These new experts impose social rules as if they are state laws, dictating what they may not eat, whom they may not marry, what is pure and impure, and what will befall them if they break these rules. Before 1854, it was customary for different ethnic groups or castes to apply their own ancient rules. Under rising Brahmin influence social behavior was regulated according to the ancient classical Hindu caste laws of Manu. In 1854, these rules were collected and systematized into a national social code for all Nepal:—The Muluki Ain (Law of the Land). Each group's allocated place in the hierarchy is spelled out in the code. Grounded in the Hindu idea of ritual purity, the Muluki Ain regulates the lives of every citizen from birth to death, just as shari'a is adopted as the legal standard in an Islamic state, and archaic Hebrew laws apply to citizens of Israel, a Jewish state.

When Hindu priests in Nepal succeeded in consolidating their authority, the political ruler—the king and for a time the line of hereditary prime ministers—became a divine figurehead. To hold divine status, a ruler needs religious sanction and this in turn requires the service and authority of priests. Thus the ruling Ranas and later the Shah monarchs found themselves dependent on priestly sanction, obliged to follow prescribed ritual procedures. Even with the restoration of limited democracy in Nepal in 1990, this alliance endured. Nepal's sacred kingship remained unassailable, reaffirmed in the 1990 constitution that defined Nepal as a constitutional monarchy. Even though democracy arrived after a hard-fought revolution, it could not easily sweep aside ancient privileges of the highborn. The 1990 secular revolution brought in some democratic processes and elections but faced the same entrenched authorities Yogmaya so fiercely campaigned against more than half a century earlier.

An important feature of Yogmaya's early success was her close association with high-caste women and men like herself. A Neupane Brahmin, most of her followers were either Brahmin or Chhetri, members of Nepal's most privileged communities. Moreover, few of them were poor. "Who else could dare do this mission but a Brahmin?" retorts ManaMaya. "Any protest from the Rai people, for example, would end in a stroke," she claims with an emphatic raising of her arm, then thumping the ground with her hand, like a kukuri weapon chopping the neck of its prey. "If *they* try, they are wiped out."

This woman was surprisingly pragmatic. "Because *we* are Chhetris and Brahmans, we are protected by the law against Brahmin murder. The government could not harm us. It could not strike Yogmaya or Mata down like they could do away with Rai and Limbu dissidents."

I had to struggle to follow this logic, and gradually I appreciated the power of the taboo against Brahmin murder. I finally grasped the profound implications of Yogmaya's call for self-reform. ManaMaya was sometimes impatient with my slowness to comprehend. "Listen to me, White Didi. Our call for change arose from within. We had to change ourselves first.

'Look again, the light is inside you.'

"That Rai woman does not know child widowhood. She does not care what our priests say. But we: we have to pay our priest a thousand rupees and a cow to watch over the burning of our father's corpse. A Rai fellow simply brews a bottle of raksi for the shaman who'll speak to her father's spirit. If we try to throw our caste away, the whole system falls apart. See, see: the Brahmin loses all his power, next his wealth!"

Yogmaya insisted that social status was a fabrication. Rules enslave a woman, all the while purporting to protect her status. "*We*," Mana-Maya emphasizes, thrusting her forefinger into her own chest, "We have to understand that we are not superior; we must reject those rules which claim we are special and separate. *We,* Brahmins, we are the ones who

Babita Katwal joined by author at Chiwabesi, en route to Majhuwabesi, (BK, 2019).

refuse to marry. It is we who refuse food from others, who order others and expect them to obey us because we think we are better. Our Sarkar could end this business if only he could break free of those priests."

Yogmaya knew that the reform-minded Brahmin rebels who came to support her felt a strong sense of responsibility. Her appeals were therefore made to her own people to abandon *their* sense of exceptionality and *their* privileges, and rid themselves of the idea of purity. Only then, she taught, would they grasp the real meaning of justice. Her religious idiom was appropriate in her time and culture too, a wise strategy few Western people appreciate.

"At that time Nepal was a religious-based regime. The best way to attack it was from inside, with its own logic," explains Nepali social critic and geographer, Harka Gurung. An early advocate of the rights of all ethnic groups in his country, Gurung is an outspoken critic of caste privileges and monopolies. Even though a secular man, he fully comprehends Nepal's deeply rooted political-religious dynamics. "Rebellion has to come from within the Hindu community," he insists. "Brahminism itself gives rise to anti-Brahminism. Yogmaya

"Yogmaya" theatrical performance flyer, after N.K. Niharika's novel, staged in Kathmandu, 2018.

was born Brahmin, and so she understood its logic. She knew the system well enough to design a credible strategy to oppose it."

ManaMaya elaborates the concept for us. "If a Rai guy marries a widow, the government doesn't care. His family will not object. But when *we* defy the law, the palace shudders. We are shaking the top of the social order. If a Rai girl runs away with a Sherpa, a month later, the couple can return to their house; their families drink *raksi* and dance all night. We? We are banished. Finished. *Bayo*," she says, slapping her hands. "If we run away with a lover, our Brahmin family performs our funeral. They consider us dead." This is why Hazur called to us: *'Look, it is inside you. See, there is nothing.'*

"When we were with our master we lost all fear of those rules and those priests. Hazur taught us to purge ourselves of fear."

It becomes clearer how her exercises in self-discipline took her beyond death; thereby she could face the privileged class and the inevitable wrath of the government. Steadily and unwaveringly, she moved towards the centre of power.

Perhaps Yogmaya's anti-Brahmin campaign is more comprehensible if we compare it to the call of contemporary Western feminists for consciousness-raising. Women wanting real change first had to reflect on their role in social institutions that placed them second. We must examine ourselves, they said, in order to understand the system we are part of and to which we contribute. Only when we know our role within Western patriarchy, can we comprehend the dynamic of our oppression. The 1970s feminist movement argued that exploitation was not the action of individual men, but it derived from a system in which both women and men were embedded together. Fighting that institutional oppression was a huge task because women had to change not only themselves but also their brothers and fathers, their teachers and sometimes their mothers too—the very people they loved and depended on.

"You are the babe in my lap, I am the child in yours."

The struggle for justice continues in industrialized countries despite their high education levels, free speech and theoretical equality under the law.

Gandhi, when mobilizing the public in the early stages of his Quit India campaign, advocated dropping caste rules. The great Indian reformer sought to unite his people by calling on his followers, many of whom were high-ranked people, to perform what they considered unclean acts: to take food from anyone, and to clean latrines. Those profound acts of defiance were difficult even for Gandhi's closest associates to accept. Yogmaya went further than Gandhi. She instructed high-caste men and women who joined her to cohabit as they wished, to remarry, to accept food from any hand. Hers was a formidable proposal, so anathema to the society around her that onlookers became fearful and denounced her for advocating what they interpreted as prostitution.

Yogmaya's understanding of caste injustices began with her own painful experience as a child. Hardly ten years old, she found herself a child widow because the little boy to whom she was betrothed died. (Editorial note: later research indicates this is incorrect; see Dipesh Neupane's 2018 book for full details.) As a Brahmin widow, she was forbidden to marry even a man of equal caste rank; she thus could never enjoy a life-partner or become a mother. Yogmaya would not accept this.

"Our Hazur eloped! She was just a girl; yet see how courageous she was." ManaMaya waits for me to grasp the significance of this outrageous action by her master. Elopement meant rebellion. Yogmaya began her life by defying Brahmin widowhood. One occasionally hears about non-Hindus eloping—not unusual in what were called tribal or hill communities. It is rare for Brahmin women, unthinkable if she is a widow.

Yogmaya not only defied the ban against remarriage. She crossed caste lines. Her lover—ManaMaya would not call him a husband—

was of another caste! When she eloped, this young Brahmin woman went into exile. She fled from the Arun Valley region altogether. (ManaMaya could give me no details about this.) "She went away," was all anyone would say. "For a long time no one heard from her."

The young fugitive crossed to north India, most likely to Darjeeling, because of its Nepali character. It offered a refuge for many earlier runaways from the north and was known as a city of lovers, refugees and fugitives. Darjeeling, according to historian Janak Lal Sharma, was the site of the Josmani religious movement at that time and he believes Yogmaya was associated with the Josmani during her stay in India.[7]

On my next visit to the Arun Valley, in February 1983, I asked Mata about that point. Her reply was curt and defensive: "Yogmaya was not part of anything else. She was alone." ManaMaya agreed with Mata. "She worked for no one."

An aged Yogmaya devotee, Lochan Nidhi Tiwari living in Kathmandu, and others we approached about Yogmaya's relationship to Josmani or any other movement all insisted Yogmaya had no teacher. They responded defensively, as if an association with other leaders might somehow diminish her achievements.

My companions at Manakamana may have worried that my primary interest might shift from their master if doubts about her unique power should arise. They could not or would not help me probe any 'foreign' phase of this rebel's life. I could not understand their stonewalling my inquires in that direction. We know she passed several years in the eastern provinces of India but any details about her activities or associations there remain mysterious, and would for years to come, even in 2019 after research into Yogmaya's history had widened considerably.

One would expect Yogmaya to have matured politically during an extended stay in India. India was in transition in the first half of the 20th century. West Bengal was a fertile political ground for young dissidents, and at the time Yogmaya stayed there she would find diverse ideologies to ponder over. Calcutta was a vibrant intellectual centre where Indian communists played an important role in the emerging independence movement. The city was also a focus of nascent anti-Brahmin philosophy promoted by secularized Hindus. At the time, no place in India matched Bengal for its political and intellectual ferment. Given Yogmaya's later political work and anti-Brahmin stand, she could have imbibed at least some of her reformist philosophy and non-violent tactics there.

Former Prime Minister B. P. Koirala told me when I met him in 1982 that when he was a lad, he met Yogmaya briefly at his home in Biratnagar, a city in southeast Nepal with close ties to nearby India (as well as with the interior of East Nepal.) "She came to see my father," he said, "so they must have spoken about politics."

The Koirala household was well known for its party activities, so this visit suggests the young rebel from Kulung (her actual natal village is Nepaledanda) was not politically naive. Unfortunately Koirala could say little about Yogmaya's visit. Except poignantly, he added: "She was not alone; she had a daughter with her. I remember, a very bright little girl," said the veteran politician. "Nainakala?" I asked. He replied "Yes, that was her name; perhaps the child was about nine years old at the time."[8] Even when I later shared B.P. Koirala's comment with my friends back at Manakamana hermitage, ManaMaya, Bhattini Aama and Mata all continued to deny their master had any outside political affiliations.

Yogmaya may have worked alone in Nepal, but before creating her own campaign, as a young woman living in South Nepal and India for a significant number of years, she must have been exposed to political issues and ideas. I hope that in time new research will clarify what if any contact she had with political parties or individual leaders there.

Eventually Yogmaya reappeared in her home village in Kulung/Nepaledanda. What motivated her decision to return is another mystery. In any case, she was not alone. "Everyone was shocked when they saw her. She had the girl Nainakala with her. No sign of any father!" (ManaMaya's report is dramatic but without reproach.)

We know however that Yogmaya's return was not warmly welcomed; she faced ostracism by some members of her family, and only with the support of one of her brothers she was able to remain there. He must have endured hostility and criticism too but he stood by his sister. He and his wife Ganga Devi accepted Nainakala as if she were their own daughter. Ganga Devi, an educated woman, tutored Nainakala while Yogmaya concentrated on her own spiritual and political development.

Yogmaya did not remain long in the village. She left her daughter with her brother and sister-in-law, and set out to explore the surrounding region. Wandering the trails, moving up and down the banks of the Arun River, Yogmaya witnessed the daily trials of her people. She saw the cracked and bleeding feet of porters carrying their contracted loads for fat merchants. She heard testimonies about abandoned little girls. She learned how peasants were dispossessed. She witnessed the vast fields belonging to men with ties to the administration. She saw how stones were mixed with grain in the market stalls, how women were forced into marriage, and later driven out, replaced by another wife. From time to time, she retreated to meditate.

<table>
<tr><td>जङ्गल् सुसोभित् बनवारि पारी,</td><td>The forest is wondrous, our mountains majestic.</td></tr>
<tr><td>पर्वत्खडा छन्, अति भारि भारी ।</td><td>Empty of houses, reserved for a hermit.</td></tr>
<tr><td>बस्ति नजिक्मा पनि छैन वाहाँ,</td><td>Thus, I pray. I meditate.</td></tr>
<tr><td>तप् गर्नलाई अति बेस् छ त्याहाँ ॥</td><td></td></tr>
</table>

"We need strength to live in the jungle." To ManaMaya, Yogmaya's solitary expeditions were a prelude to her later revelations. "She feared nothing. She needed no food to sustain her. She moved alone, from the icy rivers into the jungles and through the hills, north to Khempalung Cave, south to sacred Halesi Cave, and deeper into the mountains to the border of Tibet." This period of wandering was doubtless a formative stage in Yogmaya's development. In her verses we can see a growing love for nature and homeland.

फुल्को तवाशन् कोहि दिन् लिएर,
सूर्य: तरफ् दृष्टि वहुत् दिएर ।
लोक्का हे साक्षी तिमी हेरि लेउ,
इन्छा भए को वरदान देउ ॥

Living off the fragrance of blossoms,
Concentrating in the sun.
Oh, evidence of the world, look.
Come, favour me as you wish.

With Mata's assigned companions (Shanti Nanda, sister of Prem Narayan was one of three ascetics at the kuti who accompanied me) I visited Gaudeni Cave (earlier misidentified as Manohar Cave) a short distance upriver and across from Manakamana. Arriving there we witnessed precisely where Yogmaya had lived alone for some years. The cave is located in a steep rocky slope across the Irkhuwa River and at a slightly higher altitude than Majhuwabesi. It's a mere ledge under an overhanging rock among dense forest. Overgrown with vines and ferns, it was not visible from the trail, yet my companion from Manakamana, Shanti Nanda, located it without difficulty. She pointed out to me offerings of fresh flowers and oil on the ledge, clearly placed there not long before our arrival. (In 2019, under the supervision of Bhojpur resident Mohan Basnet and with government funding, the cave is now gated, accessible by a cement stairway, and protected by a

Gaudeni temple complex constructed in 2016 under the supervision of Mohan Basnet, (BK, 2019).

fence that encloses a new attractive temple and a park for worshipers—as illustrated in our attached photos.)

"Whoever believes in Hazur's power comes here and makes offerings." My companion Shanti Nanda spoke in a hushed tone (as together we explored the site in 1982–83). If her whispered remark was out of reverence or caution, I did not know.

Is worship of this rebel forbidden more than 40 years after she left this world?, I wondered.

"At the end of her months of wandering, Yogmaya stayed at Gaudeni. She stopped here to do her tapasya (austerities)," explained Shanti Nanda. "She fasted. She subjected herself to the bitter cold of the Arun waters. She sat with barely any covering during the winter nights. She denied herself sleep. She took a vow of silence."

Except for my intimate group of helpers at Manakamana kuti, anyone speaking openly about Yogmaya today (1980s-90s) confines their remarks to her tapasya; they avoid mentioning her political campaign. They recall her awesome defiance of nature, how she overcame sensitivity to cold and heat, hunger and loneliness. (Perhaps they're implicitly praising her defiance of Brahmanism and Rana rule?)

After she'd gained attention and recognition for her tapasya (and the self-empowerment it nourishes) Yogmaya began her political campaign more actively. Her yogic accomplishments helped her find inner power—courage to challenge the status quo. People who once scorned her behaviour now began to listen carefully to her assertions. "Some said she was a god. They made offerings to her," says ManaMaya. "From villages on both sides of the Arun, women and men came to Manohar/Gaudeni seeking her blessing, requesting advice."

Yogmaya's social trespasses were forgotten—at least this seemed so, while she directed her powers towards defying nature.

Eventually, at the insistence of the growing numbers of worshipers who sought her out, Yogmaya moved from Gaudeni to Majhuwabesi, a wide, uninhabited and forested gently rising slope close to the river. Located not far from a footbridge over the Arun further downstream, and reached from upstream by ferry (fisherman-operated dugout canoe), the site that became her centre was accessible from both sides of the river.

This is where she stayed for nearly five years and where she gave birth to *hazurbani*.[9] Under the tall trees beside the great river, Yogmaya emerged from meditation and began to utter verses, unlike anything anyone had heard before then or indeed, a hundred years later.

पक्षीहरूले अति गान गर्ने,
सुन्दै माहाँ चित बहूत हर्ने ।
स्वाँ स्वाँ गरि फेरि नदी सुसाउने,
सुन्दै माहाँ चित्त बहूत खुसाउँने ॥

So beautiful the bird's song,
It kidnaps the heart.
So gentle the river's whistle,
Our heart is again captured.

Witnessing her yogic powers, worshipers returned to their homes to urge others to come and hear the Yogi. Some reported experiencing visions; other devotees spoke of having a spiritual transformation.

Seated with the former cabinet minister from Kulung, Dambar B. Basnet, whom I met in Kathmandu in 1983, I witnessed a remarkable, enduring awe for Yogmaya. He remembered seeing her when he was a boy and was overwhelmed, sitting with Harka Gurung and me more than half a century later, as he recalled her presence with profound reverence.

Basnet was eager to share an anecdote with us, which I recorded and copy here. It's the story of an encounter between a young Tibetan herder and our Yogi.

Yogmaya visualizations are in popular use today. Her image is also featured in a government-issued postal stamp.

"It is said this lad threw a stone at Yogmaya when she was meditating at Tordhapur Cave. Realizing she was a

yogi, he apologized and begged her forgiveness. She replied:

"I am not a god; I am the one discarded and despised by society. Thus I am obliged to prove my innocence."

In that same meeting with us Minister Basnet also proffered this quote from Yogmaya:

Mohan Basnet and a villager welcome the author at Majhuwabesi. Nearby is a guest house under construction, (BK, 2019).

"I am not only aiming at that tyrant. My goal is point zero."

More young farmers arrived in Majhuwabesi to hear the Yogi; eventually Yogmaya's following exceeded anything ever seen there. Before long those gathering around her numbered nearly two thousand.

Forty years later ManaMaya remembers her experiences with the Yogi. "Knowledge of what we could achieve surged within us. We believed we might change our society and solve our problems ourselves. No one commanded us to do what we did", she insists. "Hazur Yogmaya did not lecture on the ills of government, or tell us to rebel. "The truth lay in *hazurbani*. She gave us courage. That is all," she concludes, lowering her voice as she presses her fist under her ribs and twists, pushing up—a gesture of self-empowerment.

Yogmaya was joined by her brother and Ganga Devi and Nainakala at Majhuwabesi. Nainakala was now educated and she and her aunt stayed at Yogmaya's side ready to transmit the teachings when she emerged from meditation. ManaMaya explains: "It was Nainakala who wrote down *hazurbani* as Hazur revealed them to her. Ganga Devi was there too. Ganga Devi created the music for *hazurbani*. You will find no other verses like those we sing."

ManaMaya spontaneously utters another quatrain.

मार्छन् कि भन्ने डर छैन केही,   *Why fear execution?*
आखिर काल गतिको छ भिरेको देही ।   *A body is mortal, after all.*
प्रमुका कृपाले गरि जन्म हुन्छ,   *I arrived and exist by divine grace,*
निहुँ काल् जगतिले गरि जानु पर्छ ।   *And being mortal, I'll also be gone.*

These words and their music captivated young men and women with their simplicity—their message was as stark as their structure and words. They penetrated people's social conscience, stirring their young imaginations, awakening their political longings.

गुण् दिने ता अन्तरयामि दर्शन् दिने शीव,   *The light is within you,*
यी आत्माका गुफा भित्र बसेको छ जीव ।   *And you are inside the flame.*
फुल्को थुँगो रूजि रहन्छ बासन् रूज्दैन,   *After all there is nothing;*
अगम् तत्व खोलि सके लोक् त बुझ्दैन ॥   *Look again. There is nothing.*

'There is nothing to it. Have courage,' asserts the Yogi.

Yogmaya did not order her followers to march on the palace or attack local police posts. What she advocated was simpler and at the same time infinitely profound. "She told us: 'You can change your life. You have it within you. There is no barrier but what you yourself build.'"

It is noteworthy that her verses and philosophy did not attract old men and women:- the people usually seeking spiritual guidance as they become more pious in their twilight years. Yogmaya appealed to the young. The majority of her followers were like ManaMaya, youthful and seeking change and adventure. Many were married couples with young children. "Our parents stayed away from Yogmaya. We, me and my girlfriends, Mata and her brother, came because we wished to hear new ideas." Brothers brought their sisters, women their husbands, fathers their sons and daughters. They were young and hopeful. They did not seek redemption for past crimes; they dreamed of ways to change their future.

One of Yogmaya's disciples was Prem Narayan, a young mendicant; he already had a reputation as a spiritual seeker. Some of his followers were Arun Valley Brahmins who gathered at Pashupatinath in Kathmandu during winter months. One such acolyte was Lochan

Nidi Tiwari who in 1984 met with Uttam Pant and me, and told us a story about Prem Narayan receiving a letter from Ganga Devi inviting him to the Arun Valley. That exchange went like this, he told us:

"Prem Narayan. You have been searching for god all over. But god is here in Majhuwabesi. If you want to meet god, you must come here." And Prem Narayan replied "She cannot be a god because she has many husbands. So, I cannot come there." When Ganga Devi reported this to Yogmaya, she replied "Prem Narayan is proud, but he will nevertheless arrive here within seven days." Prem Narayan was in Assam at the time that he received the second letter and overcome by a feeling that he should return home, he excused himself from his fellow sanyasi, and set out on foot for the Arun Valley. On the way he stopped at a shop to sleep and in the night awoke to see a bright light, with the sun at its center. Yogmaya appeared to him there, and asked: "What do you want?" He replied he wanted mukti (salvation). Then Yogmaya threw all the rays of the light at him which then broke into thousands of bits of paper. Then she declared: "Here, take which piece you want; but only one of them has the mukti in it." Prem Narayan feared picking the wrong piece and said, "I do not know what kind of mukti is good; you must tell me which to take." With this Prem Narayan seemed to awaken from a trance. He told the shop proprietor he must leave and he set out that very night. Before long he reached Dharan from where he continued straight north, reaching Majhuwabesi within seven days from the time of Yogmaya's declaration. Thereafter he remained one of her most devoted servants.

Lochan Tiwari also reported that Yogmaya later sent Prem Narayan to Kathmandu to petition one of the high ranking Ranas with whom she had a good relationship.[10] *"Prem Narayan assured the Rana that if he fulfilled Yogmaya's twenty-six demands, he would remain in power for twelve years. Then, when Yogmaya petitioned Juddha Shumsher after he assumed power (in 1932), she asked him: "What about my edict?" The first of these demands was prohibition of child marriage; the second was cancellation of levy against poor people. When Prem Narayan moved to Majhuwabesi to be with Yogmaya, many of his followers joined him and when he declared obeisance to her as his guru, they did too.*

Prem Narayan perished with Yogmaya. But his sister Shanti Nanda who was also a devotee of the rebel survived. I met her at Manakamana where she'd been living as a sanyasi after her brother and Yogmaya and the others 'left this world'.

"Was Prem Narayan involved in creating *hazurbani?*" I put this question to Shanti Nanda. "Did your brother help Yogmaya develop her political ideas?"

She replied, "My brother was a yogi, it is true; but beside Yogmaya he was a child."

Shanti Nanda showed me a collection of his handwritten poems, and my assistant Dharma and I examined them. Dharma translated a part of the manuscript for me and we found Prem Narayan's verses to be conventional praises to the divine; they were devoid of the rhythm, the intelligence and the political bite of his master's poems. Neither could we find any hint of political advocacy in his writings. Not unhappily, I was obliged to accept the claims of the women ascetics and ManaMaya, namely that Yogmaya was the only source of those political invocations.

Parijat concluded the uniqueness of those creations when she examined *hazurbani* in the book (addended to this volume) Mata gifted me and I later shared with Parijat. According to this leading Nepal literary figure, she knew of nothing across Nepal that paralleled the Yogi's political wit, art and audacity. An accomplished, respected political poet in her own right, Parijat declared that Yogmaya was her ancestor and her political model.

यो पैसाका चलन, भिन्न लोभ पाप रहेका,
कोहि दिन्मा हुने बात् यो अन्सारको ।
महा राज् छन् दर्बारमा हेर्न आउँदैनन्,
दुःखि जन्ले निजा निसाफ् पाउँदैनन् ॥

Raja sits in his palace.
And does not care to see
If the poor have justice–
Not even justice by chance.

Yogmaya repeatedly called for a Dharma Raj. Eventually I grasped its meaning: *'rule by truth'—justice*. In the verse above, she plays on the word 'raj' as ruler (prime minister) and also as the ideal of justice. If the ruler is imprudent or irresponsible there can be no justice, she declares. In this verse, she places responsibility for justice on the ruler. His neglect is the cause or source of injustice. Yogmaya is accusing her supreme leader of total negligence. As quiescent as these statements appear in four simple lines, they were a rude attack on Nepal's ruler. They were equal to blasphemy and certain to incite a government reaction. Consider her irony in the last line—*not even justice by chance*. 'Justice by chance' effectively means 'no justice at all'.

If these barbs aroused officials—and they did—they also alarmed the public. Some anticipated a government backlash; thus family members who'd not joined the movement urged their loved ones who followed the Yogi to abandon her, but to little effect according to ManaMaya. "We would not leave. She sought justice, no more than justice. From the beginning this was her aim."

धर्म सम्फी विचार गरी इन्साफ गरेन,
पैसा भए वहेरालाई दण्ड परेन ॥
कुल् ता हाम्रो ब्राम्हण हो छैनौ कुलैमा,
जात्ता सत्य छैन हाम्रो राख चुलैमा ॥

'Though right was on our side,
That bully escapes the law.
Brahmins, we're so unholy.
Let's leave our caste in the kitchen.

Yogmaya herself showed no signs of retreating. Having confronted the trials and forces of nature, she was well prepared to face death from any direction. Mahatma Gandhi practiced fasting during his youth in England, and in his later anti-British campaign he adopted extreme forms of fasting as a political challenge, putting responsibility for his death squarely on the shoulders of British rulers. Thus he confronted his political enemies, fearlessly testing the very people who might strike him down. This is the logic of civil disobedience that Yogmaya employed. She seemed to court a confrontation; she stood prepared to face a ruler who had wiped out opponents for demanding far less than she did.

Eventually, in fact, the dictator did order his troops into the Arun Valley to crush her movement and silence her.

Before that happened, another challenge faced the Yogi reformer and her followers—the wrath of their families and neighbours who became incensed by the group's attack on caste proprieties.

अघि मेरो जात थियो	*Before I owned a caste*
ब्राम्हण कूलैमा ।	*Belonging to Brahmin clan.*
महिले मेरो जात छैन	*Now look, I have no caste.*
राख छु चुलैमा ॥[11]	*Ho, I chucked it there in the hearth.*

Uttered in the spirit and cadence of *hazurbani*, these cheery, nimble lines belie their explosive content. The poem's brazen message is easy for any Nepali to grasp. Yogmaya exclaims: 'Chuck out the rules of marriage that divide us'; then she adds, *throw them there, in the fire.*

The fire? One can hardly imagine more flagrant disrespect to divine power. Her choice of the hearth as a dump for trash is awesome. The hearth of a Hindu (or Buddhist) home is not an incinerator. Nor is it just a cooking place. It is sacred. The hearth endows the house with sanctity. Strangers may not cook, gather, or eat here. The hearth symbolizes exclusiveness; one can find nowhere more challenging to toss caste than the household hearth. This simple quatrain advocates nothing less than to dispose of one's Brahmin caste; it implies doing away with all caste and religious edict, a very different proposition from an individual choosing to reject social norms and take up the life of a mendicant or hermit.

Those who choose to become sanyasi are respected, their anti-social behaviour tolerated in this society where such action is individualist and follows conventions of renunciation. Traditional yogis can disregard social norms because they have formally left society (including their caste status) by taking a vow of total renunciation.

Yogmaya was different. She used her self-discipline to question and challenge social norms, to defy society. Moreover she urged others to break (Hindu) social rules while continuing to live as householders.

"We began to feel we did not need our caste," said ManaMaya. "Bharat Dhoj for example refused to take the Brahmin wife his family chose for him. Then, one Brahmin widow living at Majhuwabesi took a new man as her partner." This kind of cohabitation violates a fundamental and deeply ingrained concept—Hindu purity—a principle upheld in the chastity of a Brahmin woman. This kind of union is as radical and unacceptable as incest.

ManaMaya lowers her voice speaking about this issue as the subject might invite reproach. "They said Hazur was creating a haven for prostitution. That's why some villagers came to our meetings threatening to kill our guru.

"Yogmaya met them directly and defended the couples: *I have given them this power. It is not them you assault; it is I.*"

"I was there. I heard her." ManaMaya asserts, pulling back her shoulders and placing a hand on her hip in a posture of defiance as she continues quoting her leader: "*They have done nothing wrong; it is I, I who have given them the power to do this.*"

"And they went away."

Surely the men and women in this daring assembly around the Yogi knew public criticism would not subside. To my question about lingering tensions, ManaMaya replied, "As long as we were near her we felt we could do anything. Other women and men at Majhuwabesi began living together too."

Pressure on Yogmaya from families of her acolytes continued, according to ManaMaya. "Ask Mata how her husband tried to keep her back; so she went secretly to the gatherings, taking two of her children with her. My parents told me not to go. All of us began to visit our master at Majhuwabesi after nightfall." Even then, families arrived at those assemblies to fetch their children and wives and brothers from what they believed was a den of prostitution and blasphemy; by force they dragged the young disciples home.

Yogmaya would not cease. If she was not denouncing caste, she was lashing out at the priests. Most Hindus understood how Brahmin leaders—canonical experts and ritual priests—worked with commercial interests, the ruler and the courts. Private complaints about the excesses of priests were not uncommon but only the Yogi openly voiced criticism with language like this:

यो माकुरा भित्र को होला,
कति छ है माकुरा (धागै)
धागाको (त्यो) पोला ।
यो विचार गर्ने को होला,
चैतन्य जिव जो होला ॥

Who may that spider be?
And how much silk does he hoard?
Reflecting on this
You'll have enlightenment.

Yogmaya was asking her nation to challenge the wealth of the powerful. Confront injustice, she urged them.

For the Yogi, enlightenment led to social awareness, awareness of the causal relation between privileges for an elite and injustice for the rest.

She called on her ruler to reflect, a plea which ManaMaya maintains was actually not confrontational. "She was not his enemy, you see. She did not call for his downfall. Hazur even traveled to see our Sarkar to ask him face-to-face to take responsibility for his people. 'Give us Dharma Raj,' she pleaded again and again. Hazur believed the ruler had the power to do good; she never abandoned those personal appeals."

अधम भक्ति हूं बिन्ति लेखतछू,
तिम्रा लोकको हाल् यो देखतछू
बिन्ति गर्दछु हित् छ बिन्ति यैही
तिम्रा लोकमा स्थिति छैन केही ॥

'Though I am a speck, I petition you.
Be informed of our conditions.
We have no benefits, no help.
As long as there's injustice, I'll petition you.

Yogmaya travelled to Kathmandu with the aim of petitioning the palace herself. Although unable to obtain an audience with the ruler, she insisted her message must be delivered. Later she sent Nainakala her daughter to try again but her emissary only reached the ruler's secretary. ManaMaya refers to a letter in verse which Nainakala wrote to her mother reporting the encounter, "The official asked Nainakala:

Yogmaya relics, gathered at Majhuwabesi for visiting worshipers, (BK, 2019).

Yogmaya statue newly installed at Gaudeni Cave temple complex, (BK, 2019).

'Child why do you wear this yellow cloth (her ascetic robe)? Get home, dress in red and be married.'"

The rebel Yogi was undeterred by these rebuffs. She intensified her campaign with ever more piercing attacks against cheaters and their accomplices.

<table>
<tr><td>

केहि प्राणिले मखान् बेचे पटक मिलाए,
कोहि प्राणिले मखान् किने त्यो धूप चलाए ।
धूपको वास्ना छैन एउटा कपट गनाए,
लोक् भो भुट्टो देवाहरू बिन्ति चढाए ॥

</td><td>

What swindlers sell as butter,
others burn for incense
whose odious smell... is greed.
Corruption! How it stinks.

</td></tr>
</table>

This metaphor of stinking incense poignantly captures the immorality of cheating. In modern times, merchants are known to lace their grain with sand or stones, leaving the buyer to discover this deception long after. (Such pebbles may constitute as much as twenty per cent of a sack of grain.) Though this kind of swindling was widespread few cheaters were punished. This verse describes how adulteration is exposed—as when a trickster makes his offering of incense. Like the hearth, incense has spiritual significance. Foul-smelling incense insults the divine and is a mockery of devotional acts.

ManaMaya explains: "You see incense sticks. We make them by mixing herb powder with wood and we offer their delightful fragrances to our gods. When those thieves light incense they prepare for the god, it is vile. Because of the cheating mixed in it, it stinks, so our gods are insulted.

"Are they not ashamed, defiling our god!"

In a single stroke, in four lines, Yogmaya identifies the the sinful nature of these crimes and attacks the piety of the cheaters.

A regular theme of Yogmaya is the collaboration between business interests and political power.

थितिदेखि बेथिति ता भएकै छ अइले,
त्यही थिति बिग्रनाले बिन्ती गरे मैले ॥
आमामीले पहिले कर्जा तिरिसकेछ,
साहु भन्ने लोभीले ता बाँकी भनेछ ॥

With order gone to disorder.
I pray for reason to return:
This man has paid his debt.
So why does the rich man lie?

"We all know how these injustices persist," said ManaMaya. "Before Yogmaya, no one challenged them. Our master changed all that."

At the peak of her campaign, the Yogi's local following may have numbered 2000, possibly more; they included local farmers and later, wealthy families from the capital, possibly from Biratnagar too. On her visits to Kathmandu to petition the ruler, Yogmaya stayed at Pashupatinath where she again performed feats of endurance. Hindus from India and from across Nepal converge at this holy place every winter.

Women and men from Bhojpur, Chainpur, and Nepaledanda who lived in the capital met the Yogi there and were smitten by her holiness and her calls for justice. Many joined the core of faithful supporters, leaving the city with Yogmaya when she returned to her retreat at Majhuwabesi. They included notable families of the region: Tiwari, Basnet, Pullman, Pande, Adhikari, and Chapagain.

<table>
<tr><td>

धर्मात्मी राजन तिमि धर्म घाम
ज्ञानात्मी राजन तिमि ज्ञान विचार
विवेकी राजन विवेक खुव गरियोस्
स्वराज्यको धर्म र कर्म माहा
सम्पूर्ण सारा यि छोडेर ता हा
ज्ञानु भया लौ अव देख माहा
नहोसन माहाराजको राजमा दु:ख
पाउन दु:खीले केहि चित्त खुख[12]

</td><td>

Nobel Raja, hear our plea.
Wise Raja, grant us justice.
Intelligent Raja, choose wisely.
Remove pain from this, your land;
Grant relief from suffering.

</td></tr>
</table>

As her popularity grew Yogmaya and her followers found themselves increasingly isolated. The ruler refused to respond to her appeals. Many local villagers denounced her. The young rebels may have shouted audacious *hazurbani* into the night air, ready to die with their leader, but they didn't venture into the villages to help farmers counter corruption or abuse. They did not recruit Rai, Limbu, Tamang, Magar or others who'd been cheated out of their lands and whose debts doubled and tripled, then passed to their sons; they did not go into the courts to challenge falsified land claims; they did not tutor young women to read and write; they did not boycott taxes or build bridges or rally on the steps of the courthouse. Instead they became entrenched at their retreat by the river, increasingly alienated from the wider community.

There is hardly any doubt that the authorities were closely following the activities of the rebel. The palace seemed to ignore her, but she persisted and finally adopted a strategy that courted death. Yogmaya sent a letter to the palace with clear demands: 'We insist on Dharma Raj. Allow Brahmin widows to marry. Let our people unite with whom they wish. Stop the marriage of small children. No more protection for the rich. Remove the priests, and give us laws that treat all as equals. If these demands are not met, I and my people shall die by fire.'

Within two days of the letter's dispatch, government troops descended on Majhuwabesi. ManaMaya remembered: "Yes, Hazur was ready to immolate herself."

The warning was similar to Gandhi's threat—to fast until death—to the British Raj. The Nepali government feared liability for any Brahmin's death should Yogmaya and her followers die. It would be considered murder since Hindu law itself forbids the killing of any Brahmin, for any reason. Yet the ruler was unwilling to negotiate with her and instead chose a cowardly and foolish course.

यो कलिको मुख्य आसन् सुवर्ण हो सून,	*This era rests on a craving for gold*
धिरे धिरे ज्ञानिहरूले लाउन छाड्ने छन् ।	*Which in our wisdom, we discard.*
यो कलिको सुन् हुनाले चोरि हुँदैछ,	*Leave stolen bounty to those greedy ones.*
लोक् ता भन्दा दौलथ् मेरे जोरि हुँदैन ।	*Devils, thieves, how they lust for it.*

The Yogi and her followers identified the riverbank at Majhuwabesi as the site of their immolation, then began assembling logs for their pyre. Among the hundreds involved in those preparations were Mata and ManaMaya, Bhattini Aama, Shanti Nanda and Mahili Didi. Recalling for me the awesome sight of the growing mound of wood, ManaMaya became more animated than usual: "We all joined. We carried logs from either side of the Arun to that slope at the river bank. Some were big, naked trunks washed by monsoon rains from the Upper Arun that piled up along the beaches. We chopped and tugged, and pushed. In a month we had a heap of wood reaching as high as the roof of a house."

What may have alarmed the government more than the report of the pyre under preparation was the list of two hundred and forty names attached to the notice.

"Of course my name was there," asserted ManaMaya unapologetically. "So was that of Mata. And her brother; and his wife; the children too. The Basnet family. Prem Narayan. This was our final challenge to the ruler. He had to grant us Dharma Raj. He may have refused to meet with Yogmaya but he could not ignore this."

ManaMaya's account is devoid of uncertainty or regret. She describes a logical, non-violent strategy that in theory could have worked. She was certain, as was Yogmaya and the others, Juddha Shumsher Rana would not allow them to die.

Once persecuted by the government, the rebel Yogmaya is celebrated by today's leaders. Minister of Education Giriraj Mani Pokharel is joined by local notables on his 2018 visit to Manakamana. (BT)

This approach may seem archaic to us today, but Yogmaya's strategy fit the social framework of the time. Dr. Harka Gurung pondered over this crisis as we talked about the episode and he concluded that Yogmaya was probably wise to employ a religious principle to force the ruler's hand. "Her enemy was not religion, but the abuse of religion. At that time, governance was largely according to Hindu values where the ruler felt himself sanctioned by religious edict. Any rebellious act had to be a religious one in order to appeal to his religious principles. Another strategy wouldn't have gotten them even this far," Gurung explained.

Indeed, the troops who arrived from Dhankuta in the night and marched on Majhuwabesi did not directly harm these rebels. "There were hundreds of soldiers," recalled ManaMaya. "They captured Hazur at Majhuwabesi first. They took her and everyone they could find. The Rana General had the list of names attached to Hazur's demand and thus began a hunt for all of us, sending his soldiers from village to village. They locked Hazur and the women in Siddha-Kali

Mandir (a shrine in Bhojpur town). They took the men down to Dhankuta and locked them in the jail there."

ManaMaya was among some who escaped arrest. "Word spread that the government intended to capture all of us—Hazur and everyone on the list. I hid with a neighbour and stayed with her for two weeks. The troops spread throughout the valley, searching door to door, but they did not find me." ManaMaya admits it was a terrifying time. "The whole area was under military control. Mata escaped too; she sent her husband to Bhojpur to inquire about Yogmaya's fate. We learned she was imprisoned but unharmed."

The only government version I could obtain came from Mahadev Shumsher Rana, the commander who'd led the troops into Majhuwabesi and who I was able to interview in Kathmandu. Now retired, he'd been governor of Dhankuta at that time (In 1981, when I met Mahadev Shumsher, his son was the powerful political advisor to King Birendra). The old general spoke about his mission against Yogmaya purely as a military strategy. "I wanted to surprise them, to forestall their flight or their attempt to carry out the threat. We moved on Majhuwabesi from all sides; we ambushed the group at night.

"Yogmaya was unpredictable. We captured eighty of them there, including Yogmaya. There were over two hundred names. We had the list. We found their homes and we questioned their families. With Yogmaya in our custody the young people did not know what to do, so most gave themselves up easily."

जागिरदार लोभी छन् निजा हेर्दैनन्,	*How greedy they are, discarding justice.*
मनुपर्ने शरीर हो विचार गर्दैनन् ॥	*How proud, forgetting their mortality.*
दुःखी जन हो हात जोडी सत्य पुकार,	*Oh we poor, we plead for truth.*
अर्को हाम्रो सहयता छैन विष्णु गुहार ॥	*Helpless, we pray to Vishnu.*

"Was Yogmaya dangerous?" I asked the frail looking but composed and alert old man. (His photo on page 71 was taken at the time of my visit to his home with one of Parijat's students.)

Telling this story, the former general was at ease. He was living in retirement at his son's house near the palace when he received us in a rather bare parlour surrounded by several young grandchildren. He was a very tall, thin man, with the whitest skin I have ever seen in the country. He spoke English well, with a British accent, and was proud to recall the name of his English tutor. As he talked, he lifted a little girl of about six onto his knee and, without a hint of moral concern about what he was reporting, proceeded to tell us about the capture of Yogmaya.

"They were very dangerous people," he asserted. "They were Communists, you know." Then he qualified his remark to assure me that Yogmaya was no real threat to the ruler.

"Was she anyone's agent? Was she working on behalf of an organization or party?" I asked.

The general quickly dismissed this idea. He estimated the size of Yogmaya's following at Majhuwabesi at "over a thousand." He agreed it was substantial, then he added "they were all simple villagers." (In my opinion he made this claim to minimize the degree of their threat.)

I asked him if he had ever seen a photo of the Yogi. "No", he replied, surmising that none existed. He was certain of that. We were surprised when he suddenly offered, "I think however that I have a file."

"A file?" I repeated, wide eyed in anticipation.

"Yes; from the court proceedings. I confiscated all the documents and brought them to Kathmandu. There ought to be copies in the courts too," he suggested. "But we had a file; I think it is still in this house. I will look for it. Come back tomorrow."

The next day we [11] received a message from the general informing us that the documents could not be found. The general said the house staff might have burned the paper for fuel on some chilly winter night! This and other mysterious disappearances during our inquiries in Biratnagar warned us that the history of Yogmaya still troubled many people. This led me to conclude that even forty-plus years after the uprising, the public as well as officials remained fearful and nervous. Testimonies from the old women at the riverside hermitage were permissible, but somebody gave the order that no written documentation should find its way into our hands.

ब्रिग्नेलाई मासि दिनु चोरलाई दिनु काठी,   *Kill the corrupt; behead the thief.*
धर्म संभी निसाफ् गर्नु यौटा न ढाँटी ।   *Judge with virtue, disregard lies.*
सांरथि उत्रने छन् धर्म जाग्नेछ,   *When our charioteer arrives, truth will reign.*
राजा मंत्रि भारदारलाई ठक्कर लाग्नेछ ॥   *And smash king and courtiers too.*

I returned to Manakamana after meeting the general to learn more from ManaMaya about Yogmaya's imprisonment. "They held Hazur and a hundred and forty disciples for several months. News about the capture spread throughout East Nepal; everyone was closely following the matter." ManaMaya maintained that Yogmaya's imprisonment became an embarrassment for the authorities when the Yogi and her fellow captives continued their campaign from their prison cells. She and other women were kept in a temple and a large house where day and night they sang *yogbani*, likely knowing their words could be heard through the neighbourhood. "Listening to the remarkable and enchanting *hazurbani*, townspeople stopped what they were doing and approached the prison. In Bhojpur women and men who had never before heard these gathered, enchanted by Hazur's message."

> *Bird's song kidnaps the heart.*
> *Then a gentle river's whistle holds it.*

Male followers of Yogmaya at Dhankuta jail had the same reception. *Hazurbani* floated through their cell windows across the town. "At Dhankuta," reports ManaMaya, "the troops themselves were smitten. Off duty soldiers and policemen brought their families to sit outside the prison in the evening and listen to the prisoners' recitations."

अन्त्य कालमा त्यो घुसले फटाउन लागदा,   *Fat bellies burst.*
बडो कष्ट मिलि जाला त्यो घुस निस्की जाँदा ।   *And those bribes ooze out*
महिले मात्र पचेको छ भरे पच्ने छैन,   *To poison you.*
सम्फि राख सत्य बचन् भुटो हुने छैन ॥   *So savour your riches... while you can.*

The popularity of *hazurbani* proved embarrassing for the government. A representative came forward with an offer of amnesty: they might release the Yogi and her followers in return for a promise from her, namely Yogmaya must cease her advocacy. They demanded that the group disband and quit Majhuwabesi. Most important, they were warned never to utter *hazurbani*.

Yogmaya accepted the order without protest and signed a government document forswearing her utterances and her campaign. Other prisoners followed her and one by one they dispersed and returned to their homes.

General Rana thought he had successfully ended the rebellion; gratified by his apparent achievement, he left the area.

But they underestimated Yogmaya. She would not be quieted so easily however and began plans for a final assault. This time, she would present no demand and say nothing outside her circle of devotees.

ManaMaya leaned forward to share a secret. "This time Hazur sent word only through her most trusted aides. They told us to come to the riverside at Majhuwabesi to be with her. We were to tell no one and bring nothing with us. We were to assemble after midnight.

"Oh, some of us knew what that meant. My husband told me not to go, and I stayed back. Mata decided not to go, but her brother and his wife and all their children went."

ManaMaya and the others knew details of what happened because an 11-year-old lad named Dhoj witnessed it all from his hiding place nearby and then reported the event to villagers after it was over and he had fled the scene. According to ManaMaya: "The boy had gone with his grandmother to join Yogmaya. He told us how he pulled himself from his grandmother's grasp, then ran from the gathering and hid in a tree. From there, he witnessed everything. There were sixty-nine people. Children were crying, some adults too."

The river was high and running swiftly. It was Asoj, the sixth Nepali month at the end of summer when monsoon rains are heavy. The Arun roared "chalung chalung, chalung chalung".

"Yogmaya was first; she closed her eyes and stepped into the icy, swirling water.[12] Ganga Devi and Nainakala followed her. Then came Prem Narayan. An entire family jumped next, the father tossing his screaming son into the current, then stepping forward with his wife who clutched a baby in her arms. One by one they followed. Each woman removed her jewellery before advancing into the current; each family signed its name to a document left there with the heap of jewellery.

Then there was nothing but the awesome call of the great Arun waters.

स्वप्नमा देखिएथ्यो भष्म पार्ने चाला
महादेवले लिन भयो विजुलीको भाला ॥
विजुली र बज्रसँगै असिना भई झर्लो,
त्यसैबेला जगत भरमा को को होला पर्लो ॥

In my dream, I saw destruction.
How Shiva, lifting his spear,
sent thunder, hail, lightening.
Crash. Chaos will rule, everywhere.

Yogmaya entered heaven. So did those who accompanied her into the current.

Even today some surviving members of her movement express regret that they did not join her and I suspect Mata is one of those. She had taken the vows of sanyasi to pursue a life of prayer and meditation, a noble and worthy pursuit in the Hindu tradition. Knowing her over a period of years, it became apparent to me that she regretted not taking the more radical course; she seemed a remorseful soul, pained by a failure to follow her master.

By the 1980s Mata was watching her country slip deeper into the grip of corruption, with the authority of Brahmin priests unabated, with women still mistreated and Brahmin women doomed to endure premature widowhood and live childless throughout their lives. Perhaps Mata felt more certain that Yogmaya's call for Dharma Raj was the best solution.

Notes

1   This Nepali text and others in this chapter are selected from the book *Sarvartha Yogbani* addended to this volume. English translations have been facilitated by Parijat and a number of colleagues.

2   From 1846 to 1951 Nepal was ruled by a succession of hereditary prime ministers of the Rana family. Juddha Shumsher Rana (1932–45) was in power when Yogmaya was active, but her campaign began during the rule of his predecessor Bhim Shumsher (1929–1932).

3   Hazur is an honorific title for a man or woman, secular or religious. Yogmaya's followers referred to her as Thulo (great) Hazur or Shakti (holy) Yogmaya, and to Nainakala as Sanu Hazur.

4   1940 AD. The Nepali calendar is calculated starting 57 years before the Gregorian calendar.

5   Renunciates are called sanyasi. Women renunciates are also known as bhaktini.

6   I estimate Yogmaya's birth at between 1870 and 1880, her return from banishment around 1925, and the start of her political campaign five years later. New research has established her year of birth as 1867.

7   Sharma, J.L. n.d. *Josmani santa parampara ra sahitya,* (Nepali) Kathmandu.

8   Yogmaya would have been about 45 years old at the time of this meeting, according to Lochan Nidhi Tiwari who spoke with us in Kathmandu in 1984. Nainakala was born when her mother was about 36.

9   Estimated date: the late 1930s.

10 Yogmaya lost what sympathy she had inside the palace when Juddha Shumsher came to power. If it is true that she actually met with a Rana leader, he may have been Bhim Shumsher, Juddha's predecessor who was reportedly somewhat more tolerant.

11 Murari Aryal, who also helped translate selected *hazurbani,* arranged this interview and accompanied me to the general's house.

12 Jal-samadhi: in Sanskrit—seeking eternity by immersion. This form of sacrifice in a religious context carries honour.

Manu, the Basket Carrier—Nepal 1980

A line of four men emerges from between the trees. Without breaking their stride they step into a dusty gully, then up, hardly noticing the ditch. The route they follow seems a mere path, sometimes barely a meter wide. In fact this trail is effectively a transnational roadway, the main highway between thousands of Nepal's hill villages, where consumers live, and the commercial centres of Chainpur, Khandbari and Bhojpur from where goods are distributed, starting at the roadheads in Nepal's plains bordering India .

The men walk in a line behind one another, as if trained. Or chained. Each man moves forward with head pulled down into his shoulders; yet his eyes remain upturned scanning the road for obstacles, an overhanging branch, a rock protruding from the inside wall of the road, the exposed roots of trees.

Every one of the men wears a hat, the traditional topi. Even if it's threadbare and sweat stained, with this headcover he feels dressed, despite his bare thighs and shoeless feet.

The second man in this convoy is also watchful. He must scan the path to avoid those same dangers. A third, in turn, is close on the heels of the one in front. A few metres behind them walks a younger man, hardly more than sixteen. His legs are thin and still sinewy because he's new to this work. He too is barefoot.

Manu, climbing out of the gully, is in actuality a Nepali truck. Only, this truck hauls one basket-load every trip it makes. Manu balances the load on his shoulders, taking much of the weight with his neck and back muscles, the rest with his legs and feet. Brown thighs, the heaviest parts of his body, bulge above his knees.

The cone-shaped net of bamboo is set high on his shoulders. This is the doko, fabricated by farmers here and an essential tool for them. Vendors in the capital sell a miniature replica of it to tourists who can also buy souvenir dolls each with a topi on its head and outfitted in jackets and tight-calved pants. A replica of the 'traditional' cone-basket is sewn into the doll's back.

The real basket is a handcrafted tool. Extraordinarily lightweight, its construction applies the engineering skill of these indigenous people, the knowledge of generations of craftsmen. It can hold up to 60 kilos and it may last a porter more than one season. The design is efficient and pleasing to the eye. Loaded, it needs skill and strength because a full doko is top heavy. Every farm boy and girl learns to keep a firm grip on the lines on either side of his head to stop their load swaying and tipping.

Manu clutches his line tightly. Sometimes he clenches his jaws, as if his neck muscles are tearing at his mouth, like the bit between a horse's jaw.

Despite his massive load, each porter moves smoothly. It's too early today for a smoke break. None will halt before the convoy reaches the ridge half way up the hillside. Nor will they stop until sunset and after they cross the bridge at Num, their regular sleeping point on this, the fourth day of the six-day job. They'll earn a hundred-and-twenty rupees cash for this trip.

Moving uphill, the men encounter another convoy. Only two men there, rushing downwards toward them, heading back to the roadhead. They carry no loads, so the salty tumplines lay loose across the men's chests. Whump, whump, echo the flapping empty baskets on their shoulders. The limp strap is the only ornament they wear on this job. Its flapping beat may sound gentle to some ears. To this swiftly moving team, it's an echo of compulsive labour that flails the backs of these once young and hopeful farmers.

These porters are returning to Dharan, to reload. They step quickly, but it is no dance. It's hunger. Each man runs to find work, to earn a few rupees to buy food. In just two days, he descends the space he needs six days to climb under a loaded basket. He does not wait for his friends on this route. He's hurrying to find work. Once in Dharan he hopes he'll find someone from his village as a companion when he departs with his next load back into the mountains.

Downward he rushes. The men say "One night in Dharan, then out." Dharan is no village, no town, no city. It's just a grubby depot at the roadhead. From India to Nepali cities such as Biratnagar on the border trucks arrive with supplies of kerosene, rice, sugar and biscuits. At the depots everything is loaded into go-downs, warehouses usually operated by fat men—the bosses.

"Yes hazur, no hazur, hazur hazur," replies the taciturn desperate porter.

The radios of the big-bellied men and their sons blast music into the streets; late into the night they broadcast cheery Nepali tunes that can set a man's wrists dancing. Not these porters—for them, Dharan is a hungry, cheerless place.

Hill farmers stay here only as long as it takes them to find a load— work. At night they congregate along the roadside near the warehouses, eyes scanning the street. Waiting, one man washes his alternate pair of shorts while another hand-stitches the strap on his broken sandal. The first turns to a boy he recognizes and asks who is hiring labourers tomorrow. Two others converse about their village; if they can locate a common relative, they will feel some confidence that fellow will not rob him on the road.

The waiting men sleep early; they lie within inches of one another for comfort, and for safety. When they awaken each folds his thin blanket and silently joins the line of foot-truckers, each bearing a laden basket.

Before sunrise every morning of every season the paths out of Dharan are dense with men like them—a single line ascending into un-alluring yet destined Himalayan landscape.

Every villager needs a basket: to haul fertilizer from the cowshed, to gather grass for the house animals, to trap a wayward hen or duck, to transfer seed to the field, to bear an ill relative to the clinic, chickens to market. It's the Nepali farmer's pick-up truck.

Hauling a loaded basket for wages is another work altogether; no farmer intends to become a porter. But from year to year, families who once lived from cultivating their fields cannot grow everything they need. The bartering system between villages has broken down so now everybody needs cash. The children need pencils; a radio needs batteries. The family has grown accustomed to sugared tea. For a wedding, or a funeral feast, they must serve rice which has to be imported from lower altitudes.

Cash. Where can farmers find cash?

Manu needs cash too. There's no surplus corn to sell, no extra millet.

His physical strength his only source of cash, he sets out for Dharan in search of work. One by one, farmers join others selling their hill-man's muscle.

A man's feet, not his load, betray the life of a farmer who's taken up portering. As the years pass, his neck muscles swell and his feet begin to spread and flatten. His feet are doubly wide at the front, toes permanently spread, to grip the soil, shaped by the ground he walks over under those loads. Month after month, over trails of gravel, through silt along the river's edge, pounding on boulders, kicking into grit and sand, gripping mud. The surface of his sole grows thick.

Like pads of a cow's hoof, the soles of Manu's feet turn numb, numb to cold, numb to heat, numb to gravel, numb to knife-sharp edges of rocks and the pricks of fallen branches.

But this man is not a cow. His feet are not hooves, not dead leather. Eventually the skin of his feet crack: blood vessels underneath break; raw nerves exposed in his flesh start to scream. If a wound dries one day, it splits against a rock the next, pressed under the weight of two men—himself and his load. He's got to keep walking.

Manu, the porter, hates this pain; he can never forget it. When he removes his load to take a meal at a roadside teashop, when he fords a stream, when he sleeps, he always feels his feet. He feels them more than he feels the weight of his load, more than the pressure of the tumpline across his forehead. That awful endless sting would keep him awake if it were not for his utter exhaustion at the end of the day's trek.

Sometimes, mercifully, the hurting disappears when he sleeps. Then, as soon as the load is set onto his back and his feet flatten out on the path, sharp knives in his soles return. Pus seeps from abscesses between his toes and sticks to rocks. Sand mixes with blood inside the sore.

Only three more days. Manu considers the packet of cash waiting for him. "From my hundred and twenty rupees, I keep ninety to take home." He reviews every paisa of every rupee he can spend during the six-day contract: "Four rupees for cigarettes, twelve for tea, nine for the pair of sandals, five for that cafe meal. The saved ninety rupees must cover the family's market purchases: oil, sugar, salt, matches, a piece of lumber for the doorframe, a few tablets, a meter of cloth. Beyond this, until the harvest is in, there's a steady threat of debt.

There's more on Manu's mind: "Oldest daughter is seventeen; we need her to work in the fields while I am away; she must also marry. We have been asked for her and we know the boy's family will be kind to her. It is a good chance."

Manu keeps moving—one foot, then the next. If he slows, he'd break his momentum and then need a surge of energy to resume his pace. He peers upward to a grand pipal tree a hundred yards beyond— he can rest there to adjust the strap cutting into his shoulder. He moves his feet mechanically, propelling himself over the dusty path, towards the stone shelf waiting for him beneath that tree.

Manu and his cousin Kanchha often travel together from Dharan to Dingla. Nowadays a good traveling partner is not easy to find but Kanchha is a reliable companion; they keep one another safe.

Kanchha is fifteen years younger than Manu and can carry the same weight but at a faster pace. Still, it is noon and by now Kanchha who had departed later should have caught up with Manu. Manu reaches the roadside platform and stumbles up to it. As he eases the basket off his back and onto the wall of the hillside, his neck muscles loosen. The basket secured on the stone behind him, Manu releases himself from the tumpline that bound him for two hours. The salty cord drops and rests across his collarbone; Manu expels air from his lungs with a long sigh.

The sting on the bottom of Manu's feet rises to his brain. He winces.

Another porter arrives plodding uphill. His face seems familiar. He doesn't stop but as he passes he asks, "Was that your partner down there in Basantapur, the one who was tipsy last night? He's moving fast, only an hour behind; he says wait for him at the ferry."

Manu nods to the messenger and exhales again, this time with added relief.

Sipping a glass of milk tea, his thoughts return to oldest daughter. "I cannot send her to carry baskets from Dharan. Only a few Sherpa women do this portering; it's not respectable for us—for a Rai man to send his daughter to work on the roads, carrying oil and pulses." Manu heard stories in Dharan about labour brokers and young women. Sometimes a girl stays back thinking she can find an easier contract. Manu and his friends know what happens to them. Karma's middle daughter for example never returned from working on the road last year. Four men from the village went to search for her. Even if she'd fallen off a bridge, someone would have seen her. No; when a woman disappears, it's to India; best to forget her.

"Maybe," Manu thinks, "if little Mina can find work in a carpet factory, she can earn enough to help us pay for her dowry." He'd heard about those factories in the capital whose managers are foreigners and where girls easily find work. "Europeans will protect girls. They give them free rooms too."

That's what they say. He's heard about a merchant at Chainpur who helps find jobs for farmers and he arranged for a girl's salary to be delivered direct to the family. If Manu can trust this man he might send Mina to one of those factories.

Finishing his cigarette, Manu hunches his shoulders to fix the tumpline onto his forehead. He adjusts the basket against the curve of his back, then straightens his knees and steps forward into the path.

It's another hour to Khandbari on the ridge but Manu will not stop until he reaches the flat road of the marketplace. He passes the airfield without breaking stride and starts to climb again. He sees a group approaching—they are tourists with bright green and orange packs on their backs, steel walking sticks in hand. Two old men, laughing with their Sherpa guide, approach him. Manu's first reaction is annoyance over those Nepali guides. "Those are not Arun Valley Sherpa. They are from west Nepal. None of them carries a load! They come here because a Sherpa broker pays local bosses. We must not allow them to work our trails. The bosses take a commission but what do we get? We can haul those packs, tents, blankets, tables and sun-chairs, boxes of their bathroom papers and trays of eggs."

Tourist work is leisurely and well compensated compared to hauling loads from Dharan. Some men from these eastern hills beg for a tourist contract—even for a few weeks. Not Manu. He doesn't want to take orders from any Bhotey guy. He doesn't want to see cook-boys swimming with naked foreigners at their campsites. Four months' seasonal hauling is not enough, not enough one-hundred-and-twenty rupee clumps of money in his pocket.

From out of this tourist group, a white-skinned man in a green sunhat and with a camera suddenly jumps in front of Manu. He points his camera at the Nepali and snaps a photo. He gestures for Manu to stop while he prepares to take another picture. Manu can't stop. He pushes on with the foreigner stumbling to the side, then from somewhere behind him, Manu can hear more clicking of the camera.

Maybe they're taking pictures of Manu's thick legs, or the old sandals hanging from his basket.

The tourists and their helpers disappear down the path. Manu can't think about them; his attention is on the path above where three water buffalo have appeared. A young herder boy grunts as he urges the animals on and the beasts step heavily down the rocks towards Manu, lumbering as if in slow motion. "Water buffalos are stupid creatures; stay clear of them," warn farmers. "They suddenly panic and totter in all directions; your load goes, then you." Manu steps well clear of the oncoming creatures and plods on.

He reaches a teashop set in a wide shoulder of the trail, the rest stop where he often waits for his partner. Three men are seated chatting on the bench as they casually observe Manu approach. Manu is a just a porter while these fellow are officials of some kind. Each is dressed in shoes and socks as well as his civil service uniform—a tailored suit-jacket over his beige shirt and trousers. Manu is naked except for undershorts and a soiled T-shirt. He hears no "Ho, bhariya!" no "Ali kati arak liu hos." (Come, oh porter! Have just a sip with us.) The men continue their chattering as Manu plods silently on. His body moves rhythmically, the momentum from one step helping the next. He mustn't stop.

The path widens. Another two hundred meters to the ridge where the way is smooth and free of boulders. He passes the new hospital; no electricity yet, but they have a real doctor. Doctor Hazur has as much power as the C.D.O.—chief district officer—with authority to requisition a seat on the Twin Otter for any patient in need of speedy transport to Biratnagar. This hospital and its doctor increase the prestige of the town and land prices on this side of the mountain doubled even before the building was complete. A doctor is an important fixture here.

Manu reaches the ridge where the path takes him to the east side of the mountain; the entire valley and beyond is visible from here; a magnificent panorama of the Milke Danda range defines the entire northern horizon.

Our porter does not seem to notice; at least he doesn't halt to view the grand vista beyond. He passes a row of new two-story buildings against the mountain wall. Doors on the top floor of each structure open onto a balcony. Below, shop doors face into the path. Boys and girls in soft blue uniforms seem unhurried, sauntering arm in arm, calling to other friends as they merge along the path towards the school. Some stop to stare into gallon-size glass jars posted along a shelf in front of one store. Each vessel glitters with candies, biscuits, and packs of chewing gum.

Manu smells something fragrant. Is it the flowers on the balcony ledge or the ladies standing there?

Women lean over railings of apartment balconies watching their little ones until they disappear from view, then step inside and return with armfuls of bedding to hang over the railings to catch the warming sun as it rises above Milke Danda.

A man steps from a doorway between the shops wearing a crisp cotton suit—he must be a clerk leaving for work. Manu has a blue suit like that folded inside a wood trunk at home. He can't recall if he last wore it for Dasain festival or when his second brother married. A memory escaped from his unconscious store, an image of his young self in that suit. "Watch out for Manu" neighbours shouted. "When he dances, Manu is a killer," they tease. Yes, Manu loves dancing. When he slowly pirouettes, one arm folded behind his back, the other in the air with his wrist spiralling high above, old women shout mischievously and his wife covers her face in mock embarrassment. In this momentary reverie Manu breaks his stride and as he does, his grip on his tumpline relaxes and the load teeters.

The basket! Manu steps sideways to rebalance the load. He pauses, jolted back to the present, and willing himself forward he regains his momentum. Another few yards and he reaches the bend where the town square opens before him. He'll unload at Shrestha's storeroom, then proceed downhill towards his village.

Tomorrow Manu will accompany his wife to the river with their gifts for Lord Arun. Later he will search out his blue suit. He'll find a matching topi. He'll dance at the festival.

His mind flashes through the days-long trek to count the ten days since he held his children.

Manu assures himself: yes, he did purchase new bangles for his wife and girl and a tailored shirt for baby. How they will prance happily around him.

Maya, a Little Weaver Girl—Nepal 1980

Her oldest daughter had already left for the city and now it's little Maya's turn. Maya is nine years old, a healthy and diligent child. "You are a big girl now; you can help Aama even more." Aama speaks softly, stroking her daughter's hair. "School is of no use to poor farmers like us."

The girl doesn't answer. She has heard her mother speak like this before. "Look at those boys in the marketplace. Brother Sunil sits with friends at that table playing on the carrom board; the sun moves across the sky above them, from east in the morning until it sets in the west." Where, Aama wonders, do these lads find the rupees to buy tea; she herself hasn't enough money to give the family a meal of rice, a welcome change from corn and potatoes day after day.

Aama had wanted Sunil to work in a carpet factory in the city. But he refused. "I'm an educated boy," he scowled. "Anyway, weaving is women's work. I'm going for government service so I can help our people. I need to be near our officials, near Pradhan Pancha's room, listening to the policemen, taking tea with Bahadur who distributes the seeds, and with Purna who gives out condoms and pills."

When Sunil began to study, every house sent a boy to school. Aama herself had said that Sunil should never haul loads through the mountains like his father and his uncles had. She did not want him to walk barefoot through the town, wearing only undershorts and a stained shirt, carrying a heaped load of sugar and books and cloth for other people to enjoy.

But by the time Sunil completed class six, there was no work in any town office and all the teaching posts were filled.

Aama silently makes her calculations: "We haven't enough food, no money for clothes. Last year, I sold one cow; only two goats remain. I leased some paddy to a neighbour and soon I must repay the loan I took against our own land. We might lose our fields altogether. Thank the gods for a girl like Mahili."

Aama can manage only because middle daughter found work in the city. Almost every fortnight someone arrives with Mahili's envelope. Aama might find fifty rupees there, sometimes more. She uses every paise. Because there's no wood left on the hills to burn in the hearth, families need cash for kerosene stoves. If fuel is left from last month, Aama might use the extra rupees for cooking oil, and some nutritious beans to add to chillies she prepares for the family every day. Since Maya should have an occasional egg, Aama keeps two hens. There's never enough.

She calculates, "If my Maya goes to work with her sister at the factory, I can sell the hens and buy a new water pot. Oh, but then the baby should have eggs.

"How I shall miss this tender child." Since she'd barely reached her seventh year, this girl was at Aama's side, helping with the new baby, preparing rice, cleaning the grain. Maya was happy and could manage even more work, she felt: "Teach me Aama; I learn quickly. Then you can rest." Although not strong, she never spilled grain or oil, and she could climb trees to gather leaves for her goats.

Aama smiles and watches Maya mending baby's shirt. "Yes, she is a quick learner; and she is obedient." She looks at the child's long arms. "Her skin is glossy and brown, like mine. But she is too thin; her hair is dull." She reaches out to stroke the girl's hair, flecked with dust and straw. Maya's body is slender but she has a round face with large bright eyes. She never asks for anything, already aware that food is too little for all of them to have full stomachs. Like her mother, she takes less in order to leave more for Sunil.

Aama looks at the girl's thin cotton dress, its print now faded. It pulls too tightly at her shoulders. "You are almost ten now, sweet Maya; you should have a real Nepali skirt and a satin tunic." She draws the girl towards her. The child reaches with both arms to encircle her mother's body and lets her head fall onto Aama's breasts.

"Would you like to go and live with Mahili in the city?" Aama asks, lifting the child's chin to look directly into her eyes. Maya shakes her head and gently pulls away.

"What about my Aama?"

"Aama needs you to be with Mahili. Your sister says she found work for you; soon she'll come to take you there, to teach you carpet weaving in the big city where our Raja and Rani live.

The girl steps across the room to a large earthen jar. Aama takes the baby lying nearby and lifting her blouse, eases her breast onto the child's lips while Maya refills the pot on the hearth and kneels to blow into the warm embers. She expertly stirs the embers until flames spring up, then turns to Aama to lean against her while the baby noisily sucks its meal.

Barely a week later Mahili arrives with a gift for Aama but also something special, a green and red plaid skirt, for Maya. Without removing her worn clothes, Maya excitedly wraps the bright cloth around her waist, forgetting this is a going-away gift.

"Mahili needs a helper, my little Maya. Your sister will show you many new things, and teach you to weave soft woollen carpets. Not corn husk mats like those I taught you."

Maya is silent. "You can visit me whenever you like, my cheery girl," Aama whispers.

Aama sits at the threshold of her door two mornings later cradling her infant as she watches Mahili and Maya climb the path to the main trail and turn southwards.

Maya wears her new skirt; her hair comb and a brass cup are in her bag. She needs no suitcase. Five silver rupees from Aama are folded into the cloth band wound many times around her waist. No more short frocks for Maya. She is going to work with big sister. Mahili walks ahead clutching the straw sleeping mat Aama has woven for Maya.

Visiting Kathmandu for the first time should be a great adventure for a nine-year old. Maya has never seen a city, although she once rode in a bus. She knows there are electric lights there, bicycles and cinemas too, and many shops. In the factory she'll meet other girls and boys from Dandagaon.

The journey takes four days. Somewhere along the trail Maya lost a hair ribbon and her green blouse became stained. "No matter, my sweet sister; we shall buy a pretty green ribbon when we reach Kathmandu," Mahili assures her.

On the edge of the city Maya sees a bus and cries out, "Stop bus, stop."

"Come. That bus doesn't go to our home; we live in this direction," Mahili lies to her sister simply to save bus fare although it means the girls must walk another hour.

When they arrive at a shed behind a row of shops, Maya finds herself in a spacious building whose walls are wooden boards. The room has neither a loft nor ceiling, just a roof of tin sheets high overhead. The floor is earthen, with shallow pits here and there and clusters of neatly arranged utensils—trays and glasses, a teapot, a brass tin rice pot, a small kerosene stove. Each is a hearth marking the migrant home of a family of workers.

Rolled up straw mats stand against the walls; clothes hang from nails protruding from the wall or on posts set into the earth.

Somewhere in the distance Maya hears a clacking of wooden sticks—thump, thump, thump, thu-thump, thu-thump. Is someone threshing rice? Mingled with the thump thu-thump are young voices—sometimes giggles, sometimes a shriek. They are children's voices, children's coughs and giggles, children's shrieks and songs.

The names of friends, boys and girls who left the village long ago, come back to Maya and she asks Mahili: "Where is Sunita? Where is Rani?"

"They're at work; perhaps we'll see them tonight. Let us go to buy rice, some kerosene and a new ribbon for you; this is our free day little sister."

Wherever they walk Maya can hear the thu-thump, thump, thu-thump rising above the street noise. It is not a pretty sound.

Back in the big shed the girls cook their rice and sit wordless as they eat. After washing their plates under a faucet outside Maya moves to her sister's side so Mahili can weave the new green ribbon into her hair. "Tomorrow we begin work. We will sit side by side. I will be your teacher and we will have money every week to send to our Aama." Now let us sleep. They lay on their mat clutching one another closely while the thu-thump, thu-thump swirls through the air above them.

It is still dark when Maya feels a hand on her shoulder. "Kanchhi, Kanchhi—time for work. Come. Look, I have sugared chura for you." Mahili offers the child a bowl of beaten rice and they eat hastily from the same vessel. The older sister presses her hands over Maya's head and ties her hair back. "We must go; we'll take tea in the factory."

Around her, along both sides of the shed, Maya passes humps of sleeping bodies curled under thin blankets. Later she'd learn they are night workers who'd returned from the late shift. Coughing and wheezing sounds, though muffled, rise from those huddled unseen bodies. Maya thought she heard a child crying, calling 'Aama, Aama.'

The purple sky of early morning has not yet arrived so Maya must follow Mahili along a dark path. Those sounds Maya heard all night— thu-thum thu-thump, thum, thu-thump—grow louder and Maya finds their source; it's here in the factory itself. This place is many times larger than where they sleep. It too has an earthen floor and a tin roof, and walls of loosely fitting boards. "Look, we are already at work!" says Mahili enthusiastically trying to raise her sister's spirits.

The hall they enter is divided into rows of heavy platforms on which two-meter high structures rise. Wooden scaffolds fixed onto each platform look like machines with sheets of rope joining various joists. These, Maya would learn, are looms. Carpets in various stages of completion are stretched over each machine. Maya looks down a narrow corridor where children sit at looms as if they're tied there. A single bare light bulb hangs from the roof above. "Is Sunita here?" Maya asks.

"Shush. It's not a place to meet friends. Let's begin work," whispers Mahili as she climbs onto a platform, entering this machine of rope and wooden paddles. "Come; sit with me and I will teach you what to do," says the older girl as she fastens a strap behind them, binding them both into the loom. "This rope will stop you from falling off if you should become sleepy."

More children arrive and quietly move down the corridor. Each climbs up to a loom, where they too anchor themselves. Maya smiles with her cheerful brown eyes at two girls sitting nearby. They look the same age as she is. One asks her, "Where is your village?" But when Maya begins to speak the child has already turned back to the loom, joining her partner as they reach into rows of strings stretched before them. Their little golden fingers appear and disappear once more through the strings, then clak, clak, thu-thum thu-thump, clak clak.

"Watch me, watch me," Mahili whispers. The older girl lifts balls of wool, each a different colour, from behind the loom and drops them into her lap. Pulling a rope taunt, she unwinds a ball of yarn and fixes a knot around a string fastened to the bar above her stomach. She pulls more knots, loops coloured threads up and around, then repeats the process with another colour. "Look at my feet, watch my feet," Mahili continues to work as she instructs her sister. Their loom groans like all the others—clak clak, thu-thum thu-thump.

Bewildered, little Maya gazes though the dim light. She turns from watching her sister's feet to her fingers seemingly entangled in a net of strings, then back to her feet. "You can easily do this, little Maya," says Mahili encouragingly.

It doesn't take long for Maya to feel her eyes burning and her legs numbing. Flicks of wool cover her face. "I must stay awake. I must help Mahili," she murmurs, trying to follow her sister's movements in the dim light. The older girl continues as if she herself is the loom—

uncoiling, knotting, snipping, hammering, with her feet paddling underneath.

The next day the girls again rise before the sky turns purple. They wash in the dark, roll up their mats and again file into the factory. The following day, it's the same routine; next day too. Sometimes Maya even sleeps without removing her dusty work clothes. Within a week her legs ache. She has hardly walked at all during those days.

Maya and her sister together have completed a whole carpet in just four weeks. Two boys arrive to cut it off the loom, and for the first time Maya realizes what they've actually made. How soft and lovely it is, she thinks, moving her hand over the weave. How proud Aama will be.

She wonders if she might ever have a carpet like this to sleep on.

On Saturday the sisters join Sunita and Rani to prepare their food together. "Our brother has come from the village, bringing these pickles with him. Mother makes this from roasted sesame and sour mountain lemons; we cannot find this in the city. Here, take it," says Sunita to the sisters.

Each four weeks the workers in Maya's shift receive their pay. Returning from the office with her money clutched in her fist, Mahili calls her sister and they huddle together examining it as if it were a treasure. Mahili is delighted—"Three hundred rupees! What shall we buy?"

Mahili begins to count: "We must send 100 rupees to Aama; we need 100 for our food, twenty for kerosene, thirty for a blanket for you, five for soap, and keep twenty to repay our loan from the oil seller." Maya is quick to calculate their budget. "So we have twenty-five rupees for ourselves! Please, please, let us buy pauroti from the milk shop, and take it with a glass of sweetened milk."

"And maybe an egg for you, my growing little sister."

To arrange her mother's share Mahili seeks out a trusted courier. For just five rupees he'll safely deliver the money home.

Next free morning without taking their tea, the sisters set out for the market. At a nearby tea shop Mahili surrenders four rupees for bread and milk; they chuckle as they dip the white slices into hot milk. How lovely to have a few rupees for sweetened milk!

In the street, as they continue their excursion, Maya hears the same clak clak thu-thum thu-thump rising from hidden halls and sheds and she shakes in panic.

Sensing Maya's distress, Mahili has a solution. "Next holiday, we shall visit the palace. Or, shall we go to the gates of big hotels and watch visitors come and go? Or we can take darshan of Swayambhu."

"Let us ask Devi to write a letter to Aama," suggests Maya. "What nice gift shall we send with it? A plastic ladle, some glass bracelets, maybe paper-wrapped candies?"

Months pass. The sisters spend week after week in the same encasing loom. Aama occasionally sends pickles, but there are no letters. Still, whenever the girls dispatch money home, they enclose a note with news about their friends, the children around them.

Three years have passed when one morning Maya hears a cry not far from where she sits, then the thunder of wood collapsing, then more shrieks. It is the only time in these three years that Maya remembers the thu-thump thu-thump halting. Out of the silence that day rise young, thin cries.

Mahili and others quickly unstrap themselves and run down the walkway to find five children standing immobilized, weeping. On the floor, pinned under a collapsed loom lies Rani, arms splayed and legs bent under her. A beam of wood is across her chest. More sobs spill from young onlookers. When the older girls step close to Rani and pulls the arm of the immobilized girl, another great rumble occurs and more debris collapses around them. The bigger girls jump free but Rani remains still under a mass of ropes and boards. "Rani is dead, Rani is dead," one child utters, and then others repeat the cry. Now shouts surge from behind the huddle of children: "Get out, get out all of you. Out. Quickly. To your quarters," yells a man rushing towards them.

The manager's assistant clears the room and more men arrive and hastily remove the fallen pillars and carry Rani to a waiting car. They will take her to the hospital, they announce. "Stay in your room, all of you," spits the foreman as he rushes away.

In their barracks the children awaken workers from the early shift; they all gather in a cluster waiting, hardly daring to speak.

The foreman returns and talks softly to the assembled children; "Rani is OK, not hurt badly; when she's stronger we will take her home. No reason to be afraid," he assures them and orders everyone back to work.

There they find the broken loom has disappeared; and Rani's weaving partner is nowhere to be seen. Somebody says the boss will pay her extra to work in the manager's house.

Thulo Manchha, the manager, and a Tibetan man speaking English and some foreign people visit the factory not long after the accident. "If they ask about Rani, tell them you know nothing. Nobody was hurt here," Mahili and the older girls instruct the young workers. "If we say something is wrong here, the factory will close and Aama will have no food."

The thrumming and clacking of the looms seem inexorable.

Some visitors move through the corridors taking photos and smiling at the children who grin in reply, hoping this will show how pleased they are to work here. No one is curious about their health; visitors seem occupied with comparing numbers of things—rupees, dollars, dates, colours, knots per inch, this many twin carpets and that many double sized—as they walk about. Then they leave.

The workers are afraid that if Rani really died, there would be trouble for them all. Weeks pass. The accident with Rani seems to have been forgotten; there are no more curious visitors and the big boss does not return.

One night as Maya, Mahili and other weavers are preparing their food, boys from their villages arrive. Some of them are dyers at wool factories near the river where there was trouble about workers throwing waste dye-water into the river. They'd done this for many years but now, that's forbidden; their factory might close. "It's the foreigners again," claims one boy. "They came and photographed our work and went to the river with their medicines; they found poison in the Bagmati. They say the dyes we use kill the water and that's bad for Nepal. In the future we can't wash wool in the river."

The weavers understand that if the dye sheds close so will their factory. "We'll go to Patan," Mahili tells the others. "There are factories there."

"I have searched for work there," replies an older boy. "The managers supply rice and peas but the rice is not good and the pay is low." Another adds, "They won't give us work; they say we're just children."

These boys from the dye sheds have a proposal: "We're going to refuse to work. We will tell the bosses we will not work until they allow half a day of school for every young worker." School? Maya's eyes light up when she hears the word. "Will someone teach me to write?" she wonders.

But the discussion already moved on: "There must be better lighting in the sheds. They must build a closed-in shower for every hundred workers, a toilet for every fifty. They must build sinks in our kitchens. We will ask for a kilo of rice for each worker, each week — added to our salary."

The children look at one another. "How? Who will give these things to us? What extra work must we do for the bosses?" They remember stories about girls who went to play with the bosses, who slept on real beds.

"How shall we pay for school?"

Padma, one of the older girls, stands up. "We shall not pay. They shall pay. We have a right. We have a plan.

"We are listing what we want here," and she holds the paper to show everyone. Then she explains the plan. "We shall stop working Sunday, the day after we collect our pay. We will sit outside the factory gate and not allow new workers to take our places."

A boy from a factory in Jawalakhel outside Kathmandu rises and speaks." Our weavers have been saving funds every month for the past year; we are prepared to face the difficulties, and we will help you. We will send you food. Our workers will come and sit with you, to bar entrance to the factory. The dyers from the wool washing plant will come to protect your things so no one steals your pots and bedding. They will guard this shed so you will not be put into the street. You will be safe."

Maya feels confused. But she sees a sparkle in the eyes of these older boys and girls. Mahili rises to sit beside Padma and smiles back at Maya: "Yes, Maya. You shall really study at a school; soon Aama will be so pleased because you can write her to tell her about our all friends here."

EPILOGUE

When I set out to prepare this edition I had not imagined that so many new questions about these two extraordinary women would reoccupy my thoughts. So compelling are these Nepali rebels that they refuse to leave me; I am driven to more deeply examine their characters, to assess their strategies, to learn what others wrote about them in intervening years, to assess public reaction to news about them, and to consider how their reputations are stimulating attention or impacting changes underway in Nepal today.

Enormous advances have taken place across Nepal since I first began assembling these histories. I need to take those into account too. Alas, none of the developments—in the political structure, in caste dynamics, in women's status, and in ethnic identity politics— seem in any way related to the campaigns of Yogmaya and Durga Devi. Nevertheless, not unreasonably, I felt that I couldn't prepare this book without re-evaluating these women's work in the context of recent transformations in the country.

Some issues like corruption and exploitation of vulnerable communities are actually more widespread today than when these women raised their voices to challenge the authorities and overturn abuses. Early campaigns directed at similar injustices are testimony of the depth of these problems in Nepal. Whether or not those early calls for justice succeeded, reviewing them can be useful for activists, reformers and politicians as they move forward.

Recent years have seen a range of projects launched in the name of Yogmaya Neupane. None, as far as I am aware, yet addresses issues of corruption, injustice, women's rights or structural inequalities endemic in the country. This is troubling. Are Yogmaya's and Durga Devi's historical examples of the search for justice worthless?

If we really believe Yogmaya was noble and worthy, brave and outstanding, then we have a challenge: to adopt strategies and find ways through Nepal's hard won democracy to somehow implement her ideals—in social, legal and artistic programs, not in monuments and conferences.

Almost a century has passed since the height of Yogmaya Neupane's career, more than seventy years in the case of Durga Devi Karki Ghimire. The possibility of useful empirical study recedes with time, even as these women's reputations may become better known.

The daring novel *Yogmaya* arrives at an especially critical and promising time. This semi-fictional history and a subsequent eponymous stage adaptation demonstrate the value of more creative interpretations; I elaborate on this in my article "Literature Can Displace Anthropology" (translated into Nepali; https://www. kantipurdaily.com/koseli/2018/10/06/153879427213244251. html). These sahasi women's lives and their personalities offer venerable ideals, abundant drama and awesome personalities that can stimulate others' creative energies. The story is far from over.

My experiences with these historical figures and with contemporary Nepali friends profoundly altered the course of my own life, my global political perspective in particular. So I want to close with an excerpt from my prologue to *Heir to a Silent Song* describing my prescient first visit to Parijat.

I should first explain how I came to hear Parijat's name because it actually emerged from my association with Yogmaya. And I was still in the Arun River Valley!

Dharma Shrestha working with me at Manakamana told me that there was another politically driven Nepali patriot, also a woman committed to securing her peoples' freedom. "Her name is Parijat. She is a poet," he explained. "Her verses are circulating around the nation—

recited by brave young people in their irrepressible search for justice."
My curiosity was aroused, although I really didn't know what to expect
from a meeting with this dissident bard. And I certainly had no inkling
about how she (along with Yogmaya and Durga Devi) might influence
my own inchoate political views.

Reaching Kathmandu from the eastern hills, I was led to Parijat's
residence by a young worker at the Panorma Hotel (no longer a feature
of Nepal's capital, and never very panoramic) where I lodged while in
the city. This lad, likely after overhearing me mention my search for
Parijat to someone on the phone, approached me and blurted, "She is
my auntie; I'll take you to her." I welcomed his invitation particularly
since inquiries to Nepali professors I knew had yielded nothing of the
dissident's whereabouts.

Parijat's cottage was located among paddy fields sheltered by a
thick grove of bamboo near Naya Bazaar on the periphery of
Kathmandu. With my arrival at the gate of her home I was initiated
into a whole new relationship with Nepal.

*One hot afternoon in 1981, returning to Kathmandu from my second visit
to the hills of East Nepal, I carried with me a treasured copy of Sarvartha
Yogbani- a slim, sepia-colored volume entrusted to me at Manakamana by
one of Yogmaya's surviving disciples. This was a collection of the rebel's
utterances, sharp political invocations, which had been strictly banned
following her martyrdom. How many people outside East Nepal knew of its
existence forty-one years later (when dissent and opposition to the ruler was
still forbidden) and if the verses in this extraordinary collection had any
parallels, I was uncertain.*

*If there was someone comparable to the Bhojpur rebel, I might find her
in a modest, brick cottage in Meipi, a quiet corner of Kathmandu Valley to
where I was headed that day. Here resided a political opponent to the ruler,
a poet and writer who together with a small group of dissidents dared to
challenge the absolute authority of the king.*

*I was told her verses were not unlike Yogmaya's in their power to inspire
young people's call for reform and for justice. I was keen to learn what she had*

in common with Yogmaya whose utterances had stirred an earlier generation of Nepalis to call for freedom.

As I made my way through the fields around Meipi in what was then the outskirts of Nepal's capital, I had no feeling of any danger I might encounter. Nor of the reward that awaited me. I trustingly followed this young lad of 12 who seemed proud to simply lead me to the house of his esteemed auntie. Apart from her being a popular poet, I knew nothing about Parijat. Nor did I have any awareness at that time of what threats and punishments she and other political dissidents faced.

This was a decade before the popular revolution of 1990 which led to limited political reform, and before the rise of the Maoist guerrilla movement. Meanwhile a nascent struggle for democracy was underway, centered at the poet's residence.

The path where the boy took me passed through thick green fields of paddy, then ended at a clearing where a red brick dwelling stood. Parijat was expecting me, I'd been told. But no one waited for me at the threshold. Instead, some 15 meters from the door, a man sat on a stool outside a low wooden fence across the clearing. He was dressed in a police uniform, and it immediately became clear that he was not there to protect the famous dissident, but to monitor who passed in and out of her residence. Authorities knew this cottage was a place where activists congregated—some arrived directly from prison; others gathered here for strategy meetings; visitors came in search of succor, a few weeks' employment, a loan, to collect bulletins for distribution, seeking counsel, a meal.

This was the house of an 'enemy of the king', and anyone passing through that innocent ramshackle gate which stood before me would be reported to Nepal's security services.

I was not prepared for a confrontation, yet neither was I intimidated. Perhaps my newfound solidarity with Yogmaya, possibly the presence of that volume of poems tucked inside my shoulder bag urged me on.

I knew the policeman would register my presence, and send my name to an office in the Singha Durbar.

The boy who led me here had already reached the doorway. I hesitated for barely an instant; then I lifted the latch on the swinging wooden gate and walked forward, as if propelled by Yogmaya herself.

Acknowledgements

So many people assisted me in the course of this extended journey starting in the early 1980s during my original research forays, then in preparation of *Heir to a Silent Song*, and during the past decade as we keenly follow new developments around the public's growing awareness of Yogmaya Neupane.

My initial thanks go to novelist Neelam Karki Nikarika whose unconventional approach opens exciting and unlimited possibilities for scholars and the public to pursue the subject of Yogmaya; her work also invites me to rethink issues and my initial approach to our Nepali rebel woman. Niharika is a worthy descendent of Yogmaya, an unarguably major figure in history whom other women inexplicably had largely chosen to overlook. Her entry into this narrative is heartening and promising.

How encouraging it is that Mandala Book Point, a leading publisher, continues what The Centre for Nepal and Asian Studies at Tribhuvan University undertook with the 2001 publication of *Heir to a Silent Song*, launched thanks to its Executive Director Prof. T.P. Mishra, Deputy Director Prof. Nirmal Man Tuladhar and our esteemed colleague Dr. Harka Gurung.

My deep gratitude goes to Nirmal Tuladhar, currently Chair of Social Science Baha, for his assistance in overseeing its publication. He, Padma Tara Tuladhar and I have been consulting on vicissitudes of Yogmaya over several years, a testimony to our enduring and fruitful friendship.

I've had the pleasure of working with Nirvaya Subedi, a writer and culture critic. Independently drawn to Yogmaya's story, he's become a trusted colleague, generously assisting me with translations and offering valuable comments during this book's preparation.

Long ago, before anyone else grasped the benefit of these extraordinary histories, national poet and democracy activist Parijat urged me forward. She reinforced initial encouragement received from Harka Gurung, Nepal's renowned geographer and intellectual; this, even at a time when such investigations were politically risky in Nepal. Although neither of them is with us today, they'd be proud of where their trust and insights have led. The same applies to the thirty-two women at Manakamana kuti on the Arun River shore who hosted me, trusted me, and taught me. Among them ManaMaya and Vishnumaya Dahal proved indispensable to my grasp of the issues.

Contemporary scholars—Drs. Dipesh Neupane, Matrika Timsina, and Govinda Mansingh Karki, and Ninu Chapagain—all currently engaged in original research into Yogmaya Neupane's history, generously acknowledged the value of my work to their own pursuits, and later, when we eventually met, warmly received me. We continue to engage in discussions about Yogmaya.

Matrika Timsina reconnected me with Dharma Shrestha with whom I'd lost touch following our work at Manakamana. Since our reunion in 2015 we meet as often as possible, in the U.S. and in Nepal.

In the preparation of this manuscript I've had technical assistance from Sandesh Tuladhar who also updated the map, and perceptive comments by Shreeya Rai. Maria Toft arranged an online bibliography of my articles on Nepal (see p 223, Online Sources), advised on the title and designed the cover. The 2018 and 2019 photographs of newly embellished Yogmaya historical sites along the Arun River are provided by Babita Katwal and Bhupal Thapa. (These same places were completely deserted lacking any landmark or building when I visited them in the 1980s.) Nirman Shrestha arranged for the Google map of Majhuwabesi, and Nirdesh Tuladhar helped assemble the photographic entries. To all, I owe my boundless thanks.

In late 2019, I had the pleasure of Babita Katwal's sturdy, cheerful companionship on our journey to Majhuwabesi and Gaudeni Cave where Mohan Basnet warmly received us. I'm grateful to them and to Rajendra Thapa, Sankhuwasabha ethnographer, who accompanied me to Marwa where Durga Devi's Ghimire relatives generously shared new details about her with us; they affirm that much more can be learned about her career. I am honoured to have the trust of these fine people and indebted to them for their support.

These many helpers constitute a kind of panorama of my enriching, sometimes hazardous, occasionally anxious, frequently interrupted, yet sustained and ever-evolving career in Nepal—at lofty Solu monasteries and restless Kathmandu neighbourhoods, in the industrious Tarai plains, over forested mountain ridges, and along white-sandy banks of the formidable Arun River—with welcome new associates and my long-standing colleagues.

Throughout these many years Sukanya Waiba, sister of Parijat, kept me informed about Nepal's vital political developments and the country's awakening interest in Yogmaya. I thank her for her unfaltering friendship.

Madhab Lal Mahrajan, Executive Director of Mandala Book Point, extended his personal attention to this publication.

I am grateful to all for their enduring encouragement and warmth.

Note on spellings and photo illustrations

In this volume I adopt a conventional rendition of Nepali place names and terms; some may differ slightly from what I used in the 2001 edition. Because of a personal attachment to *yogbani* (and *hazurbani*) I italicise them throughout the text; otherwise I use standard font for Nepali words and drop all diacritical marks.

Photographs accompanying the text are from the early period of research 1980-1985 and from 2018-2019. Although the quality of some is not ideal, I include them so that readers can compare the historic sites as recorded earlier, then forty years later. I also want to share with readers, images of some of the personalities discussed and quoted in the book. Photos with captions ending in BK and BT are courtesy of Babita Katwal and Bhupal Thapa respectively. The 2013 mural inspired by Yogmaya's story was photographed by Nirvaya Subedi. Other photos are by the author whose photo archive from her 1980s tenure in Majhuwabesi and Sankhuwasabha, and from other parts of Nepal, and in Tibet, are posted on www.barbaranimri. com. Her complete collection is archived in digital form in the Nepal Picture Library, Kathmandu under "Barbara Nimri Aziz Collection/ Yogmaya". To contact: mail@nepalpicturelibrary.org.

Bibliography

Nepali and English publications on Yogmaya and Durga Devi

Books

Aalok, Pawan, ed. 2013. *Bahumukhi Byaktitwa Ki Dhani Yogmaya* (a collection of previously published articles on Yogmaya). 2070 B.S. Kathmandu: Nepal Shrashta Samaj.

Aziz, Barbara Nimri. 2001. *Heir to a Silent Song: Two Rebel Women of Nepal.* Kathmandu: Center for Nepal and Asian Studies (CNAS), Tribhuvan University.

Bhandari, Lekhnath, ed. 2002. *Yogamaya 1860–1941. Sarvartha yogavani; Yogamaya Nyaupane.* Kathmandu: Vaikalpika Samuha (2059 B.S.).

Chapagain, Ninu. 2018. *Sarvartha Yogbani ra Pragatishil Yogmaya,* (Sarvartha Yogbani and the Progressive Poet Yogmaya). Kathmandu.

Mansingh Karki, Govinda. 2012. *Samaj Sudharak Yogmaya.* Kathmandu: Sajha Prakashan, (2069 B.S.).

Neupane, Dipesh. 2018. *Amar Jyoti Yogmaya.* Kathmandu: Yogmaya Foundation.

Neupane, Dipesh. 2014. "The Synthesis between Social Protest and Nirguna Bhakti in Yogmaya's Sarvartha Yogbani." Unpublished PhD Thesis. Tribhuvan University.

Niharika, Neelam Karki. 2018. *Yogmaya*. Kathmandu: Sangrila Books. (Recipient of Madan Puraskar Literary Award, 2018.)

Pant, Uttam. 2019. *Yogmayadham*. Kathmandu.

Timsina, Matrika. 2013. *Nepali Santa Paramparama Yogmaya Ra Sarvartha Yogbani*. Kathmandu: Pairabi Publication, 2070 B.S. (With a short introduction by BN Aziz.)

Selected Articles

Aziz, Barbara Nimri. 1993. "Shakti Yogmaya: A Tradition of Dissent in Nepal." Charles Ramble and Martin Brauen, eds., *Anthropology of Tibet and the Himalaya*. Zurich: Ethnological Museum of the University of Zurich. (From Aziz' 1990 lecture presented at the conference on Tibet and Himalayan Studies, Zurich.)

_____ 1994. "Durga Devi: A Woman's Tale from the Arun River Valley." Michael Allen, editor, *Anthropology of Nepal: Peoples, Problems and Processes*. Kathmandu: Mandala Book Point. (From Aziz' 1992 lecture presented at the International Conference on the Anthropology of Nepal, Kathmandu.)

_____ 1989. "Buddhist Nuns." *Natural History,* Magazine of The American Museum of Natural History, New York. March, pp. 40–49.

_____ 1978. "Ani Chodon: Portrait of a Buddhist Nun." *Loka 2,* A Journal from The Naropa Institute, Boulder. Pp. 43–46.

Neupane, Dipesh. 2013. "Renunciation in Sarvartha Yogbani." *Patan Pragya Research Journal*. February 2013.

_____ 2013. "Samajik Yoddha Yogmaya." *Gorkha Patra Daily, 28.09.13.*

_____ 2013. "Yogmaya as Star of the Darkest Age." *Adarsa Smarika*. 2070 B.S.

_____ 2012. "Social and Political Lampoon in Yogmaya's Sarvartha Yogbani." *Molung Research Journal*. July, 2012.

_____ 2012. "Spiritualism and Religious Fervor in Sarvartha Yogbani." *Pursuits, A Journal of English Studies*. July, 2012.

_____ 2010. "Yogmaya's Sarvartha Yogbani as the Embodiment of Spiritual Illumination and Enlightenment—The Path of Buddha." *Ganesh Man Darpan.* 2067 B.S.

Karki, Padma Singh, http://annapurnapost.com/news/132861. Op Ed. योगमायाको गन्तव्य "Yogamaya's Legacy." July 22, 2019

Online Sources

Selected Online Articles on Nepal 2015-2020. Earlier writings on Himalayan history and culture can be accessed on HYPERLINK "https://barbaranimri.com/blog-nepal" \t "_blank" barbaranimri.com/blog-nepal

https://en.wikipedia.org/wiki/Yogmaya_Neupane

https://www.peacewomen.org/content/nepal-yogmaya-neupane nepals-first-female-revolutionary.

https://www.counterpunch.org/2020/04/27/have-nepals-people-managed-a-healthy-breakthrough-in-the-covid-19-crisis/

https://www.globalresearch.ca/nepal-turn-around-realize-your-neighbor-china/5708101 (2020/03/30)

https://www.counterpunch.org/2019/01/16/how-long-can-nepalblame-others-for-its-woes/

https://www.counterpunch.org/2019/01/04/can-nepal-realisticallylook-to-china-as-an-alternative-trade-partner/

https://www.counterpunch.org/2018/08/31/literature-candisplace-anthropology/

https://www.kantipurdaily.com/koseli/2018/10/06/153879427213244251.html

https://www.asia-pacificresearch.com/migrant-labor-a-central-pillarof-nepals-grim-economy/5628220

https://www.asia-pacificresearch.com/nepals-economy-cancontented-tourists-match-desperate-migrant-laborers/5628213

https://www.counterpunch.org/2018/06/29/becoming-ademocracy-the-example-of-nepal/

https://www.counterpunch.org/2018/06/29/becoming-
ademocracy-the-example-of-nepal/

https://www.counterpunch.org/2017/11/24/an-allegedcommunist-
and-prostitute-in-nepals-grade-ten-schoolbooks/

http://www.globalresearch.ca/womens-art-and-other-work-
innepals-hill-country/5602583

https://www.globalresearch.ca/nepal-womens-art-andpolitics/
5603623

https://www.globalresearch.ca/womens-artand-other-work-in-
nepals-hill-country/5602583 (First published in Heresies,
Journal of Feminist Art and Politics. 1978, Volume 4, pp 43–45.)

https://www.counterpunch.org/2017/07/07/democracy-in-nepal-
passes-a-second-test/

https://www.counterpunch.org/2016/06/17/china-or-india-does-
nepal-have-a-realistic-choice/

https://www.counterpunch.org/2018/06/29/becoming-a-
democracy-the-example-of-nepal/

http://www.counterpunch.org/2016/05/10/one-happy-man-
anepal-case-study/

http://www.counterpunch.org/2015/10/26/nepals-democracy
landmark-a-constitution-leads-to-instability/

http://www.counterpunch.org/2015/06/08/nepal-earth-
tremorsfading-monsoon-looming/

http://www.counterpunch.org/2015/05/29/demolition-
dilemmasacross-nepal/

http://www.counterpunch.org/2015/05/26/schoolboy-looks-
tonepals-army-with-new-pride/

http://www.counterpunch.org/2015/05/18/awaiting-the-
nextrumble-in-nepal/

http://www.counterpunch.org/2015/05/13/three-women-insearch-
of-munas-house-a-nepal-guide-to-gongabu/

http://www.counterpunch.org/2015/05/11/nepal-signs-ofprogress-
if-not-hope/

http://www.counterpunch.org/2015/05/06/dispatch-from
kathmandu/

Introducing Hazurbani

Hazur: master—Yogmaya: *bani:* her message. Here, we include one volume of Yogmaya's utterances as printed in the original Nepali [1]. This is a photo offset of the booklet gifted to me by Mata Damodara Giri, who headed Manakamana Kuti during the years when I visited there. The volume was published in 1940 in Kalimpong, India by Mani Press not long after the passing of Yogmaya.

This is not a comprehensive collection, but it is the only book I was able to obtain at the time and I drew heavily on it for my research on the teachings of Yogmaya, their creator [2]. All the translated poems cited in Chapter 5 derive from this collection.

From the time of Yogmaya's 'entry to heaven' and until well after 1990, although the oppressive Rana rule had ended twenty years before, unlimited political expression in the country was not possible even under the Shah monarchy. Clandestine copies of this and other collections of Yogmaya's work may have existed, but the work was essentially unavailable. Whoever owned a copy kept it hidden. Banned during the Rana period, broadcast of *hazurbani,* either orally or through these texts, was equally dangerous during Panchayat rule (1960–1990). One colleague, making inquiries about Yogmaya after seeing the collection I obtained in 1981, claimed that volumes similar to this were in the possession of some surviving members of Yogmaya's movement (in Kathmandu and in East Nepal). Whether or not any were made available to him, I'm uncertain.

The political message of *hazurbani*, although some verses may be less explicitly political than others, is self evident within the text. We are delighted to include translations of 33 of those poems in Chapter 5 of this edition; you will easily grasp how they unequivocally demonstrate the art and message of their creator.

But there is much more to be revealed by *hazurbani*. For anyone interested in political philosophy, women's history and Nepali literature in general, this work promises further benefit.

The pithy, often witty, and poignant quality of Yogmaya's creations demand that this collection be made widely available. We reproduce it in its entirety to introduce her teachings to the largest possible audience. Any Nepali-speaking person can now have immediate access to her philosophy and enjoy and appreciate her intelligence and daring. Activists, authors, philosophers, even bureaucrats can find the verses insightful. With inclusion of the entire 1940 volume here, we hope to stimulate translation into other languages for writers, teachers, women advocates, political activists, and scholars worldwide.

My personal introduction to *hazurbani* was through oral transmission. During my first two visits in 1980 and 1981, living with the custodians of Yogmaya's legacy in Manakamana in East Nepal, I was unaware of this book's existence. I heard *hazurbani* being sung by Manakamana residents who knew them well:—women who fifty years earlier lived through their creation and dissemination at the height of Yogmaya's political attacks against Rana tyranny. I collected some of their recitations on audiotape and transcribed these with the help of my assistant, Dharma Shrestha. Before the translations were complete, even with my rudimentary knowledge of Nepali, I could experience the enthralling power of Yogmaya's words.

I've always believed the music of *hazurbani* was as equally important as the text. Although not a musicologist, from my earlier experiences across Nepal I suspected their uniqueness the very first time I heard *bani* uttered by Bhattini Aama and ManaMaya, her colleague at Manakamana. They recited countless verses from memory for me, and explained that their distinctive rhythm was in fact crafted by Ganga

Devi, Yogmaya's sister-in-law. It is also said that these verses embody characteristics of East Nepal's regional hill music as well as distinct local idioms. In this respect, they are cultural treasures emanating from the very area where Yogmaya grew up. The superior quality of the poetry is now affirmed by many of Nepal's literary authorities, and their positive impact on anyone who has read or heard them is unarguable and affirming. I expect these verses will eventually find many admirers; they may even inspire the creation of contemporary *bani*.

Reactions to the collection, particularly from politically oriented citizens, speak for the verses' ideological appeal. Their social relevance lives on even now, a century after their creation. Nepalis from the Bhojpur region have long held these verses dear. As time passes, we expect *hazurbani* will find favour throughout Nepal's many communities.

When poet Parizat, Harka Gurung, Murari Aryal, Khagendra Sangraula and other savants and writers first read these verses, all unhesitantly embraced them for their literary value, their charm, and their political sagacity.

With the implementation of (some degree of) democracy after 1990 in Nepal, we expected the emergence of a deeper and wider appreciation of Yogmaya's contributions. (Now in 2020, as summarized in Chapters 1 and 2, we have abundant evidence of widening knowledge of this Nepali rebel and poet). Matrika Timsina is leading the way with his analyses of these verses and we anticipate others will follow as the public becomes increasingly aware of what this remarkable woman can teach us about Nepal and the pursuit of justice.[3]

Yogmaya's political agenda was not entirely clear to me at first. Even so, I suspected these verses would definitely and unequivocally reveal her teachings. In pursuit of their significance in the context of Nepali history and literary traditions, I carried them to Kathmandu from the hills where I'd been gifted them; I showed them to a colleague who immediately grasped their value. Next, the pre-eminent poet Parijat recognized Yogmaya as a literary figure of stature and she included this book in a conference she convened in 1984 focused on literature by Nepali women.

I have hardly met a Nepali who, reading this work for the first time, is not exhilarated by it. One man, upset that he continues to face family criticism over his inter-caste marriage, told me how helpful and moving he found a particular verse in this collection. He read the verse to his wife and daughter in order to help them understand his personal feelings about his decision years earlier to shed his orthodox Brahmin beliefs.

One Nepali writer examining these verses recalled to me that he'd seen some of them in his youth 35 years before. He'd been impressed by them at that time and was eager to take a closer look now that we'd made them available. He agreed to assist us by translating some verses for this book. As he began this work, he told me, he was overcome with pride and gratitude to their creator.

In view of the corruption that is so rampant in Nepal today (on-going in 2000, possibly more severe in 2020), we read Yogmaya's early attacks on corruption with renewed appreciation. Her words offer us a powerful non-violent weapon with which to fight today's many injustices.

Almost a century after their creation, living in a very different era from Yogmaya's, we can feel her contemporariness. She speaks to universal issues that transcend time; her language is fresh, her wit invigorating.

We include this collection for readers because of our commitment to wider dissemination of Yogmaya's teachings and creations.

Notes

[1] Although the text may contain some grammatical or typographical errors, we reproduce it as it was originally printed.

[2] Now in 2020, 40 years after this copy was made available to me, and 80 years after its publication, no other collection of Yogmaya's utterances, in verse or in prose, has surfaced. The search for them should nevertheless continue.

[3] See Matrika Timsina, Ninu Chapagain and Bhandari et al, in our bibliography.

Appendix II

Sarvartha Yogbani.
Nepali Text, 1940, Kalimpong.

श्री

सर्वार्थ योगवाँणी

लेखक—
भक्तियोग माया

प्रवन्ध—
चिन्ता मणि

प्रकाशक—
डम्बर बाहादुर क्षत्री

(सर्वाधार स्वरक्षित)

ठेगांना
पृ० ४ नं०
दिङ्ला मजुवा ब्याँशि
नेपाल ।

मुल्य—जिर्णोद्धार

श्री भूमिका

ॐ नमः शिव शक्ति सत्य सचेत शरणा गत,
संसार रूपि समुद्रबाट पार हुने उत्तम मार्ग,

श्री भक्ति योग मायाको शुक्ष्म वर्णन, वाँहा नेपाल पूर्व ४ नम्बर मजुवा सिले कौडिन्य गोत्र न्यौपाने ब्राह्मण कुल्म जन्म भै, शन्सारका हरेक ब्यबहारि रस लाई चाखि, मान्व ब्यवहार गर्दैं जाँदा बैराग्यको बिजा रोपण भै मानव तिर्थस्थान श्री बद्रि नारायण; उत्तर ख्याम्पालुङ हिमालय आदिमा समेत जाँद मन्भा सान्त नभै अरूण वरूण श्री इन्द्रा वति सङ्गम मजुवा त्रृवेणि घाटमा रहि श्री सङ्क्रेश्वर भगवानको आधार्ति उग्र तपस्या तर्फ बढ्दै जाँनु भो । तपस्याको वर्णन गर्न लाई हामी— अशिक्षा द्वारा बिचार न भएका मानव तनवाट वर्णन गर्न के शकौंला ।

ठन्डिमा जल शैया गर्मिमा पञ्चाग्नि आश्रय गरि इत्यादि कष्ट देखाउँद कहिले अन्न पानी त्यागि गुफाको आधार गर्न कहिले कहिले निलाहार रहने, कहिले श्री गङ्गाजीका सेवाद्वारा फलाहार रहने कहिले गाईको दुध मात्र कहिले अमलाका दाना मात्र, कहिले फुलको वाशन मात्र, कहिले हावा मात्र आहारा गरि आइ लागेका लोकापबसदलाई सहन गर्दैं श्री गङ्गबहादुरलाई तपो- बलको बिचार दिदैं समिपमा रहेका दुःखि जनबाट सेवा लिदै तपोबल योग सक्तिद्वारा खुलेका भविष्यमा हुने बाँणि सुन्ने लिखे राख्ने लेखने कोहि नहुँदा मानव तन्मा सम्बन्धकि गङ्गा देविबाट गरिएका सेवाद्वारा त्रृकाळ्का भजन बाह्राँलाई कृपा गरि बक्सियो

(ख)

ओ भविष्यका लागी हुने वाणि सर्वत्र नावालख निरक्षरि वर्ष
८ की पुत्री नैनकलामा आफ्ना मुखारविन्दबाट सुम्पि दिनु भो ।
प्रभूका कृपाले उनलाई नभुलि लिन करै लाग्यो सो वाणि श्रवण
गर्ना साथ कस्तै पत्थर हृदयमा पनि सत भावनाको विजा रोपण
हुने सो वाणी १४ वर्ष पछि लेखता पनि नभुलिएका हुँदा सर्वार्थ
योग वाणी लेखिएका प्रख्यात छन्, तपस्याको आनन्द लिन लागे
पछि श्री नरेन्द्र वहादुर द्वारा मजुवा व्याँसि टापुमा १ कुटि बनियो
र त्यसैमा आश्रम गर्नु भो' पूर्व तपस्याका तपोरश सारालाई वर्ताउन
लागनु भयो सो तपोरश यो माहाँभारतदेखि लिएर विन्ध्याचल सम्म
कड्रौं नरनारी पर्यन्त नियमित रूपसंग सामान्य पठित जन्देखी
लिएर ठुला ठुला अभाह २ जनहरूमा पनि प्रकाश भयो आसाममा
ब्यवहार गरि बस्तु भएका श्री पं० प्रेमनारायण सारा ब्यवहार
छाडि अर्ध रात्रीमा उठी श्री भक्तिजीका चरणमा दाखिल भई भक्त
दास बन्नु भयो । तपोवल सत शब्दले ब्रह्माण्डमा खलबल मच्चिन
लाग्यो । भक्तहरू छानिन खिचिन लागे । वाहाँका भक्तहरूको नाम लेख्न
लाई लामो लेखाई पर्ने हुनाले माहाँनन्द, रत्नमान, पहल्मान् डिल्लि
बाहादुर, डम्बरबाहादुर आदि दम्पति सहित सारा दुःखी हरिभजनका
भोका प्रभू चरणका दाश घेरैं स्त्री, पुरूष, बाल, बृद्ध चरणमा दाखिल
हुन आए । ॐ नमः शिव शक्ति सत्य सचेत शरणा गत । भज्ञे
शब्द गंकन लाग्यो सत शब्दका ध्वनिले गर्दा झुठो असत खल्वलिन
लाग्यो हरेक लोकापवाद पनि आई परे । अघि भएको देव दानवकां
खेला जस्तै खेला पनि हुन लाग्यो ।

जस्तै श्री मोहिनिबाट एउटै घड़ामा राखियेको चिज बाड़िये-
को थियो कसैलाई अमृत पर्न गयो कसैलाई बिष पर्न गयो
जस्ले जस्तो पाछनु थियो सो सो पाई भक्तहरू कृतार्थ पनि भये ।
त्यस्तै खेला पनि हुन लाग्यो एता चरणका दास मैं श्री गङ्गाजी
पं० प्रेम नारायण गङ्ग बाहादुर, नरेन्द्र बाहादुर, टेक बाहादुर, डिल्लि

बाहादुर, चमेलि, शिव भक्तिनि पं० गोपिकृष्ण लगायत सारा आफ्ना भक्त दाव्राँ वाव्राँ राखि हरि भजनमा आल्हाद भें तपोरश वर्षाई भक्तका शरिरमा करकमलका छाप लगाई भक्तका हार बनाई हृदयमा लिनु भयो तपोरश योग शक्तिका आनन्दको सीमा रहेन वर्णन गर्ने हामी अशामर्थ छौं केवल अन्तःकरण पुग्नु सक्तैं न प्रभू शरण………………

हरि भज भनि सारालाई चेताउन लाग्नु भयो लोकबाट स्तुति निन्दा बराबर आउँदथे स्तुति निन्दा एकै रूपबाट पान गर्नु हुन्थ्यो राजधानिमा समेत चेताउँनु पर्छ भनि पं० प्रेम नारायण लाई पठाउँनु भयो श्री ३ चन्द्रमा सुचना गर्दा गर्दै स्पर्स हुन नपाउँदै वाहाँ मुक्त हुनु भयो । श्री ३ भिमका पालामा बिन्ति पत्र द्वारा श्रवण गराउँदा गोकर्ण उत्तर बाहिनि गुफामा राखने हुकुम भै पं० प्रेमलाई गुफामा राख्नु भयो, बिचमा नेपाल वाशि धेरै भक्ति बनिए भक्त श्री ३ पद्म, श्री गु० भरतराज लोचन निधि समेतबाट सेवा गरिनु भयो श्री ३ मा भने वार्तालाप हुन नपाउँदै वाहाँ पनि मुक्त हुनु भयो पुर्ववत श्रवण हूँदा श्री ३ जुद्धका पालामा श्री पं० प्रेमलाई राजदरवारमा लगि श्री भक्तिजिको वर्णन श्रवण गराउँदा श्री भक्तिजिले पठाउँनु भयेको सुचना पाँव्ने धर्म पालना गर्छु भन्ने सत्य कबोल भै त्यसको चिन्न १ फुल्को थुँगो श्री भक्ति जिमा चढाउँन हस्तरूपि पात्रबाट दिनु भयो, सो प्रतिज्ञा चिन्न साथै लिई श्री पं० प्रेम श्री भक्तिजिका चरणमा दाखिल भै पुर्व वर्णन बिन्ति गर्नु भयो । तेस पछि पूर्वाश्राम छाडि त्रिवेणिमा आश्रम लिनु भै पानि मात्र जलाहार गरि ३२ दिन रहनु भयो सो ब्रत समाप्ति वाद १९८८ साल भाद्र श्री कृष्ण जन्माष्टमिका रात नदिले सो आश्रम लिनु भए पछि इन्द्रवति पार गौरखपुर भन्ने जगा मा आश्रम गरि तपष्या गर्न लाग्नु भयो सो गौरखपुर भन्ने जगा

श्री गङ्ग बाहादुरले ले॰ नरेन्द्र बहादुर द्वारा माता शिव कुमारि प्रितये भनि गौचरन रखाउँनु भयो र श्री आबाल ब्रह्मचारि षड्रानन्दको आश्रम दिङ्ला पाठशाला राम मन्दिरमा, ७ रात्रि आसन । लिनु भै पूर्वाश्रम गौरषपुरमा पाल्नु भयो र साग सिस्नु पिठो फाँक मुठि मानु औ लात बात मनो इच्छा भिक्षा कार्तिक शुक्ल पुर्णियाँ सम्ममा दिनु होला भन्ने भिक्षा पत्र लेखि श्री ३ मा र ठाउँ ठाउँमा समेत सुचना पठाउँनु भयो आज सम्म सत्य कबोल धर्म पाल्नाको चिन्न न देख्ता उत्तर टोढ़ापु हिमालयंमा तपस्या गरि बस्नु भई पुरा बर्ष दिनपछि पूर्वाश्रम मजुवा व्याँसिमा आसन भयो र स्वयं आफै नेपाल राजधानीमा गई श्री ५ मा सुचना गछुं भनि पाल्नु भई वाहाँको इच्छा श्री ५ मा थियो तापनि वाहाँ जाने रूल छैन, जानु हुँदैन भनि अरू ब्यवहारि भक्तले रोकी श्री ५ मा दर्शन दिन मनाहि गर्नु भयो भक्त बत्सल ईश्वर हुँदा भक्तका वचन स्वीकार गर्नै पन्यो श्री ३ का हुकुमले श्री पशुपति निकट बक्त्र घरमा आश्रम भयो हरेक शास्त्र वेदान्त ब्रह्मज्ञानादि भक्तिजि छेउ आई चल्न लागे निन्दा स्तुति बरोबर चले हरे तँलाई दण्ड दिन दिलाउँनका लागि मेरो ज्यू और धन आज अर्पण गरें भनि कुनै भक्तले श्री भक्तिजी छेउ बिन्ति गरेका तिन दिन मै वहाँले यस्थुलबाट बाहिर जाँने बाटो लिई शरीर छाड्नु भयो र नेपाल बाशि कोहीमा भए पनि पैदा भयो बड़ा दशैं श्री दुर्गाष्टमिका दिन श्री भक्तिजि र वाहाँ- का पूर्व वाशि भक्तलाई श्री पसुपति मन्दिरमा राखने हुकुम भं श्री ३ महाराज जुद्धको श्री पशुपति नाथमा सवारि भै श्री भक्ति छेउ बसि दोहोरा वार्ता हुँदा जस्का राजमा उदय भयो सो सूचना राष्ट्र पतिमा दिन हाजिर छु लेउ गर यदि नगरे जस्को पालो आउँछ उसैले नगरि छाड्ने छैन भन्ने समेत आज्ञा हुँदा मैले के गर्नु पर्छ तपाईंलाई के चाहिन्छ भनि हुकुम हुँदा केवल सत्य धर्म भिक्ष्या पाउँ भनि वर्णि ३ पटक सम्म निस्कदा सत्य धर्मको भिक्षा

दिव्ये गर्छु तपाईं जस्ता सत् पात्रको आशिर्वाद पाउनु पर्छ भन्ने
समेत स्तुति भै श्री ३ जुद्धवाट सत्य धर्म भिक्षा पाई श्री ३ पद्म
श्री ३ मोहन समेतका सेवाद्वारा पूर्वाश्रममा पाल्नु भयो धेरै दिन
सम्म बाटो हेर्दा पनि धर्म सत्य प्रतिज्ञाको ख्याल नरहेको विचार
भयो त्यस पछि अग्नि प्रवेश द्वारा प्राण त्यागने भै विचार लिएको सुरू
हुँदा जिल्लाबाट फौज आई पालो पहरा वसि रोकावट भयो हामी
२४० जना भक्त, श्री भक्तिजि साथै सति भै अग्नि प्रवेश गरि
प्राण त्याग गर्छौं हामी आफु खुशि जान तयार भयेका हुँदा सर्कार-
बाट रोक टोक, नहवोस् यदि वुढा पुराना थोत्रा भैसकेका अँन
कानुन लगाई हाम्रो सत्य कबोल्लाई वाधा डाल्नेमा सो डाल्ने
उपर नव्या उपवृद्ध कानुन चल्नेछ भन्ने समेत सूचनाको विन्ति
पत्र पठाए पछि भक्तिजी सहित, १०।१२ जना भक्तहरूलाई पक्राड
गरि जिल्लामा लगे । तेस्का क्यै दिन बाद भक्ति भनाउदिलाई
पाटिमा राखि कैद पर्‍यो भनि सुनाई दिनु अरूलाई धन्कुटा झेल-
मा थुन्नु भन्ने प्रभाड्गि भै सो विन्ति पत्र समेत वापस आये
पछि श्री मे॰ ज॰ माधव शम्सेर दम्पति सहित, फौज गोली गट्टा
लिई तपो भूमिमा गै ५।७ जनालाई पक्राड गरि कसैलाई छाडि
बाँकि जम्मा ११ जना लाई १९९५ साल कार्तिक २७ गतेका
दिन धन्कुटा झेलमा बन्द गरि राखे, त्यस पछि—

नाबालख वर्ष ११ को फटिक बाहादुरलाई छाडि दिनु अरू-
लाई नेल ठोक्नु भन्ने हुकुम प्रभाड्गि आयो, त्यसका ३ मैना बाद
भक्ति सहित खास्नी मानिसलाई छाडि दिनु अरूलाई ३ वर्ष कैद
गरि छ । छ मैनाको फरक गरि छाडि दिनु भन्ने हुकुम बमोजिम
पुर्जि पाई हरि किर्तन स्थान झेल्लाई बनाई आनन्द पुर्वक बसे
पछि सर्कारिया डिट्ठा बिचारि अफिसर सिपाहि २।३ सौ झेलमा
पनि आउँन लागे । झेलमा बस्ने समेत भक्तले योग सक्तिको बिचार
भै धन्य धन्य धन्य सम्झि स्तुति गर्न लागे त्यस पछि रत्नमान

झेल्मै मुक्त भये, थुनिएका १५ मैनामा छिल्लीबाहादुर, ईश्वर बाहादुर, सुर्जे बहादुर, भक्तबहादुर ४ भाई छुटे । टेक बाहादुर झेलबाट जबर-जस्ति भागे । श्री पं० प्रेम नारायण १८ मैना वाद र बाँकि भाई ले० नरेन्द्र बाहादुर, पहल्मान, गोविन्द पुरा ३० मैना भए पछि हामि मर्ने छैनौं यदि मन्च्यौं भने अरुन सवाल बमोजिम बुझाउँला भन्ने अङ्गाले कागज गराई छाडि दिए । धर्म भिक्षा सत्य कबोलको बदला झेल नेल्मीले धन्य प्रभू कि माया १९९८ साल आषाढ़ ३१ गते शनिबार हरि शयनि एकादशिका दिनमा श्री भक्तिजी सहित ६८ जना जल समाधि मै परमधाम जानु भयो । बाँकि १२।१५ जना वाहाँका भक्त आमा बिनाका पुत्र आँखा बिनाको स्थुल जल बिना-का माछा जस्ता मै आज सम्म रहेका छौं तर कामैमा बसेका सम्झेका छौं, त्यस पछि तपोभूमिको सेवा गर्दै श्री ब्रह्मचारी माहा-नन्दजी रहनु भयो, नेपाल उत्तर वाहिनि गुफामा वाहाँको देहान्त भये पछि, हाल श्री ब्रह्मचारी पद्मलाल जि तपोभूमिको सेवा गर्दै रहनु भयेको छ, भविष्यका लागि जो हुनु पर्छ दैव ईच्छा ।

विज्ञापन

———

संसाररूपि वृक्ष रहेछ । त्यो बृक्षमा दुइ प्रकारका फल फलेका रहेछन् । १ पाप २ पुण्य सो फल चार प्रकारका रसले पूर्ण भरिएका रहेछन् । कस्ता रस भनि बिचार गर्दा १ धर्म, २ अर्थ, ३ काम, ४ मोक्षले पूर्ण भई अत्यन्त स्वादिष्ट भएका अणिमा मणिमा आदि अष्ट सिद्धिका गुणले युक्त भएका यी दुइ स्वादिष्ट रस लाई पान गर्ने २ प्रकारका पक्षी रहेछन् । १ जीवात्मा २ परमात्मा, यी दुइ पक्षी जलजा आदि चौराशि लाख योनिमा प्राणीहरूका आधार भई २ स्थान बनी रहेका रहेछन् । १ जिवित २ मृत्यु जसले मनुष्य भन्ने नाम भईकन यी दुइ पक्षीको बिचार गरेन भने मानव जन्म धिक्कार छ भन्ने श्रुति आदिमा कहिएको छ ।

त्यसर्थ सज्जन बृन्द प्रति यी पुस्तिकामा दृष्टि दिई योग शक्ति अमृत रसको पान गरिबक्सिने छ भन्ने सहर्ष आशा गर्दछु ।

शुभेक्षु—चिन्तामणि ।

श्री

ॐ नमः शिव शक्ति सचेत शरण गत ॐ

———

ॐ श्री शक्ति सत्य शरणा गत मा हुँदामा,
पाञ्चाय नादि सब देव, प्रशान्न तामा ।
आकाश बायू पृथ्वि अनि जल,
सूर्यः सबै देबर पित्रृ को बल ॥

१

बेद मन्थ व्याकरण र छन्द माहाँ,
पुण्यः पवित्र जति तिर्थ र ब्रत माहाँ ।
ऋषिहरू सकल ध्याँनि र ज्ञाँनि माहाँ,
जोछौ जति सकल मान्यत यो जगत्मन ॥

२

जोछौ जति सकल खुसि रहिदिनु होस्,
हुन् ई अनाथ भनि दृष्टि खोलि दिनु होस् ।
चौधै वरष् व्यतित भोत थिएन ईन्छा,
दिनू भयो अहिले जाहेर गर्ने शिक्षा ॥

३

नाँउ ठाँउ गाँउ पनि लेख्छु केही,
दया गरूनाथ, परिपूर्ण एही ।
उत्तहौँ खण्ड कन जम्बु दिपको,
भारत् भुमी मुख्य पवित्र नैहो ॥

पर्वत माहाँ मुख्य भनेर भन्छन्,
हिमालयै देखि नदी बहन्छिन् ।
नाउँ अरुण हो सँगमा बरुण छन्,
इन्द्रा वती फेरि त्यहि मिसिन्छिन् ॥

५

गिरि कुट प्रमाणानि सुस्वादूनि मृदूनिच,
तेषां बिशीर्य माणानां सुरसेना मृते नच ।
अरुणो दश बर्णेन अरुणो बय बर्तते ॥
नदी रम्य चला देव दैत्य राज प्रपूजिता ॥
अरुणा ख्या माहाराज बर्तते पाप हारिणी,
पूजयर्न्ति चतो देवि सर्बे काम फल प्रदाँ ।
तप्का बलैले कनयोग माहाँ,
चले बहुत् शब्द सुहार माहाँ ।
शरीरको धर्मछ बोल्नु पर्ने,
हुने कुरा जोछ कशौनटर्ने,

६

त्रृवेणि घाट को पनि शक्ति नाउ छन्,
अरूहरू घाट पछि हुने छन् ।
इन्का सबै नार्म पछि रहन्छन्,
इन्द्रा वति घाट त्यहि मिसिन्छिन् ॥

७

शिब पोखरि लिङ्ग समेत् खडा छन्,
पछि याहाँ क्षेत्र ठुला हुनेछन् ।
त्याहाँ बढा पत्थर छन् रहेका,
गुफा मनोहर अति बेस्भएका ॥

८

जङ्गल सुसोभित बनवारि पारी,
पर्वत खड़ा छन् अति भारि भारी ।
बस्ति नजिक्मा पनि छैन वाँहाँ,
तप गर्नेलाई अति बेस छ त्याँहाँ ॥

९

त्रब्राणि घाट र त्रिबेणि भए ई क्षेत्र,
शक्तिर मुक्ती पनि छन् पवित्र ।
दुर्गा पुरि घाट भए इसात,
म्नानादिले पाप सबहुन्छ नाश ॥

१०

सूर्य्यः उपस्थ अनि चन्द्र पस्थ,
मन्मोह आनन्द ईचार खास ।
बैराग्य मन्मा बहुतै उदाई,
पागल सरि भैं बनमा कुदाई ॥

११

बैराग्य मन्मा यो लिएर बस्न,
इध्रमाँहाँ भारि सुरथ कस्न ।
यस्तो भुमि फेरिं ह वैन काँहीं,
बिश्वास्ले गर्दामा बहुत आँहीं ॥

१२

पक्षीहरूले अति गान गर्नें,
सुन्दै माहाँ चित्त बहूत हर्नें ।
खाँ खाँ गरि फेरि नदी सुसउने,
सुन्दें माहाँ चित्त बहुत खुसाउँने ॥

१३

यस्तो   सुशोभित्मा   वशेर   भक्ती
ॐ शीव सत्य शरणा गत लेउ शक्ती ।
दुःखै   जति   संझि   बहुत्   रूवाई
तप्   गर्न   ईच्छा   मनमा   उदाई ॥

१४

यक्ता जनम्की पनि हूँ स्त्रि जाती
कुल्मा पनी हिन्छु बहूत भारी ।
उस्मा   पनि   फेर्बय   आज   गैगो
संझन्छु सन्ताप् अति झिर्ण भैगो ॥

१५

कस्ता   तवले   अबके   मगर्नू,
अनारि हूँ नाथ कसोरि तर्नू ।
अघी पनि जन्म कती लिय्यें हूँ,
चौराशि लाख् जन्म विती सके हून ॥

१६

चिन्थ्यें प्रभुलाइ व काँ म भुल्थ्यें,
सन्सारिबिषे धेर कशोरि डुल्थ्यें ।
हानाथ् प्रभूले बहुतै डुलायौ,
शन्सार विषे धेर बहुतै भुलायौ ॥

१७

यस्तै   तवले   बहुतै   पुकारी,
गछु तपस्या अब तिम्रो भारी ।
तप्को निव्याँ दिन्छु तपस्या गर,
ल्यौंला शरण्मा तिमि लौ नडर ॥

१८

भन्ने यो स्वप्ना पनि केहि दिँदा,
आत्मा विषे तपशको तविधान मिल्दा ।
लौनाथ् जगत्को सब आस छोड्छ,
पाशा जति छन् ई चुड्राइ तोड्छ ॥

१९

आशा इ पाशा सब छाड्रि दिव्ये,
खालि फगत् एक सत नाम लिव्ये ।
छाड्ने भव्ये प्राण शरण लेउ,
रोक् टोक् मलाई न लगाई देउ ॥

२०

अन्त स्करण् एहि लिएर मन्मा,
बस्तु भयो डर नमानेर मन्मा ॥
कोहि दिन किनार्मा कोहि दीन बन्मा,
ॐ शीव सत्य शरणागत यो छ मन्मा ॥

२१

फुल्को तवाशन् कोहि दिन लिएर,
सूर्यः तरफ् दृष्टि वहुत् दिएर ।
लोक्का हे शाक्षी तिमि हेरि लेउ,
इच्छा भए को वरदान देउ ॥

२२

क्यै दिन धुप्को पनि बास्ना लिने,
फगत् जल्ये मात्र पिएर हुने ।
एक् पातको अङ्ग चिरेर आदी,
खोचो बनाइ छुद खाने रक्ति नमागी, ॥

२३

दिनमा   दुईटा   अमला   तखाई,
ब्यतित्   भयो   कार्तिक   मैनालाई ।
कैले   गुफामा   यक   मास   बस्नू,
निर्वाण   भै   यो   व्रतमा   रहनू ॥

२४

यक्   वर्ष   दिन्का   दुई   भाग्   लगाई,
गर्ने   विधी   आफ्नु   रितु   जनाई ।
गर्मि   भए   मा   पनि   अग्नि   ताप्नू,
ठण्डि   भए   मा   जल   भित्र   पस्नू ॥

२५

यति   हुन   ई   कष्ट   तपस्का   भनेर,
बित्यो   वर्ष   चौध   को   शक्ने   गनेर ।
कृपा   भो   प्रभूको   तपस्का   सकइले,
खोलेकै   छ   वार्ता   विचार   गर्छ   जस्ले ॥

२६

ढाँचा   चरित्र   रती   छैन   ईन्का,
दया   भो   प्रभूको   बितेछन   कुदिन्ता ।
ढाट्नु   र   छल्नू   रति   छैन   भक्ती,
सदा   सम्झिलेउ   हरी   शिव   शक्ती ॥

॥२७॥

प्राक्तन्छ   पालो   त्यसलाई   दिन्छू,
मता   भित्र   हुन्छू   समुझ्नै   रहन्छू ।
दिन्छू   म   लिन्छू   अभिमान्   नराख,
जती   प्राप्त   हुन्छ   तिमि   बोल   खाश ॥

२८

कपट् केहि मनमा कहिल्यै नलिनू,
कोही केहि भनोस् तबि शान्ति लिनू ।
रिस् राग् र शेखी कहिल्यै नगनू,
सदा चिन्त नित्य मञ्जी माहाँ धनू ॥

२९

ललाट् बाट प्राणः आखिर तिम्रो लिउँला,
ईच्छा जो छ तिम्रो त्यो पूर्ण गरूँला ॥
यस्तो प्रभूको छ आडर भएको,
केहि डर नमानेर प्रख्यात् गरेको ॥

३०

सर्वज्ञः वेत्ता सदा शिव् प्रकाश,
निर्गुण् स्वरूप् हो सगुणै छ खाश ।
अहो यो कलौमा तपस् गछ् कस्ले,
जगत्लाई बाँध्यो यहि मोह बस्ले,

३१

तपस्याले गर्दा याहाँ वेद् पाए,
पूर्वै थियो कल्पित गाथ गाए ।
तपस्या गरी मन्त्रले लोक् बनाए,
ब्रह्माण्ड यो जो छ खडा गराए ॥

३२

तपस्या गरी देव लोक्मा गएका,
तपस्या गरी अष्ट दिक्पाल् बनेका ।
तपस्या गरी चित्र आकार बनेको,
तपस्या भई क्षेत्र आदि बनेको ॥

३३

तपस्याले गर्दा सबै तिर्थ बर्त,
तपस्या गरी आत्मा बिषय भर्ता ।
तपस्याले गर्दा सबै देह बन्ने,
तपस्याले गर्दा प्रभूलाई मिल्ने ॥

३४

तपस्याले गर्दा असत् शान्ति हुँने,
तपस्याले गर्दा भय भ्रान्ति मिल्ने ।
तपका प्रतापले परम् प्राप्ति मिल्छ,
तपस्या गरे नाम उत्तम् रहन्छ ॥

३५

तप्का प्रताप्को बलवान जान्नू,
अन्धी समान्को हो भनी नठान्नू ।
तप् पूर्ण हुँदा गगने छ थर्कने,
ब्रह्माण्ड कंपित् भई लोक् डराउँने ॥

३६

तप्को अवाज् यस्तो भनेर औंले,
बयान् सबै गर्न शकिन्छ कैले ।
तप्को प्रताप् चिन्न कती नशक्नू,
दोष् दीनु ता ब्यर्थ हरे नशक्नू ॥

३७

नबिद्या नसाख्न नअभ्यास थीयो,
तप्का प्रताप्ले त आत्मा उदायो ।
इच्छा हुँदामा इन बाँणि हेनू,
एक् बार सुजन्हो यहि पाठ गनू ॥

३८

पर्नें छ आखीर अवश्य मन्नू,
तृष्णार शेखी रति क्यै नगन्नू ।
क्यै बातको छेड छ विज्ञ माहाँ,
दोस्ता नदिनु केहि हामि माहाँ ॥

३९

युग् लोकको यो चलन् हो कहेको,
साँचा हुन् यी बाँणी जति हो भएको ॥
आशा छइन रति केहि हाँम्रो,
चलख्वलोस लोक माहाँ यो राम्रो ॥

४०

इच्छा छईन रति केहि याहाँ,
धर्मैं चलोस् लौ सब लोक माहाँ ।
हाजिर छाँदैछौं हरि नाम् कहेर,
सन्ताप् जति हुन् लोकमा सहेर ॥

४१

धेयैं भई यो सत नामगाई,
दया हवस् नाथ् सब लोक लाई ।
सम्पूर्णलोक्को करूणा गरि योस्,
धर्मैं जगत्मा अबता छरि योस् ॥

४२

आनन्द को ज्योति जगाई याहाँ,
प्रकाश् गराएर निरास रूपमा ।
नित्यैं प्रभू को कन दास् भएर,
सब् हेन्न पाउँ म दृष्टि दिएर ॥

४३

आचार बाँणी र नियम हेर्दा,
आत्मा विषे केहि बिचार गर्दा ।
नास्‌ बान्‌ जगत्‌ हो भनि जानि लिन्छूँ,
ऐश्वर्य लोक्‌को सब छाडि दिन्छूँ ॥

४४

भजन्‌ अति भारि बिचार गर्दा,
तप्‌का प्रभाव्‌ले बर वाक्य मिल्दा ।
लोक्‌मा सबैले अब दोष्‌ नदिउँ,
ईश्वर सगै छन्‌ सधै शंझि लिउँ ॥

४५

वर्षैं ब्यतित्‌ बाइस भैगो औले,
तपस्याको बल्‌ यो भनि सक्‌छु कैले ।
आधार जतिले इनिको गरेथ्यौं
इन्‌का शरण्‌मा जति जन्‌ परेथ्यौं ॥

४६

क्याबात्‌ दया भैगो बहूत राम्रो,
सन्ताप्‌ रहेन अब केहि हाम्रो ।
हरी भजन्‌ ता दिन केहि भैगो,
उन्नाइस्‌ सहे साल अठास्सिमा हो ॥

४७

मैना आषाढ्‌ हो तिथि पूर्णिमामा,
वार्भौंम योग्‌ कर्ण यि मिल्दिदामा ॥
गुरूहरूले सब दृष्टि दींदा,
भूःखर्ग आदि सब देव सहाय हुँदा,

४८

इच्छा यहि भो इनि भक्ति माहाँ,
खाने जति चिज् सब छोड्‌न माहाँ ।
आकाश देखी जल बिन्दु आयो,
जल्‌देखि ब्रह्माण्ड खड़ा गरायो ॥

४९

जल्‌बाट सम्पूर्ण साखा बनायो,
त्यो जल्‌ले यो सम्पूर्ण जगत् भरायो ।
त्यहि जल् रहेछ सबै खानु लाउँनू,
जल्‌को चलन् सर्व कती बताउनू ॥

५०

यती बुझि यो जल्‌को जमेको,
अनाज बस्तू जति चिज् बनेको ।
त्यो चिज खाँदा केहि दोष लाग्ने,
त्यो चीजले प्राण् पनि त्याग्नु पर्ने ॥

५१

अभक्ष अस्पर्श पनी त्यहि हुने,
तेहि चीज उत्तम् फलाहार बनिने ॥
तेहि चीजलाई कन बिष् भनिन्छ,
तेहि चीजको औषधि त्यो बनिन्छ ॥

५२

त्यहि चिजले हुन्छ जगत्‌मा खाँचो
त्यहि चिजको दोष् अति हुन लाग्यो ॥
त्यसैले हँसाउछ त्यसैले रुँवाउछ,
त्यसैमा छ इच्छा त्यो आफै खुवाउँछ, ॥

५३

आफूले त्यो आफै छ खाइ रहेको,
त्यसैको चलन यो छ सारा चलेको ।
त्यसैले यो गर्दा छ जगत बलेको,
जगत सर्व जम्मा आहारा बनेको ॥

५४

आहाराको राहा भनि सक्छु काहाँ,
आहारै चलेको छ यो जाहाँ ताहाँ ।
एकै थोक लिन्छु सबै छाडि दिन्छु,
यो फेदै पिइन्छु यसैले जिइन्छु ॥

५५

जाहाँ तक रहन्छु ताहाँ तक कहन्छु,
शरिर छाडि दिन्छु म ता शुद्धि हुन्छ ॥
जति खाने फल फूल अनाज छाडि दिर्वे,
हरे नाथ दया होस एकै नाम लिर्वे ॥

५६

हरी भक्त जो छौ रति भन डर,
जो आफ्नु छ इच्छा तिमीहेरू गर ।
हरिभक्त आल्हाद भै मुक्ति हौला,
आनन्द भै त्यो पदमा रहौला,

५७

फरक नपारी कन मुक्त हुइने,
आनन्द सागर सहजै तरिने ।
इच्छा हुँदामा सब दुःख छुट्ला,
दया हुँदामा सब आश टुट्ला ॥

५८

येस्ता बचन् अमृत सुन्न पाई,
बस्यौ कोहि भक्त हरी नाम गाई ।
यि भक्तिको आश गरी रहेका,
हरी नाममा नित्य सुरथ् कसेका ॥

५९

भन्छन् त कोही ब्यवहार छाड्छ,
तिरा पछेड़ा कन लागि जान्छ ।
शान्त रहू बाबु हड् बड् नगर,
कल्याण हुन्छ रति भर न डर ॥

६०

हे बाबु शान्त सब शान्त शान्त,
अन्तस्करण यो छ माहाँ एकान्त ।
चड्का गरी बोल्न पनी नहुने,
भक्ति थिनि हून र बोल्नु हुने ॥

६१

शान्त स्खभाव् को बचनै नजान्ने,
आफु समान्को गम मात्र ठान्ने ।
याहाँ तक् भएको यति यादू छ याहाँ
पश्चात् के गर्छ अब दैव काहाँ ॥

६२

हेरौं जगत्मा अब के त हुन्छ,
देख्ता सबैको पछि चित्त रून्छ ।
धैर्यः रहू लौ पछि बाग्ने हेर,
लोक्मा हुने भो रमिता अब बिघ्न घेर ॥

६३

सजीब को हो बिचेतूमा नपनू ,
सज्जन्को सङ्गत् कहिल्यै नछाड.नू ।
आत्मा विषे नाम हरिको बिचानू ,
प्रणब् माहाँ मन्त्र बहुत् पुकानू ॥

६४

यो मात्र लोक भरिमा बुझ बाच्चे होला,
अर्को उपाय गरिने त काहाँ बचौला ।
यो घेर बिन्ती कति गर्नु अैले,
तागत् पुगे पो गरि सक्छु मैले ॥

६५

अन्सार मिल्दा यति हो लेखेको,
एक् भक्तका छिद्रले यो देखेको ॥
दिवानिशि दृष्टि दिई इनि वाणि हेनू ,
कस्तो हुनेछ दिन दीन बिचार गनू ॥

६६

झूटा हुँदैन इनि वाँणि बिचार गर्दा,
पर्दैन आपत्ति अवश्य टर्ला ।
योग्देखि वाँणी कन निस्किदामा,
पात्रै नपाई कन राख्न नपाउँदामा ॥

६७

बाल्ख् थिईन छोरी त सम्मु माहाँ,
सुम्पी दिनु भो उहि पात्र माहाँ ।
अक्षर् वाचक् उनिमा थिएन,
कृपा हुँदामा नलिई भएन ॥

६८

चौधः वरष् ब्यतित भो र नभुल्दा माहाँ,
ईच्छा उदाइ लेखियो अरुणा किनारमा ।
दिन्मा घड़ी एक् सबले बिचानूँ,
बिचार पुगे दुःख हुँदैन तनूँ ॥

६९

पद्को त स्वार्थ गुरू हो यो मिलेको छैन,
आत्मा बिचार गरदा मिल्नै परेन ।
अठाशि साल महिना भो आषाढ़ यी मा,
लेखी समाप्त भई गो रविबार दिनैमा ॥

७०

तपोभूमि माहात्म्य

१६

[श्री गणेशाय नमः]

प्रात भजन

श्री ॐ नमः शिवाय

ॐ नमः शिव शक्ति सचेत सत्य शरणागत ॐ

ॐ शिव ३ ॐ शिव ३ ॐ शिव ३ शिव ३

ॐ विष्णु ३ ॐ विष्णु ३ ॐ विष्णु ॐ विष्णु ३

ॐ ब्रह्मा ३ ॐ ब्रह्मा ३ ॐ ब्रह्मा ३ ॐ ब्रह्मा ३

ॐ शक्ति ॐ शक्ति ३ ॐ शक्ति ३ ॐ शक्ति ३

ॐ सत्य ३ ॐ सत्य ३ ॐ सत्य ३ ॐ सत्य ३

ॐ गुरू ब्रह्मा शक्ती सत्य ॐ नमो नमः २

ॐ गुरू शक्ती सत्य ॐ नमो नमः नमो नमः २

ॐ आत्मा ब्रह्म महात्मा ब्रह्म परमात्मा ब्रह्मः

ॐ गुरू शक्ती सत्य ॐ नमो नमः नमो नमः २

ॐ सीर ब्रह्म गजुर ब्रह्म माहाँ मुख्य अलग तिमि

एक ब्रह्म ॐ गुरू ब्रह्म शक्ति सत्य ॐ नमोनम २

ॐ गुरू शक्ती सत्य ॐ नमो नमः नमो नमः ३

ॐ ज्योति ब्रह्म जुक्ति ब्रह्म माहाँ मुक्ति साचा

वाचा पुण्य पवित्र तिमि एक ब्रह्म ॐ गुरू ब्रह्म

शक्ति सत्य ॐ नमो नमः २............

ध्यानका ध्यान माहाँ ज्ञान माहाँ तत्व माहाँ तपस्या

तिमि एक ब्रह्म ॐ गुरू ब्रह्म शक्ति सत्य ॐ नमो

नमः २ शक्ति भक्ति माहाँ मुक्ति माहाँ जुक्ति घोर मन्त्र

अघोर मन्त्र दिक्षा गायत्रि तिमि एक ब्रह्म

ॐ गुरू ब्रह्म शक्ति सत्य ॐ नमो नमः २

आत्मा रूपी घट घट वासि अन्तर्यामी गुरू अविनासी
विश्व मूर्ति ज्योति स्वरूप सच्चिदानन्द तिमि
एक ब्रह्म ॐ गुरू ब्रह्म शक्ती सत्य ॐ नमो नमः २
ॐ गुरू शक्ति सत्य ॐ नमो नमः २ निरञ्जन निराकार
निरामय आत्मा सुद्धि समुज सुद्धि प्रकाश ब्रह्म ॐ
गुरू ब्रह्म शक्ति सत्य ॐ नमो नमः २ चार युग्का चतुर्मुं खि
ब्रह्मा चारवेद अष्ट सिद्धि तिमि एक ब्रह्म ॐ गुरू ब्रह्म शक्ति
सत्य ॐ नमो नमः २ चार वेद अठार पुराण नव ब्याकरण तिमि
एक शुद्ध ब्रह्मको चाकर तिमि एक ब्रह्म ॐ गुरू ब्रह्म
शक्ति सत्य ॐ नमो नमः २ चार जात छतिस वर्ण अनन्त सोभाय
तिमि एक ब्रह्मको लिला ॐ गुरू ब्रह्म शक्ति सत्य ॐ
नमो नमः २ ब्रह्मा विष्णु माहादेव तृ देवता तिमि एक ब्रह्म ॐ
ॐ गुरू ब्रह्म शक्ति सत्य ॐ नमो नमः २ चन्द्र सूर्य सारा तारा
ज्योति गुरू एक ब्रह्मको देख ज्योति ॐ गुरू ब्रह्म शक्ति
सत्य ॐ नमो नमः २ अनन्त ऋषि ऋषेश्वर सारा तपि
योगान्तर तिमि एक ब्रह्म को इच्छा ॐ गुरू ब्रह्म शक्ति सत्य ॐ
नमो नमः २ अनन्त धूप अनन्त दीप अनन्त फूल अनन्त सुबास
तिमि एक ब्रह्म ॐ गुरू ब्रह्म शक्ति सत्य ॐ नमो नम २
अनन्त स्वर्ग अनन्त कैलास अनन्त बैकुण्ठ आकाश
पाताल ब्रह्माण्ड तिमि एक ब्रह्म को इच्छा बाचा ॐ
गुरू ब्रह्म शक्ति सत्य ॐ नमो नमः २ ब्रह्माण्डय भित्रका
तिर्थ ब्रत पुण्य पवित्र होम यज्ञ स्वाहा स्वध्या कर्म धर्म तिमि
एक ब्रह्मको ब्रह्माण्ड भित्रको चलनमा ब्रह्मो ॐ गुरू
ब्रह्म शक्ति सत्य ॐ नमो नमः ! ॐ जगदीश्वर ईश्वर
महेश्वर बौद्धेश्वर दशम अवतार तिमी एक ब्रह्मको आदि शक्ति
सारथीका लिला ॐ गुरू ब्रह्म शक्ति सत्य ॐ नमोनमः २

गुरू शक्ति सत्य ॐ नमोनमः नमोनमः २ शिव शक्ति सत्य ॐ
नमोनम २ गुरू शक्ति सत्य ॐ नमोनमः २ धर्म स्थापन ब्रह्म ॐ
धर्म स्थापन असत खारण सारा विकामाॅरन सारा सेखिझारन
प्रभू भुभार्टारन धर्म उतारन धर्मि युग बनाउँन धर्मैं चलन्
चलाउन प्राणि धर्मि गराउन स्वधर्म प्रति पालन सारा विकारमारन
आत्मा उज्ज्वल पारन ब्रह्म ज्ञान सारन ॐ गुरू ब्रह्म शक्ति सत्य
ॐ नमोनमः २ गुरू शक्ति सत्य ॐ नमोनमः २ धर्म स्थापन
विष्णु धर्म स्थापन अशत खारन सारा विकामाॅरन सारा सेखि-
झारन प्रभू भूभार्टारन धर्मि युग बनाउन धर्मैं चलन् चलाउन
प्राणि धर्मि गराउन स्वधर्म प्रतिपालन सर्व विकाखारिन आत्मा
उज्ज्वल पारन ब्रह्म ज्ञान सारन ॐ गुरू ब्रह्म शक्ति सत्य ॐ
नमोनमः २ गुरू शक्ति सत्य ॐ नमोनमः २ धर्म स्थापन शिव
स्वरूप धर्म स्थापन असत खारन सारा विकामाॅरन सारा सेखि
झारन प्रभू भुभार्टारन धर्म उतारन धर्मि युग बनाउन धर्मैं चलन्
चलाउन प्राणि धर्मि गराउन स्वधर्म प्रति पालन सारा विकाखारिन
आत्मा उज्ज्वल पारन ब्रह्म ज्ञान सारन ॐ गुरू ब्रह्म शक्ति
सत्य ॐ नमोनमः २ गुरू शक्ति सत्य ॐ नमोनमः २ गुरू
शक्ति सत्य ॐ नमोनमः २ शक्ति भक्ति जि धर्मस्थापन ॐ
धर्म स्थापन असतखारन सारा विकामाॅरन सारा सेखि झारन प्रभू
भुभार्टारन धर्म उतारन धर्मि युग बनाउन धर्मैं चलन् चलाउन
प्राणि धर्मि गराउन स्वधर्म प्रतिपाल्न सारा विकाखारन आत्मा उज्ज्वल
पारन ब्रह्म ज्ञान सारन ॐ गुरू ब्रह्म शक्ति सत्य ॐ नमोनमः २
गुरू शक्ति सत्य ॐ नमोनमः २ ब्रह्म ब्रह्मा २ सब घठ बासि
एकै ब्रह्म २ निर्गुण ब्रह्म स्वगुण ब्रह्म २ निर्गुण स्वगुण एकै ब्रह्म
२ स्वजीव निर्जीव एकै ब्रह्म २ स्वर शब्द एकै ब्रह्म २ समुज
चिन्तन एकै ब्रह्म २ हं ब्रह्म स्वहं ब्रह्म २ जप ब्रह्म अजप ब्रह्म २ अकार

उकार एकै ब्रह्म २ शक्ति भक्ति जि एकै ब्रह्म २ जुक्ति मुक्ति एकै ब्रह्म २
श्री गुरू ब्रह्म शक्ति सत्य २ ॐ गुरू ब्रह्म शक्ति सत्य २ साचा
वाचा सत्य शाक्षि २ ॐ गुरू ब्रह्म शक्ति सत्य २ साचा वाचा
सत्य शाक्षि २ ॐ गुरू ब्रह्म शक्ति सत्य २ ब्रह्म जोति जाग
जाग २ आत्मा ज्योति जाग जाग २ महात्मा ज्योति जाग
जाग २ शुद्धि ज्योति जाग जाग २ ब्रह्म धुनि जाग जाग २
वेद धुनि जाग जाग २ सत्य ब्रह्म धर्म छिट २
शिव गुरू धर्म छिट २ बिष्णु ठाकुर्धर्म छिट २ साँचो धर्म २
साँचो धर्म २ दया धर्म २ दया धर्म २ साँचो धर्म लोक
लाई २ दया धर्म लोकलाई २ नित्य शुद्धि भक्तलाई २ शुद्धि
समुझ भक्तलाई २ नित्य जागा भक्तलाई २ सर्वत्र नघाऊ भक्त
लाई २ सत्य प्रकाश भक्तलाई २ सत् शक्ति शरण लेऊ २
ध्यान्दिष्टिले हेरी देऊ २ आफ्ना भक्त खीचिलेऊ २ ब्रह्म बेग्ले
खीचिलेऊ २ ब्रह्माण्डय नघाई लेऊ २ सारा बिकारखारि लेऊ २
सेखि सङ्का मारि देऊ २ शुरथ हाम्रो लगाइ देऊ २ भक्तका
जिव को मेटि लेऊ २ आउनु जानु मेटि देऊ २ बिचबाट नफिकार्ाउ २
नीज घर्मा पौचाई देऊ २ सारा भवन थर्काई देऊ २ सत् शब्दले
डगाई देऊ १ आकाश पताल थर्काई देऊ २ असत्लाई हर्काई देऊ २
श्रीष्टिको चलन फर्काई देऊ २ रामराज्य पारि देऊ २ कर्मका बन्धन
काटि देऊ २ आउनु जानु मेटि देऊ २ शत् शक्ति शरण लेऊ २
लिएको लियै पारि देऊ २ २ यो मायालाई चिनाई देऊ २ अमृत
रस पियाई देऊ २ आफ्ना भक्त जियाई देऊ २ झिल्का पारी नउडाउ २
बृंदा पारिन झार १ वाशन भई घुस्न पाउ २ प्रकाश भई देख्न
पाउँ २ शुद्धि प्रकाश पारि देऊ २ काल बाहिर पारि देऊ २
माया वस्तु चिनाई देऊ २ यो मायाले घुमायो २ यो मायाले
फिराउँछ २ यो मायाले गिराउँछ २ माया चिन्न सक्छ को २

माया तिरो अगम् हो २ माया चिम्रे मुक्ति भो २ सत् शक्ति
शरण लेउ २ कार्य सिद्धि पारि देउ २ रक्ष पालक् होईदेउ २
चञ्चल् चित्त रोकि देउ २ बिजुलि मनलाई खीचिलेउ २ गर्भका
दुःख सम्झाई देउ २ अन्त्य कालका दुःख् सम्झाउ २
चौरास् जन्मका दुःख् सम्झाई देउ २ दुःख् सुख् देखि फुर्सद
देऊ २ उच्चा निम्बा खारि देऊ २ एकामय पारिदेउ २ रामराज्य
पारि देउ २ सत् शक्ति शरण् लेउ २ लिएको लियै पारि देउ २
नित्य जागा पारि देउ २ सत्य प्रकाश् पारि देऊ २ सत् शक्ति
शरण लेउ २ भुल् चुक् छ ता माफ देउ २
सत्य ॐ सत्य ॐ सत्य ॐ सत्य ॐ सत्य ॐ सत्य ॐ
सत्य ॐ

[इति प्रातः]

सायम

ॐ नमः शिव शक्ति सचेत सत्य शरणागत ॐ
सत्य ॐ सत्य ॐ सत्य ॐ सत्य ॐ सत्य ॐ
ॐ शिव ३ ॐ शिव ३ ॐ शिव ३ ॐ शिव ३
ॐ विष्णु ३ ॐ विष्णु ३ ॐ विष्णु ॐ विष्णु ३
ॐ ब्रह्मा ३ ॐ ब्रह्मा ३ ब्रह्मा ३ ब्रह्मा ३
ॐ शक्ती ॐ शक्ती ३ ॐ शक्ती ३ ॐ शक्ती ३
ॐ सत्य ३ ॐ सत्य ३ ॐ सत्य ३ ॐ सत्य ३
ॐ गुरू ब्रह्म शक्ती सत्य ॐ नमोनमः २
गुरू सक्ती सत्य ॐ नमो नमः नमो नमः २
ॐ सीर ब्रह्म गजुर ब्रह्म महाँ मुख्य अलग तिमि
एक ब्रह्म ॐ गुरू ब्रह्म शक्ति सत्य ॐ नमोनमः २
शरण लेऊ २ माहाँ दया गरि देउ २ आफै अघि सरि देउ २

शुद्धि कार्य भरि देउ २ सत् ज्योतिमा सारि देउ २ शुद्धि प्रकाश् पारि देउ २ भय भ्राँति खारि देउ २ असत् लाई मारि देउ २ सब्को सेखि झारि देउ २ भूमिको भार टारि देउ २ लोक्मा धर्म सारि देउ २ धर्मि राज्य पारि देउ २ प्रजा धर्मि पारि देउ २ साँचो धर्म लोक लाई २ दया धर्म लोकलाई २ नित्य शुद्धि भक्तलाई २ शुद्धि शमुज् भक्तलाई २ सत्य ॐ सत्य ॐ सत्य ॐ सत्य ॐ झूट्टा होम् ४ असत् होम् ४ विकार होम् ४ जन्म होम् ४ मर्न होम् ४ गर्भ वास गरदेउ होम् २ सत्य ॐ सत्य ॐ सत्य ॐ सत्य ॐ शरण लेउ २ सारादेब दृष्टि देउ २ ज्योति गुरू दृष्टि देउ २ शक्ति भक्ति राजी होऊ २ ब्रह्मा विष्णु जागारौ २ महादेव जागारौ २ चन्द्र सूर्य जागारौ २ तारागण जागारौ २ महा सागर जागारौ २ भन्द हावा जागारौ २ पृथ्वी माता जागारौ २ ऋषि मुनि जागारौ २ सारा तपि जागारौ २ तीर्थ व्रत जागारौ २ पुण्य पवित्र जागारौ २ जप तप जागारौ २ मूल मन्त्र जागारौ २ खाहा स्वधा जागारौ २ तत्व तपस जागारौ २ ध्यान ज्ञान जागारौ २ माहाँ मन्त्र जागारौ २ घट वासि जागारौ २ अन्तर्यामि जागारौ २ अविनासि जागारौ २ साँरथि जागारौ २ अग्नँशक्ति जागारौ २ जल ज्योति जागारौ २ शक्ति भक्ति जागारौ २ सारा जगत् जागारौ २ सत् का शब्द जान्न देउ २ बिचबाट नफिर्काउ २ शूर्थ हाम्रो लगाइ देउ २ निज धर्मा पाँचाइ देउ २ सारा भव्रन् थर्काइ देउ २ चौध लोक थर्काइ देउ २ आकाश पताल थर्काइ देउ २ असत् लाई हर्काइ देउ २ सृष्टिको चलन फर्काइ देउ २ स्वर शब्दले डगाई देउ २ सत्य ॐ शरण लेउ २ सारा देव खड़ा रौ २ असत मार्न खडारौ २ झूट्टो मार्न खडारौ २ सेखि झार्न खडारौ २ सारा देव जागारौ २ पृथ्वी माता जागारौ २ सत् का शब्द जागारौ २ शक्ति भक्ति जागारौ २ सत् शक्ति शरण लेउ २ भुल् चुक् छ ता माफ देउ २

जगत् भित्र तिमि छौ २ तिमि भित्र जगत् छ । आखिरिमा होइन केहि ।। हेदैँ लाँदा छैन केहि ।। ज्योति भित्र तिमि छौ ।। तिमि भित्र ज्योति छ ।। आखिरिमा होईन केहि ।। हेदैँ लाँदा छैन केहि ।। जल भित्र तिमि छौ ।। तिमि भित्र जल छ ।। आखिरिमा होइन केहि ।। हेदैँ लाँदा छैन केहि ।। खालि प्रभुको तत्व हो ।। तत्व चिन्न सक्छ को ।। तत्व चिन्ने उतृगो ।। तत्व चिन्ने मुक्ति भो ।। हावा भित्र तिमि छौ ।। तिमि भित्र हावा छ ।। आखिरिमा होइन केहि ।। हेदैँ लाँदा छैन केहि ।। वेद् भित्र तिमि छौ ।। तिमि भित्र वेद् छ ।। आखिरिमा होइन केहि ।। हेदैँ लाँदा छैन केहि ।। सर्वत्रमा तिमि छौ ।। तिमि भित्र सर्वत्र ।। शब्द भित्र तिमि छौ ।। तिमी भित्र शब्द छ ।। आखिरिमा होइन केहि ।। हेदैँ लाँदा छैन केहि ।। सारा प्रभुको तत्व हो ।। तत्व चिन्न सक्छ को ।। तत्व चिन्ने मुक्ति भो ।। आकाश् पाताल् हवोइन ।। जल ज्योति रहोइन ।। सारा जगत् लय भो ।। लय भाको हैनेंको ।। सूरथमा वसि देउ ।। तार खबर कहि देउ ।। सत् शक्ति शरण लेउ ।। सत् शक्ति शरण लेउ ।।

ॐ सत्य ॐ सत्य ॐ सत्य ॐ सत्य ॐ सत्य ॐ सत्य
ॐ सत् शक्ति शरण लेऊ हरिः ॐ तत्सत्

तपोभ्रमि वर्णन

इति

———————

श्री भक्तिजी का योग वाणि

ॐ नमः शिव शक्ति सत्य शचेत शरणागत

श्री शक्ति सत्य शरणागत पर्दछू,
भक्त वाक्य संक्षेपमा बिस्तार गर्दछू ।
गिद्को जस्तो भाषा आयो ब्राह्मण् के सुन्नून्,
पैल्हा दोष् छ ब्राह्मणलाई होइन न भनून् ॥
१

त्रिजातिको भाषा हुँदा गिद्का जस्ता छन्,
मालुम् गरि बुझ् न सके अर्थ असल् छन् ।
भाषा सुनि न भुलनु अर्थ बिचार,
अन्तस्करण् बुझ्न सके छुट्ला बिकार ॥
२

पुरोहित्को बुद्धि हेर निक्‍क लिने युक्ती,
यौटि गौले बार जग्गा कैल्हे हुन्थ्यो मुक्ती
यौटि गौमा बार जग्गा भन्छ ताप्यौँ ताप्यौँ,
तिनि गौले बिन्ति गरिन् पाप् बिप्रमा साप्यौँ ॥
३

यौटा घर श्राद्ध खाई अर्का घरमा आँटे,
ग्रहहरू बिन्ति गर्छन् पुरोहित्ले ढाँटे ।
विद्या लिनु ब्राह्मणले व्यशासनका धनी,
बनियाँका काम्मा लागे उत्तम् मणि पनी ॥
४

ब्रह्म चिन्हे ब्राह्मण भनी उत्तम गराए,
ब्राह्मणहरू सत्य छाड्दा देव डराए ।
बैश्य साहू अघि छँदा सस्तो गरायो,
ब्राह्मणहरू बेपारि छन् भाउ हरायो ॥

५

ब्राह्मणको बेपार देख्ता बैश्य डरायो,
बैश्य बेपार के लाई गरोस् फाइदा हरायो ।
लोभ बढि ठग्दै ल्यायो मालुम् न पाउँने,
यति छोटा खेल्मा पनी कत्रो सुआउँने ॥

६

शंकरजिका भेद् बाणिमा कुञ्चै पर्दा हून्,
युग् भरिको आयु दिए कसो गर्दा हून ।
सम्झ मन्मा अमृत सरी गिता पढेको,
जानि जानि ब्राह्मणले के काम् गरेको ॥

७

अघि ब्राह्मण भारि पण्डित् सुदामाजि थिए,
दुःख थिए तै पनि ति कुन बेपारमा गए ।
निति शास्त्र बिचार गरी ज्ञान्का भरमा रहे,
दुःख सुख कर्म चिनी धर्म थाँदा भए ॥

८

धन्य ऋषि सुदामाजी धर्म छोड्रेनौं,
आफ्नु धर्म न छोड्नाले दुःख पाएनौं,
नृग राजा धनि थिए माहा दानी भए,
तैपनि ती सरा सरी खोइ स्वर्ग गए ॥

९

मनको भ्रमण नछुट्नाले झन् क्षेपारो भए,
त्यां अधिका भक्त कामूले पिछे स्वर्ग गए ।
गौरी शंकर व्यर्थ बेच्यौ बिचार नगरी,
सारै गोशा हुनु भयो शंकर श्री हरी ॥

१०

महाँराज्का जागिरदारलाई कुछ दोष दिवें,
जस्तो मनमा उब्जा भयो सोहि बतार्वें ॥
येसै बात्का पिरोलाले धेरै प्राणि रोउला,
अनाथ्हरू विन्ति गर्छन जान्ने कसो होउला ॥

११

धर्म सम्झी विचार गरी इन्साफ गरेन,
पैसा भए वरेह्हा लाई दण्ड परेन ॥
कुल् ता हाम्रो ब्राह्मण हो छैनौं कुलैमा,
जात्ता सत्य छैन हाम्रो राख चुलैमा ॥

१२

येसै बातको अर्थ न लाई धर्ता पावैनौ
पैसा धेरै पायौ भने बेर ता लावैनौ ।
धर्म थाम्ने निसाफिले यति चाल पाउन्,
कुन् कुन् जात्ले जुन् जुन् ल्याउछ जात्मा मिलाउन् ॥

१३

बिग्नेलाई मासि दिनू चोरलाई दिनु काटी,
धर्म संझी निसाफ गनूं यौटा न ढाँटी ।
साँरथि उत्रने छन धर्म जाग्नेछ,
राजा मंत्रि भारदारलाई ठक्कर लाग्नेछ ॥

१४

होइन मैले बोले को ता योग् छ चलेको,
बिचार गर्ने सज्जनलाई तत्व खोलेको ।
हरिजिले आँटेको काम् नभई छोड्दइन,
जान्न त म जान्ने होइन फेर ता परोइन ॥

१५

धन्य हरी कृपालु को दया भएछ,
सूर्यबाट दुर्पिन् हेर्दा वेला गएछ ।
रिस् र सेखि सत्य मैले होइन गरेको,
जगत् भरको दुःख मैले देख्छु भरेको ॥

१६

छाड् बाबु पाजि काम् यो बियाज् बढाउँने,
भगवान्मा ल्यो लावो बिन्ति चढाउँने ॥
अमृत्सरि वाँणि चले योग्मा भए जती,
धेर दौलथ् छाड्नु पर्दा होउला के गती ॥

१७

गर्दा गर्दै लाँदा माहाँ हुँदै जाँदामा,
कुन् कुन् बिरता पर्नेछन् लौ पाप्का फाँदामा ।
भन्नु होला यस्तो भाषा कस्ले गुनेछन्,
भगवान्का भक्तजन्ले यस्तो सुनेछन् ॥

१८

स्वपनामा देख्न लाग्यें सागर मथेको,
भगवान्का शक्ति बिनो होइन कथेको ।
भन्नु होला यस्तो भाषा कस्ले गुनेछ,
हेर्नु होला कुछ दिन्मा कस्तो हुनेछ ॥

१९

स्वपनामा देखिएथ्यो भष्म पार्नें चाला,
महाँदेव ले लिनु भयो बिजुलिको भाला ।
बिजुलि र बज्रसंगै असिना भई झर्ला,
त्यसै बेला जगत भरमा को कोह्होलो पर्ला ॥

२०

हावा चल्ला बृक्ष ढल्ला पानि बगाउँन,
सृष्टि सफा गर्नु हुन्छ धर्म जगाउँन ।
भन्नु होला यो बात त्यस्लाई कस्ले बतायो,
तपसका प्रभावले शक्ति यो आयो ॥

२१

आज मलाई भन्नु भयो धर्म हरेको,
त्यसै बेला सब थोक को सं योग परेको ।
धर्म छाड्नु क्या हो भने आफ्नु नियाँ छाड़ी,
ब्राह्मण हरू बन्न लागे शुद्र जात का जोड़ी ॥

२२

ब्राह्मण भई सर्व चिज्को बिक्रि गरेको,
मालिक भई दुःखिहरूको वृत्ति हरेको ।
अहिले गर्छौ भलादुमिहो आफ्ना खुशइले,
भित्र जरा हालि सक्यो लोभि घुसइले ॥

२३

अन्त्य काल्मा त्यो घुसले फटाउला धाँदा,
बड़ो कष्ट मिलि जाला त्यो घुस निस्की जाँदा,
अहिले मात्र पचेको छ भरे पच्ने छैन,
सम्झि राख सत्य बचन झुटो हुने छैन ॥

२४

जत्ति कमाउ सम्पत्ती प्यारि घरैमा,
दौल थिया पर्नें भये ज्यम डरैमा ।
घुमाई घुमाई दुष्टहरू दुःख दिने छन्,
राक्षस् जस्ता दैत्यहरू इज्जत् लिने छन् ॥

२५

थितिदेखि बिथि तिता भएकै छ अइले,
त्यहि थिति बिझ्रनाले बिन्ति गरेँ मैले ।
आसामिले पहिले कर्जा तिरि सकेछ,
साहु भन्ने लोभिले ता बाँकि भनेछ ॥

२५

दौल थिया हुनु भयो त्यहि निर्धा बाटै,
आसामिले कर्जा तिर्‍यो तमसुक्छ ठाडै ।
छोरो थियो बालख बाबु मरेछ,
लोभि साहु माग्न गयो तिर्नु परेछ ॥

२७

हेर्न केटा तमसुक्मा येति बड्डेको,
अन्तरयामि प्रभु देख्छन् धर्म छाड्डेको ।
लोभर अन्यायका अक्षर लेखेको,
आफु सत्य भगवान्ले रछ देखेको ॥

२८

होइन मैले बोलेको ता योग् छ चलेको,
बिचार गर्ने ज्ञानिलाई आत्मा खोलेको ॥

२९

श्लोक बद्ध

जन्म   नर   अन्न   पच्चीसा   लायो,
साना   ठुला   पाथिहरू   चलायो   ।
लिनू   ठुला   दिनु   पर्दा   त्यो   सानू,
अधम्   त्यो   हो   कुंभिपाक्   बाश   जान्नू ॥

३०

त्यस्को   फल्   ता   आज   के   भन्नु   मैले,
सम्पूर्ण   कष्ट   भनी   सक्छु   कैले   ।
कहीं   सक्नु   छैन   बड़ो   कष्ट   पाउँला,
सदा   यम   दण्ड   पिई   दिन्   बिताउला ॥

३१

फेरि   जन्म   हुन्छ   बड़ा   दूःखि   कुल्मा,
हिजै   नष्ट   भईगो   लिँदा   दीदा   धर्म   ।
एक   बाक्रौ   योनि   कदापि   यो   होइन,
बिना   दैव   इच्छा   जनम्   ठर्ने   छैन ॥

३२

धर्म   नष्ट   पारी   फेरि   काहाँ   जान्नू,
जन्म   हुन्छ   याहिँ   भिक्षा   माँगि   खानु   ।
शरिर   हुन्छ   रोगी   नराम्रो   छ   हेर्दैं,
सबै   प्राणि   हेर्लन्   बड़ा   नेत्र   तर्दैं ।

३३

बताउँछु ज्ञान् म सबै चित्त लाउ,
जन्म हुन्छ याँही धर्म खूब् मगाउ ।
जगत्मा म भ्रष्ट एकै नाम लिन्छू,
चलन्को यो धर्म म सम्झाई दिन्छू ॥

३४

मार्छन् कि भन्ने डर छैन केही,
आखिर काल गतिको छ भिरेको देही ।
प्रभूका कृपाले गरि जन्म हुन्छ,
निहुँ कालू गतिले गरि जानु पर्छ ॥

३५

गई तिर्थ बस्ने र ज्ञानीहरूले,
एक् सत् पुकारून् भने हीत मैले ।
बहुत् बिन्ति लाउन् सत शब्द गाउँन्,
प्रभू छन् कृपालू धर्म खूब् मगाउन् ॥

३६

नहीं धर्म लोक्मा डुबेको छ शोक्मा,
छोड़ी धर्म दिदा परे दुःख भोग्मा ।
प्रभू सत् कृपालू त खाँनि दयाका,
म ता देख्न लाग्यें प्रत्यक्षई भएका ॥

३७

केही दोष दिन्छू सुनि लेउ ऐले,
झुटो ता यो होइन देउ माफ् सबैले ।
सरकारका इ अड्डा अदालथ् रहेका,
लोक्को निन्या हेर्न राखि दिएका ॥

३८

लोभ्‌ले गर्दा धर्मको नष्ट पारी,
नियाँ त्यस्को थियो लियो घुस् हकारी ।
दोहोरा त्यो दण्ड त्यसैमा लगायो,
थियो जित्ने मुद्दा त्यो मुद्दा हरायो ॥

३९

यसै लोभ्‌ले गर्दा अन्याय परेको,
मालिकहरूले आशा राखे नौ भरेको ।
प्रभू देख्न लाग्यें त्यो निर्धो मरेको,
मालिक्‌हरू हो यो के काम् गरेको ॥

४०

बाबा बिन्ति भन्छ ममा दोष् नराखी,
निब्बा छाड्‌ि दिए घुशैमा तयारी ।
कलियुग्‌का मालिक् घुशैमा छन् राजी,
कलियुग्‌को बुद्धी कति कब्बा पाजी ॥

४१

दोस्रो भाषा

योगि जन्‌को चलन् केहि बिस्तार गर्‌छु,
उच् निच्छ माफ दिनू शरण पर्‌छू ।
योगि जन्‌ले आशन् बाँधी बस्ला बनैमा,
आफ्ना मालिक् माहाँदेव जप्ला मनैमा ॥

४२

शिद्ध त्यो हो कैलाश् जान्छ नगई छोड्दइन,
सबै योगि कैलाश् जालान् भन्नु पर्दैन ।
बनका गौरि शङ्कर नभई योगि भएन,
मनका गौरि शङ्करजिको यादै रहेन ॥

४३

बनका गौरि शङ्कर मागि भर्न लागे झोला,
मनका गौरि शङ्करजिलाई खुम्काइसके होला ।
रूद्राक्ष ता योगि जनले एउटा लाए हुन्छ,
द्यौन बाबा द्यौन बाबा बर्षैनि त्यो भन्छ ॥

४४

यौटा लाए पुगि जान्छ घेर के गर्नू,
दुनियाँकै स्वभाव् लिन्छ अप्ठारामा पर्नू ।
दुनियाँको चलन्दाना योगि के गर्दछ,
ज्ञान्को बिचार नगरि त्यो त्यसै दगुर्दछ ॥

४५

योगि झोला बन्न लागो भित्रि पत्रै पत्र,
त्यो सम्पत्ति लुकाउँन बन्नु किन नत्र ।
योगि जन्को चलन यस्तो धर्म काहाँ जाग्नू,
ईश्वरमा सत्य सुरथ् कुन दिन तिन्को लाग्नू ॥

४६

माया त्याग्न सजिलो छ लोभ् छ त्याग्न कोटी,
लोभि चित्त भयो भने कर्म हुन्छ खोटी ।
कशि जस्तो माया रछ रज्ज जस्तो लोभ् छ,
जाहाँ माया बस्न गयो त्यहिं लोभ्ले छोप्छ ॥

४७

अरकाको चिज् हो भनी बिचार गरोइन,
लोभि चित्त भयो भने धर्म हेरोइन ।
यस्तो स्वभाव् बस्यो भने दुःख पाउँनेछ,
संसार तरी जादैन त्यो यार्हि आउँनेछ ॥

४८

बाबु त्यस्को मरि गयो काहाँ गएछ,
कुल्को माया नमर्नाले छोरो भएछ ।
आमा त्यस्कि मरिकन दोस्रा कुल्मा सरिछ,
दोस्रा कुल्कि कन्या भई जन्म लिईछ ॥

४९

माया जिले संयोग् पारि फेरि घुमाई फर्काई,
त्यो अधिकी नातिजिकि प्यारि हुन आई ।
यतै हुँदो घुम्द छन्ति यार्हि खेल्दा रछन,
मुक्ति पद्को रस्ता छोपि येतै ठेल्दा रछन ॥

५०

मुक्ति हुने युक्ति हेर छैन कसैमा,
आफ्नि प्यारि मायाजिका परे बशैमा ।
घर्कि माया त्याग्यौ भने अर्कि हुने छन,
चारै पट्टि तिनै माया फर्कि दिने छन ॥

५१

तिनि माया हसाउँछिन् प्रिति बढाउँछिन्,
शेखि गर्नें सिद्ध जन्को जन्म भसाउँछिन् ।
हे दैव कृपालु माया तिम्री सिपालू,
मायाजिको चरित्र म कत्ति निकालू ॥

५२

मृतक् हुने दिनको दुःख कहन्छु म थोड़ा,
लेखेको छ मन्थ हरूमा बिचार गर्नु होला ।
सबै बात कहन्न म झुट्रो हुने छैन,
सबै दुःख कहुँ भने सुनि सक्नु छैन ॥

५३

मृतक्स्यलाई फिर्नेहरू भन्छन् आज मर्‍यो,
कर्म अनुसार त्यसलाई बड़ो दुःख पर्‍यो ।
चार पाउ कसि कसि डल्लो गराउँछ,
बन्धुवर्ग सुनुन् भनि उम्र कराउँछ ॥

५४

काँढावाला लट्टि लिई लागि हाले हान्न,
नाँगो छ त्यो बस्त्र छैन दुत्ले लागे तान्न ।
कुटि कुटि चूर्ण भैगो निक्लँदैन श्वास,
छोरो चाँहि भन्छ वाहाँ गछु क्षत्रो पास ॥

५५

कुटि कुटि निलो पारि दुत्ले घिच्याउँछ,
नाताहरू सुनुन् भनि उम्र चिच्याउँछ ।
फर्सा भालाहात्मा लिई च्वास्स च्वास्स घोच्न,
त्यो शरिरको खुन झिकी कुंभि पाक्मा थप्न ॥

५६

पापिहरूको खुन झिकि कुण्ड भरेको,
कुहेको छ गन्ध चल्ने किरा परेको ॥
यमराज्का दुतहरू जम्मा भइ जान्छन्,
कुंभि पाक्मा थप्न भनि तेस्लाई लैजान्छन् ॥

५७

बहँदो छ शरिर भरी धारा रगत्को,
दुत्ले भन्छ कमाई तेरो यै हो जगत्को ।
डरलाग्दा छन् दुत्हरू सातो हरिदिन्छन्,
बिच्छिलाई डस्नु भनी हुकुम् गरि दिन्छन् ॥

५८

कालो साँप्ले डस्ता डस्तै तालु फोरि दियो,
यमराज आई फेरी तालु जोड्डि दियो ।
दण्ड लिन दियो देह मर्न नपाउँने,
यमराज निठुरि छन् दया नआउँने ॥

५९

ल्याउ यस्को खाता हेरौं कस्तो रछ काम,
कुन् दिन् भज्यो यस् चोर्ले खोई हरी नाम ।
हेरि सक्यौ बहि पत्र छैन हरी नाम,
जन्मे देखी आज सम्म लोभि तेरो काम ॥

६०

कति थियो धन तेरो साँचिस् कुन् दिनलाई,
कति थिए सन्तान् तेरा छोरा नाति भाइ ।
कस्ले लिन्छ शरण् तेरो अहिले याहाँ आई,
यसो भन्दै दुतहरू थुक्छन् त्यसलाई ॥

६१

तेरो बुद्धि बिग्रियो (त) दोष नदे कसैलाई,
छैन तेरो कल्याण् गर्ने अहिले याहाँ आई ।
हेर्दा माता जाति छ त्यो केहि गर्दैन,
भित्र भने चोर बुद्धिको संगत् छोड्डैन ॥

६२

त्यसका निति लाइदियौ पुराण् स्वर्ग तर्दैँन,
निर्धो होला यजमान् र धेर दान् गरोइन ।
लोभि होला पुरोहित् र चित्त परोइन,
यस्तो ढड्याङ पर्ला जसूका पितृ तरोईनन् ॥

६३

पुरोहित ले सन्तोषि भई दक्षिणा हो लिनू,
यजमान्का पितृ तर्नें आशिर्वाद दिनू ।
शान्त स्वाभाव् लिनसके धर्म पलाउला,
आफ्ना ज्ञाति बंशादिमा बासन् चलाउला ॥

६४

पण्डितले चाल् पाउँनु गड्डुर लाउँनु,
धेर कर्ममा नभुल्नु प्रेतमा नहुल्नु ।
यो बात् सुन्दा पण्डितको चित्त दुख्नेछ,
भक्तजिका दृष्टि पर्दा नर्क सुक्नेछ ॥

६५

श्री शिवलाई बासन् चल्ने ज्ञान्को धुप होल,
चोर बुद्धिलाई पयट लाई बाहिर निकाल ।
ईश्वर बस्ने हृदयमा चोर बुद्धिको भाला,
दुःख पाउँने जिव्को गति सम्झि लोभि चाला ॥

६६

चटक् जस्ता संसारमा खप्ना जस्तो खेल्छ,
प्राणिहरूका हृदयमा तृष्णाको भेल् छ ।
सम्पत्तको त्यो तृष्णा कुछ घटाउ,
भगवान्का भजन् पट्टी चित्त लगाउ ॥

६७

बेला बखत् भने सब को आयो होला बित्तै,
सम्पति ता याँहि बस्छ जानु पर्छे रित्तै ।
सबै चिज पग्लने हो सबै याँहि बिल्छ,
ठुला भाग्य सत् सङ्गत्ले आनन्दि पद् मिल्छ ॥

६८

भगवान्को भजन् गरे बुद्धि पाइन्छ,
ठुलो भाग्य सत् सङ्गत्ले उत्रि जाइन्छ ।
कल्प बृक्ष बिरूवालाई जंगलले ढाक्यो,
यो हो भनि नचिन्दामा पत्कर हुन आँट्यो ॥

६९

कल्प बृक्ष बिरूवा आत्मा माहाँ छन्,
जंगल सबू नाश गर्दा तब देखिन्छन् ।
कल्प बृक्ष बिरूवा चिन्नु यसो गरी,
एक वटा पत्ता होला सम्झ बेस गरी ॥

७०

गिता पढ़्दा ज्ञान् ता हुने तत्व नबुझिने,
अगम् चिज्को मालुम् नभई मुक्ति नमिल्ने ।
गुण ता दिने अन्तरयामि दर्शन् दिने बिष्नू,
शिवजिका नामबाट छ उक्लने लिस्नू ॥

७१

गुण दिने ता अन्तरयामि दर्शन दिने शीब,
यी आत्माका गुफा भित्र बसेको छ जीब ।
फुल् को थुँगो रूजि रहन्छ बासन् रूज्दैन,
अगम् तत्व खोलि सर्के लोक् ता बुझ्दैन ॥

७२

बासनका महिमाले मसला ता किन्छन्,
भक्तहरूको स्वभाव पनी भगवानले चिन्छन् ।
भगवान्को नाम् मध्ये बिष्णुको नाम् जबर,
लेखि सर्के बिन्ति पत्र छाड़े तार खबर ॥

७३

आयो मेरो तार खबर मन्त्रिहरू धरि देऊ,
आफू सत्य महादेवले यसको निसाफ गरि देऊ,
गिद्को जस्तो भाषा आयो सवाल सुनाई देऊ ।
के के भन्छन् कुन् कुन् जन्ले त्यो बात यहाँ लेऊ,

७४

अघि पनि रामचन्द्रले यसै भनेथें,
धोबिदेखि दुष्ट बचन त्यो ता सुनेथे ।
धर्म स्थापन गर्न भनी औतार लिएथे
लङ्का पति रावणलाई मारि दिएथे ॥

७५

अहिले पनि भुभाईनें चाला लिनु भो,
हो कि होइन शङ्कर जानुन् संक्षेप् दिनु भो ।
बैकुण्ठमा जाने ईच्छा लिएँ मनैमा,
आफ्नि सिता लक्ष्मिलाई त्यागे बनैमा ॥

७६

रामचन्द्रका हुकुमले बनमा जाँनु भो,
निम्या पुगि लक्ष्मिजि ता स्वर्ग जानु भो ।
अहिले पनि भुभाईनें चाला लिनु भो,
हो कि होइन शङ्कर जानुन् संक्षेप् दिनु भो ॥

७७

काला बस्त्र पोल्दै हिंड्‌ने बिचार गर को हो,
अघि बिर धनुर्धारी गाँडिडब् लिने जो हो ।
जान्न त म जान्ने होइन यत्ति भने अहिले,
युधिष्ठिरका वंश होलान् भन्ने ठान्छु मैले ॥

७८

कालो बस्त्र सत्य भन्छू सब्‌ले मोलुम् पाउँनू,
गायत्रको जप् गर्ने ले कहिले नलाउनू ।
गोयत्र ता लक्ष्मिजि हुन् श्वेत भूषण् लिन्छिन्,
कालो बस्त्र कालो गाजल् तिन्ले त्यागि दिन्छिन् ॥

७९

होइन मैले बोलेको ता योग् छ चलेको,
बैराग् लिने जनहरूमा तत्व खोलेको ॥

८०

श्लोक

अघी बिष्णुजीले गायत्र दिनु भो,
ब्राह्मण् नष्ट हुँदा उ आफै लिनु भो ।
गायत्रको जप् यो साँचो छैन याह्राँ,
गायत्र पहुँचिन् बिष्णुका समिप्‌मा ॥

८१

बिप्रादिलाई जपता लोभको दिनू भो,
गायत्र माता प्रभुले लिनू भो ।
रूद्राक्ष देखिछ इबि उठेको,
प्रत्यक्ष धर्म शिवले लुटेको ॥

८२

चार युग मध्ये कलि युग अध्यारो,
कलिका पदार्थ करेलो पघेरो ।
यिन तीन युगले अमलिए मिठो,
कलियुगको अम्मल काँचो पातको तितो ॥

८३

यिनै तीन युगले कलिलाई ढाँटे,
कलि युगको बस्त्र छ कालो र पाठे ।
यिनै तीन युगले बाँधे यस्तो रोहा,
कलिको गहना रंगिएको लाहा ॥

८४

शरिर छन् कलिमा कुप्रा निधार टेढ़ा,
धर्मः युग्मा होलान् यिनै बेस्त्व रूप्का ।
कलि युग्मा शास्त्र श्री कृष्ण चरित्र,
धर्म युग्मा शास्त्र माहाँ ज्ञान पवित्र ॥

८५

कलि युग्को स्वभाव्बि चार गर्छु यस्तो,
धर्म युग्को स्वभाव् फटिक् झल्के जस्तो ।
धर्म युग्को स्वभाव् कहन्छु म थोड़ै,
नारी जन्ले विश्वास् मानुन् है अघोरै ॥

८६

सुन्दर सपेत्का पहिरेर सारी,
हात्मा लिएका अति श्वेत झारी ।
मधुर बचन्ले गरि बोलि दिने,
झाँक्को स्वभाव् नारिहरूले लिने ॥

८७

हि हि गर्ने हाँसो रहदैन जान्छ,
एक् बार मुसुक्क हाँसो यां रहन्छ ।
रहदैन स्वभाव् अघोरी अबोला,
मधुर बचन्को स्वभाव् फिर्ने होला ॥

८८

लक्ष्मिको स्वभाव् छ धर्ममा रहेको,
सारा लोक् सुनन् यो अधम्ले कहेको ।
प्रभू अन्तरयामि आफू जान्नु होला,
जातकी म छु स्त्री स्वभाव्की अबोला ॥

८९

को हो लायो लोक्मा म जस्ती अभागी,
तबि बिन्ति गर्छु (म) दयाका लागी ।
हितै भन्छु मैले हितै जानि लेउ,
भक्ति अधम् हूँ शुभाशिष देउ ॥

९०

यो प्राण् त्याग्नलाई खि जाती छु आँटी,
साँच्चो बिन्ति गर्छू रति भर नढाँटी ॥

९१

दोस्रो भाषा

सूर्यजिका वरिपरि साँवा रहन्छन्,
लोक्मा साक्षि सूर्यजि छन् साँच्चो कहन्छन् ।
कसुर हेरि दण्ड दिन्छन् बेसि दिदैनन्,
सूर्य जिता साँच्चो बोल्छन् घुस् ता लिदैनन् ॥

९२

लोक भन्छ ज्वालामुखि बिक्रि गरें धेर,
बिष्णु ठाकुर घुम्नु हुन्छ गोशा भई हेर ।
धेरै दिन भो सम्झाउँदैछु लोक टेर्दैन,
ज्वाला आफै प्रकट हुन केहि बेर छैन ॥

९३

ज्वाला उत्रि अग्नि रूप ले जगत जलाउलान्,
ज्वाला उत्रि जल्यो भनि कस्ले मालुम् पाउलान् ।
धेर दिन भो सम्झाउदैछु पत्यार मानेनन्,
हित का बचन् दिर्वें मैले लिन जानेनन् ॥

९४

भगवान्को शक्ति मैले अन्सार कहेको,
कसो गरि हेर्नु मैले भस्म भएको ।
सारथि सारथि हो हो मेरो नाम,
ज्ञान्का गर्भ भित्र म छू बुझ मेरो काम ॥

९५

ज्ञान्का गर्भ भित्र म छू खाँनु पर्दैन,
यो ज्ञान्बाट उत्रे पछि नखाई हुँदैन ।
यस्ता चौराश लाखौं खटाउ खाँदा अघाईदैन,
नखाई र नअघाई राजि हुइदैन ॥

९६

सारथि साँरथि हो हो मेरो नाम,
ज्ञान्का गर्भ भित्र म छु सम्झ मेरो काम ।
ज्ञान्का गर्भ भित्र म छु बोल्नु पर्दैन,
यो ज्ञान्बाट उत्रे पछि नबोलि हुँदैन ॥

९७

एकै शब्द बोल्न नपाई जगत् रहँदैन,
साँरथि साँरथि यो हो मेरो नाम् ।
ज्ञान्का गर्भ भित्र म छू बुझ मेरो काम्,
ज्ञान्का गर्भ भित्र म छू खेल्नु पर्दैन ॥

९८

यो ज्ञान्बाट उत्रे पछि यो खेल् थामिदैन,
गुड्ड गुड्ड खेल्नु पर्ने जगत् पक्का छैन ।
होइन मैले बोलेको ता योग् छ चलेको,
इच्छा गर्ने संगत् संग शब्द खोलेको ॥

९९

यो संसारको रित जो छ विन्ति चढाउँला,
ब्रह्मा विष्णु महेश्वरको आसन् डगाउँला ।
सत्य शिव माहाँदेवको ध्यान् म धरूँला,
बिष्णु ठाकुर्ने झिकाझ के को छोड्ला ॥

१००

अन्तरयाँमि ईश्वर सित यैत पड्.दैछू,
दुष्ट बुद्धि झुट्टो कर्म त्याग् म गर्दैछू ॥
अन्तरयाँमि ईश्वर सित यैत पढूला,
शक्ति चल्ने विद्या न पि के को छोड्ला ॥

१०१

अन्तर्यामि अबिनासि मालिक् भित्रै छन,
ब्रह्मा बिष्णु महेश्वर ता कर्म दिने हुन् ॥
शक्ति शालि अबिनासि मालिक दोश्रा छन्,
अविनासि को हुन् भने कर्म मेट्.ने हुन् ॥

१०२

अन्तर्यामि   अविनासी   देख्छु   यसोरी,
ब्रह्म ज्योति मस्तक भरी मर्थे कसोरी ।
यो शरिरमा रह्यू यिन बिहोस मा होइन,
झुट्टो रति कहुइन बिचेतमा छुइन ॥

१०३

ईश्वर   उत्रेश्वर   शब्दमा   शक्ति   नलोई,
हत् पत् गम्ता पाउने छैनौ सेवा न दीई ।
सेवा टहल् सन्सारमा जस्ले जान्नि गर्ला,
अन्त्य काल्मा सम्झनाले सन्सार त्यो तर्ला ॥

१०४

सबै   रस्ता   खुल्ने   रछन्   रोक्का   परोईन,
भ्रान्मि सबै उड्ने छन् दोष् केहि रहोईन ।
रूद्र कण्ठ एक मुखि ले अजि गरेछन्,
अजि सुन्दा भगवान्को आसन् डगेछन् ॥

१०५

ब्रह्मा   विष्णु   शिव   तिनै   जम्मा   भएछन्,
त्यै दिन्देखि लोक्मा खबर गर्दा रहेछन् ।
देवाहरू बिन्ति गर्छन् भुभार धेर भयो,
उत्रि देउ बिष्णु ठाकुर लोक्मा बेर भयो ॥

१०६

कोहि   प्राणिले   मखान्   बेचे   कपट   मिलाए,
कोहि   प्राणि   मखान्   किने   त्यो धूप चलाए ।
धूप्को वासन् छैन एउटा कपट गनाए,
लोक् भो झुट्टो देवाहरू बिन्ति चढाए ॥

१०७

ब्राह्मणले सत्य धर्म सब छाडि दिए,
जगतमा भ्रष्ट कर्म सब गर्दा भए ।
त्राहि त्राहि पच्यो प्रभू झुट्टा कर्मैले,
सारा लोकमा छाड्थ्यो प्रभू साँचा धर्मैले ॥

१०८

यसो भन्दै देवताहरू जोडले कराए,
बिष्णु ठाकुर गुस्सा भई सब्लाई अराए ।
योगि जन्ले दृढ गरी शङ्कर पुकारून्
माझ मिद्धान् पर्न लाग्यो सत्य उतारून् ॥

१०९

सत्य जपि ध्यान गरि देउ चार वेद्का सोजि,
आफु आत्मा गर्नु हुन्छ ब्रह्म ज्ञान्को खोजि ।
सत्य जपि ध्यान गरि देउ बिष्णुजिका सोजि,
आफु आत्मा गर्नु हुन्छ माहाँ ज्ञान्को खोजि ॥

११०

सत्य जपि ध्यान गरि देउ शिवजिका सोजि,
आफु आत्मा गर्नु हुन्छ शक्ति ज्ञान्को खोजि ।
सत्य जपि ध्यान गरि देउ हिमाल्यका सोजि,
आफु आत्मा गर्नु हुन्छ तपि ज्ञान्को खोजि ॥

१११

सत्य जपि ध्यान गरि देउ सूर्यजिका सोजि,
आफु आत्मा गर्नु हुन्छ प्रताप ज्ञान्को खोजि ।
सत्य जपि ध्यान गरि देउ चन्द्रमाका सोजि,
आफु आत्मा गर्नु हुन्छ अँविज्ञान्को खोजि ॥

११२

सत्य जपि ध्यान गरि देउ समुद्रका सोजि,
आफु आत्मा गर्नु हुन्छ सागर ज्ञानको खोजि ।
शक्तिदेखि कृपा हुँदा मैले पाएको,
आफ्ना भक्त दुःखमा पर्दा सुचन दिएको ॥

११३

सम्पुर्णको मै हूँ एउटा बोल्ता बसेको,
गुरूजिको मर्जि हुँदा छु सब्मा पसेको ।
फौज मेरा धेर छन् जम्मा बिच्मा रहन्छु,
एकै छिन्मा हराउछु एक्ला म हुन्छु ॥

११४

ब्रह्मा बिष्णु महेश्वर ता एक स्वरूप हुन्,
म मात्र ता हुइन भन्ने मालिक दोश्रा छन् ।
बिष्णु गुप्त भाको अहिले चौकोट्टि साल भएछ,
ब्राह्मणको साँचो धर्म तब उडि़ गएछ ॥

११५

भगवान्ले साँचा भक्त राखे हुनन् काहि;
बिष्णुस्वरले उत्रने छन् आफ्ना भक्त माहि ।
लोकले भन्ला बिष्णुस्वरलाई कुन प्रमाण्ले जान्नू,
आफ्नु विश्वास् बस्छ जाहाँ बिष्णु उनै मान्नू ॥

११६

उनै बिष्णु पुकार्दा म दुःख टर्नें छ,
धिरे धिरे भक्तदेखि धर्म सर्नें छ ।
सानु कम्मर कलिलो बर्ण सिधा उभीए,
सारा चौरास् काँधमा राखि अल्गिएका थीए ॥

११७

सामु बिन्ति तिन्का गर्दै काँधमा चढ्दै थीए
छैन जगत् भवन् भो फगत् तमासा हेर्दै थीए ।
क्या हो कोनि देख्छु यस्तो भने कसो होला,
सिद्ध मुनि ज्ञान वान् ले सुने सेखि गर्ला ॥

११८

गौका धनि गुवालालाई दया हुँदैन,
गउ राम् छिन् गुवालिमा झट्ट फुकाउदैन ।
चरन् सम्झि जङ्गल् छैन रुन्छिन् धुरू धुरू,
शिवजिमा बिन्ति गर्न जान्छिन् खुरू खुरू ।

११९

गाई जाँदा गोरू पनि सँग गएछ
गोरू जाँदा दुनियाँमा दुःख भएछ ।
दुःख पर्दा गाई सबै कैलाश गएछन्,
दुःख देखि देवताले दया गरेछन् ।

१२०

देवताहरू बिन्ति गर्छन् गोरू फिराउन,
मर्जि भयो गाई साथ गोरू फिराउन ।
छाड् देउ सवाल् पुगोस् नेपाल् सब्ले मालुम् पाउन्,
माहाराज्मा मालुम् हवस् मन्त्रिहरू जानुन् ॥

१२१

पत्यार परे आफ्ना राज्मा धर्म चलाउलान्,
धर्मि राजा भन्ने लोक्मा नाउ कमाउलान् ।
पृथ्वि मनि रछ ठुलो तलाउ जमेको,
त्यहि तलाउले रछ जम्मै चौरास थामेको ॥

१२२

धर्म सम्झि सत्य मान सेखि नगरी,
नहिँ चौरास् डुबाई देलान् सङ्कर श्री हरी ।
तलाउ मनि दोस्रो किसिम् बन्दो भएछ,
त्यहि भित्र पाताल् पुरि शहर रहेछ ॥

१२३

उज्यालो छ सुन्दर सबै शहर देखिँदा,
प्राणिहरू ससाना छन् देह छ रीता ।
मधुरै छ शब्द सब्को बाणि ललीता,
क्रोध सेखि छैन रत्ती छैन ममता ॥

१२४

सारा मैले राम्रा देखें स्त्रि पुरूष नारि,
जय शब्द गर्दा रछन् बलि राजा भारि ।
कुछ घड़ि त्यहि बसि नेत्र धुमाएँ,
सिद्ध रूपि तपस्विको दर्शन त्यहि पाएँ ॥

१२५

नमस्कार त दुबै जनको बराबरी भयो,
मेरा मनमा सिद्धलाई सोध्ने लहड़ गयो ।
कत्ति सम्म बस्नु हुन्छ पाताल् पुरीमा,
याहाँदेखि उठि गुरू पाल्नु हुन्छ काहाँ ॥

१२६

सिद्ध रूपि तपस्वि हुन् साँचै बताए,
भगवान्कि भक्ति भनि तिनले मालुम् पाए ।
बिष्णुजिको मर्जि हुँदा बसेकोछु याहि,
बिष्णु लोक्मा प्रकट् हुँदा उत्रि जान्छु बाहि ॥

१२७

शिद्ध रूपि तपस्वि हुन् धेरै नबोल्ने,
जाहि ताहि प्राणिसित तत्व नखोल्ने ।
शिद्ध रूपि तपस्विको मनको ईच्छा पाएँ,
जाहाँ सम्म ईच्छा पाए खबर बताएँ ॥

१२८

साना खाल्का माकुराले धागो छाड़ि दियो,
त्यो धागामा सारा चौरास् झुण्डिएको थियो ।
क्या हो कोनि देख्छु यस्तो शङ्का गरौला,
विचार गरि चिन्यौ भने सनसार तरौला ॥

१२९

श्लोक

इता छन् यिनैमा लहै दिन दिनैमा,
यिनैको नमस्कार छ है छिन छिनैमा ।
यि ता छन् यिनैमा यिनैमा उनिन्छू,
यिनैका कृपाले म यिनै बनिन्छू ॥

१३०

यिनैलाई भज्छू यिनैलाई जप्छू,
यिनै दिन्छिन युक्ती र पो थुन्न सक्छू ।
यो माया छाड़ी जउन् पस्ला झाड़ी,
मिले पूर्ण ब्रह्मा उता जान्छ पारी ॥

१३१

कस्तै बिकट् होस् असल् हो इ जान्छ,
एकै छिनमा हाजिर ब्रह्म लोक्मा रहन्छ ।
निराकार भन्नू रति छैन काहीं,
देखिन्छ झल् झल् सब लोक वाहीं ॥

१३२

अग्ला अटाली सहर झल्किएको,
घेरैं छन् तलाउ अनेक् टल्किएका ।
छन् बृक्ष उज्ज्वल् छ छायाँ तलाउमा,
अत्यन्त सुन्दर बयान् के लगाउमः ॥

१३३

बृक्षः उपर पक्षि गाना गरेका,
बुझियो अगम् तत्व सुन्दा खोलेका ।
त्यहि एक छ उच्चा फटिक्ले चिटेको,
दश लाख योजन् छ त्यो अल्गिएको ॥

१३४

पर ब्रह्म प्राप्त हुकुम् शिघ्र पाई,
उतै ब्रह्म बेग्ले लिने झट् उठाई/छा
त्यसै उच्चा माहाँ चढ़ि हेर्दा ताहाँ,
देखिन्छ लोक् सर्व नजीक माहाँ ॥

१३५

उनै ब्रह्म बेग्ले खिचेर ल्याउछन,
सम्पूर्ण लोक ता नजिक्मा देखाउछन ।
कोहि नजाने छ उ ब्रह्म लोक् माहाँ,
सबै जन भुलेछौ यहि शोग भोगमा ॥

१३६

त्यो ब्रह्म लोक् ता अगम् हो अपार,
मेरो नमस्कार पुगोस् बार बार ।
मनुष्यहरू हो सबै के भएका,
गति आफ्नु आफै नचिनि रहेका ॥

१३७

सबै डुलि डुली कति सुख खोंज्छौ,
निसिब् ता सँगै छ के को भाग्य रोज्छौ ।
ज्वाला र मुग्दार भए अमोल्का,
के हुन्छ कोनि र म देख्छु उल्का ॥

१३८

इ दाना वेन्न त दुगुछ काशी,
हरे काशि साक्षि भरे पछ फासी ।
एक मुखि रूद्राक्ष उडि गए छन,
शङ्कर माहाँ केहि अरज गरे छन ।

१३९

अरज कठोरको छ काहाँ खपौला,
रूद्राक्ष बेच्नं त काहाँ बचौला ।
यो बिन्ति गछु म दयाका लागी,
रूद्राक्ष बेच्नेछौ सारै अभागी ॥

१४०

धर्मैंको ढोका बिचमा छ सानू,
ढोका नछिरेर हुँदैन जानू ।
भक्ति सुकेका सहजैमा छिरे,
ठुला शरिरका अहङ्कारि फिरे ॥

१४१

भक्ति मलिन्द्रा सहज्मा ति फड्के,
क्रोधि घमण्डि अभिमानि अड्के ।
भक्ति अभक्ति कन छानि लिए,
रूद्राक्ष बेच्नेलाइ अति कष्ट दिए ॥

१४२

त्यसै बखत्मा म सुरथ् पुगेछु,
बम् बम् सदा शीव पुकार दिएँछ ।
भूःलोककि प्राँणि तिमि किन आयौ,
कस्ले बतायो र यो थाहा पायौ ॥

१४३

ईच्छा के छ मन्मा सव ई बताऊ,
मालिक् ता मन्चि हूँ अब ता नडराउ ।
शङ्कर प्रभूको यति मर्जि पाव्ये,
मैले पनी झट्ट पाउ समाव्ये ॥

१४४

शङ्कर प्रभूले गरि द्रष्टि दिनू,
भस्मै घसेको छ ललाट् माचिनू ।
बालुवा माहाँ छ त्यो चिनि मिसेको,
यही टिप्न मैले मिह्निनत् गरेको ॥

१४५

बालुवा मिश्री त चिनि छुट्याई,
पाछु यसैको अब लौ मिठाई ।
माथ्मा सदा शिव छन् यहि भोग लगाउला,
यस्को यसैले यो पियास् मेटाउला ॥

१४६

यो कलिको मुख्य आसन् सुवर्ण हो सुन,
धिरे धिरे ज्ञानिहरूले लाउन छाड्ने छन् ।
यो कलिको सुन् हुनाले चोरि हुँदैछ,
लोक् ता भन्छ दौलथ् मेरो जोरि हुँदैन ॥

१४७

मृतक् हुने दिन्मा पनि त्यहि सुन खुवाउछन्,
स्वर्ग जाने भए पनि येतै फिराउछन् ।
सम्पत्ति ता शत्रु मान्ने सन्ताप् भिराउने,
देख्न लागे हरि नाम् यो मति फिराउने ।

१४८

धिरे धिरे यो कलिको स्वभाव टार्ने छन्,
माहा राज्का पल्टन् सबै सपेत पार्ने छन् ।
जान्न त म जान्ने हुइन यति भने लौ,
अहिले हत्पत् गर्नु छैन पछि बुझ्ने छौ ॥

१४९

यो पैसाका चलन् भित्र लोभ पाप रहेछ,
खाने लाउने चिज वस्तु घट्तो भएछ ।
पहिला मार्लान् कम्पर्नानिलाई पिछे मार्लान् मोहोर,
मासि देलान् पैसा चलन् निक्लि जोला फोहोर ॥

१५०

यो पैसाका चलन् भित्र लोभ पाप रहेको,
कोहि दिन्मा हुने बात् यो अन्सार कहेको ।
महा राज् छन् दर्बारिमा हेर्न आउदैनन्,
दुःखि जन्ले निन्या निसाफ् सिधा पाउदैनन् ॥

१५१

जागिरदार लोभि छन् निघा हेर्दैं नन,
मानु पर्ने शरिर हो बिचार गर्दैं नन ।
दुःखि जन हो हात जोड्डि सत्य पुकार,
अर्को हाम्रो सहायता छैन बिष्णु गुहार ॥

१५२

आफै बिष्णु लक्ष्मिले कल्याण गर्ने छन,
चैतन्य जिव खुलेकामा दर्शन दिने छन ।
होइन मैले बोलेको ता योग छ चलेको,
थामि सक्नु नहुदामा शब्द खोलेको ॥

१५३

बिम्बनलाई बिम्बकि छु भनि सक्छु काहाँ,
तै पनि केहि बिन्ति गर्छु बिष्णु शरण माहाँ ।
हरि शङ्कर माहादेवले शिक्षा दिनू भो,
मेरो पनि चित्त बुझ्यो जात्ता लिनू भो ॥

१५४

मेरो जात्ता शङ्करजिमा शरण पर्न गो,
तत्व खोलौ मर्जि छैन बुझ्न सक्ला को ।
कस्तै ज्यात्रा तमास् गरुन हेर्ने म आवैन,
भगवान्को दया भए लोक्मा म आवैन ॥

१५५

भगवान्को दया भए जन्म लिवैन,
कस्तै दौलथ् सुख भन्नु चित्त लावैन ।
छैन मेरो चित्त याहाँ लगे हरेर,
आफु बिष्णु दर्शन दिन्छन बिच्मा झरेर ॥
एकान्तमा बसेकै छु बिन्ति गरेर ॥

१५६

दोस्रो भाषा

गोरषा राज मै तपस गर्दछु,
सत्य शीव कै ध्यान म धर्दछु ।
साँचा धर्म कै खोजि गर्दछु,
विष्णु ठाकुर कै पाउ पर्दछु ॥

१५७

मन का मालिक्मा पेच पो पछर्र की,
तम गुण पाल्दा हुन त्यो अघि सर्छ की ।
सेखि देखि ता बहुत डर्दछु,
हरिका आड़मा बात गर्दछु ॥

१५८

रिस का पेचमा पर्नु पर्दैन,
यो देह मर्ला के शक्ति मर्दैन ।
सुनेर बुझ्नु हो भित्र ज्ञानले,
मस्त छौ कि कोइ झुट्टा मानले ॥

१५९

बिन्ति गर्दछु सर्कार माफ्नु होस,
अब ता धर्मको स्थिति बाफ्नु होस ।
लोभि लुध्ध चाल सकल टुट्नेछ,
उल्का लोकमा ज्यादा उठ्ने छ ॥

१६०

लोभि	चाल्ले	दुःख		पाउछ,
अबत	धर्मको	यूग	आउछ	।
दुष्ट	बुद्धिकां	सेखि	गिनें	छ,
अबत	धर्मको	यूग	फिर्नेछ	॥

१६१

सुनन	सत्य	नाथ्	बिन्ति	लीनु	होस्,
अबत	धर्मको	योग	दीनु	होस्	।
सकल	घट्	घटै	ज्ञान	छिट्नु	होस्,
अबत	धर्मको	ढोल	पिट्नु	होस्	॥

१६२

लोक	लोभि	भो	धर्म	छैन	गो,
तिमि	बिना	प्रभू	धर्म	सार्नें	को	।
झुट्टा	बातले	अत्याचार	भयो,
सकल	दुखि	छन्	भूभार	घेर	भयो	॥

१६३

सत्य	शक्ति	नाथ्	सकल	जान्दछौ,
तिमि	त	भक्तको	बिन्ति	मान्दछौं	।
आफ्ना	लोकको	हाल	हेर्नु	होस्
बिन्ति	गर्छु	नाथ्	श्रृष्टि	फेर्नु	होस्	॥

१६४

सकल	प्राणिले	धर्म	छाड्	दिए,
सत्य	फिर्दो	हो	क्रिपा	गर्दिए	।
सत्य	छोड्दा	धर्म	गइ	गयो,
तिर्थ	ब्रत	सब्	न्यर्थ	भइ	गयो	॥

१६५

झुट्टा बातमा सब अघि सर्दछन्,
पछि त दुष्टले बिहिजत् गर्दछन् ।
साँचो छोड् दिए र झुट्टो बोल्दछन्,
पछि त दुष्टले दुर्मत् खोल्दछन् ॥

१६६

अधम भक्ति हूँ बिन्ति लेख्तछु,
तिम्रा लोकको हाल् यो देख्तछु ।
बिन्ति गर्दछु हित छ बिन्ति यही
तिम्रा लोकमा स्थिति छैन केही ।

१६७

सत्य नाथ कै पस्छु धाममा,
अहिले पो रहें यस्ता काममा ।
बिषय दुःखका छाड्यो मानले
मग्न छू म ता तिम्रा ज्ञानले ॥

१६८

आफ्ना लोकको रक्षा गर्नु होस्,
धनको भाग्य सब दैव हुनु होस् ।
धनका भाग्यमा दुष्ट लाग्दा हुन्,
ज्ञानको भाग्यभा शत्रु भाग्दा हुन् ॥

१६९

धनका भाग्यले पोल्दै ल्याउदो हो,
ज्ञानको भाग्यभा गुण पाउदो हो ।
धनका भाग्यले सेखि गर्दो हो,
ज्ञानको भाग्यभा मग्न पाउदो हो ॥

१७०

धनका   भाग्यले   यमपुर   भर्दो   हो,
ज्ञानको   भाग्यभा   स्वर्ग   सर्दो   हो ।
धनका   भाग्यले   प्रेत्मा   सर्दो   हो,
ज्ञानको   भाग्यभा   शिव लोक्   सर्दो   हो ॥

१७१

सुनन   सत्य   नाथ्   बिन्ति   लीनु   होस्,
अब   त   ज्ञानको   भाग्य   दीनु   होस् ॥

बौलाहाका   छाटले   उर्ऌे   आफूँ   आटले,
मुलुक   खायेछ   ढाँटले   यो   अर्काका   राजमा ॥

आएकि   छु   काजमा,
नौलै   छु   र   जान्दिन   झुट्टो   बिन्ति   मान्दिन ॥

१७२

हरिका   तिर्थ   हुन्   महिमा   गर्नेलाई,
जान   लागे   सब्   वार्दि   मर्नेलाई ॥
अघि   त   निर्धाको   सम्पती   हरे,
क्षत्रमा   बसेर   खर्च   त्यै   गरे ॥

१७३

घटिया   काम्   नभै   दौलथ्   जम्दैन,
होइन   भन्नता   कोहि   पाउदैन ।
सम्पति   हुनेको   तिर्थमा   छ   फल्,
दुखिले   गर्दछौ   आत्मा   चिन्ने   बल् ॥

१७४

हरि त नित्य छन् हृदयमा संगै,
मुक्ति छैन की तिर्थमा नगै ।
अधम भक्ति हूँ र बिन्ति लेख्तछु,
मुक्ति दिने नाथ. सब ठाउ देख्तछु ॥

१३५

काशि क्षत्रमा गै बस्तछन् नुहाई,
कस्ले देख्तछ ति कृष्ण चन्द्रलाई ।
महिमाले गरी बस्छन् क्षत्रमा,
हरि ता उत्रिये हाम्रा नेत्रमा ॥

१३६

देख्तछु हरी शकल लोकभरी,
काहाँ जानु हो भ्रांन्ति मन्गरी ।
जान लागे सब काशि मर्न लाई,
इच्छा गर्दछन्देह फेर्न लाई ॥

१३७

वाहिरि बिद्या हुन् लोभ्मा पार दिने,
भित्रि बिद्या छन् ज्ञान सार दिने ।
आफ्ना चित्तमा पसेर हेर्नु होस्,
हरिको नित्य ध्यान बसेर गर्नु होस् ॥

१३८

अर्को दोख्रो काम् साँचो छैन क्यै,
आत्माको बिचार गर्दछु म यै ।
आत्मामा पसी पिरोलो लाउनेको,
अमालि काम् लिदा गर्न लाउने जो ॥

१७९

अमालि काम् लिदा कति बिग्रि गो,
काशिराजले प्यादा छाड् दियो ।
चित्तमा पसी खान लागि गो,
डर देखाई देखाई ढान लागि गो ॥

१८०

माया त मर्दैन आफ्नि प्यारिको,
आफ्ना साथ मा जान तयारि भो ।
अधम भक्ति हूँ लेख्दिबें यती २,
सकल जान्ने छौ बिन्ति लाउ कती २ ॥

१८१

होइन मैले बोलेको ता योग छ चलेको,
दुख मान्ने भक्त जन्लाई संक्षेप् कहेको ॥

१८२

चौरास् भित्रै डुल्छन सबै चौरास् बाहिरको,
चौरास् बाहिर डुल्न जान्ने ब्रह्म लोक्मा गयो ।
चौरास् भित्रै हेर्छन् सबै चौरास् बाहिरको,
चौरास् बाहिर हेर्न जान्ने ब्रह्म ज्योति भयो ॥

१८३

चौरास् भित्र खान्छन् सबै चौरास् बाहिरको,
चौरास् बाहिर खान जान्ने माहाँ तपि भयो ।
अक्षर भित्रै बोल्छन् सबै अक्षर बाहिरको,
अक्षर बाहिर बोल्न जान्ने अन्तर्यामि भयो ॥

१८४

आयु भित्रै देख्छु सबै आयु बाहिरको,
आयु बाहिरको सम्झि राख एउटै सुन्ना हो ।
उहि हो सुन्ना उहि हो निर्गुण् दोस्रो होइन केहि,
निर्गुण् अहिले चाहिदैन सगुण बताउ येहि ॥

१८५

अबि नाशि निराशमा नित्य वाश गर्ने,
अबि नाशि को हुन भने कर्म नाश गर्ने ।
अबि नाशि जाहि ताहि बस्तै वस्तइनन,
निराशमा नभै त्यस्को कर्म माल्तइनन् ॥

१८६

सारा कर्म तोडि यस्मा चित्त लगाउ,
हितका बचन सुनाइ दिएँ सब ले मालुम् पाउ ।
अर्जि गर बिन्ति गर आशा छोड़ेर,
सत्य भक्त भए जाउला रस्ता लिएर ॥

१८७

छाप यिनका जाहाँ लाग्यो ताहाँ लाग्यो चीनु,
हुकुम् भइ गो त्यस्लाई रस्ता खुला गराई दिनु ।
मस्तक्बाट निस्केको जिव् प्राप्ति हुन्छ वाहि,
छैन त्यस्को देह याहाँ रहदैन काहीँ ॥

१८८

विष्णु देखि थोड़ै मुनि माहादेव् को रूप,
माथ्मा मुकुट् नाग् (को) माला ठूलो शिर छ खूब ।
कोहि भन्ला हो हो यो बात् कोहि भन्ला होइन,
दुबै रकम् नबोल्ति याहाँ हुने छैन ॥

१८९

कोहि भन्ला हो हो यो बात् होइन भन्ला जस्ले,
सम्झि राख केहि दुःख भोग्नु पर्ला त्यस्ले ।
होइन मैले बोलेको ता योग छ चलेको,
इच्छा गर्ने सज्जन जन्मा तत्व खोलेको ॥

१९०

गजल

पुर्खा मेरा सुन्ना भवन् पृथ्वि मेरि माता,
(यी) पृथ्वि भित्र जम्मा जति सम्बन्धिका नाता ।
जाति मेरा आत्मा गुरू सागर मेरा साखा,
आकास् मुनि पृथ्वि माथि बास् हो मेरो खाशा ॥

गुरू मेरा अन्तर्यामि बिन्ति कति लाउ,
यहि सुन्ना खला भित्र चेत् भई बस्न पाउ ॥

डुबि डुबि स्नान गर्छू सन्ताप् हर हर,
शिवजिको ध्यान् म धर्छू नित्य खर खर ।
हरि हरि हरि ॐ सत्य ॐ हरी,
आखिरि तनमन सुम्पेकै छु हरिलाई नगरी ॥

हरि मेरा मन भरी लाई गर मनपरी,
हरि हरि हरि ॐ सत्य ॐ हरी ।
तन मन मैले सुम्पेकै छु हरिलाई नगरी,
हरि मेरा मन भरिलाई बनाउ साफ गरी ॥

हरि हरि हरि ॐ सत्य ॐ हरी,
हरि हरि हरि मन भरि तिम्रो नगरी ।
बस हरि साफ गरि तिम्रो मन परी.

यां सम्झना समृचारि भइ झट्ट पौंचि गइ गो,
सुरथ् माथि सवार गरि याद आउनु भैगो ।
बस्नु भयो हृदयमा याद मेरा आई,
यि गुण् दिन लाग्नु भो है साचा मलाई ॥

१९१

हृदयमा सूर्य प्रकट् लागे झल मल,
चन्द्र माजि उदाउनु भो मेरा घट्मा बल ।
गुरू मेरा घट्मा प्रकट् सम्झ नबिचारि,
जाला मेरो चित्त काहाँ ल्यौं ल्यौं लछारि ॥

१९२

बसोस् चित्त थिर सित सत नाम् यो पढ्दै,
जावस् मेरा सङ्करजिमा सुरथ् खुब बढ्दै ।
गुरू मेरा अन्तर्यामि सत नाम् पढ़ाइ देउ,
ब्रह्मा बिष्णु महेश्वरले शक्ति चढ़ाइ देऊ ॥

१९३

प्राण मेरो ओहोर दोहोर गर्छ बारम्बार,
या प्राणको मूल अड्डा नाभि हात्ति सार ।
नाभिदेखि बढ़ि प्राण मन्तक् सम्म गैंगो,
मस्तक्देखि फिरि उधो नाभि सम्म भंगो ॥

१९४

नसा मासि जागेका छन् प्राणका रसैले ।
अगम् तत्व छिटियो लोक्मा बुझेन कसैले ॥

दोस्रो शब्द

धर्मका राजा उत्रन लागे लोक हो अब ता बेर छैन,
कलिको कर्म चञ्चल भयो लोक हो आयु ता धेर छैन ।
भक्तका दर्शन हरि नाम् बिना लोक हो मुक्ति ता मिल्दैन,
शिव हरि सत्य मनमा लिए लोक हो दुष्टले छुदैन ॥

१९५

आखिरि जन्म भइ गयो नरमा लोक हो नमरि हुँदैन,
शिव हरि सत्य मनमा लिए लोक हो दुःखले छुदैन ।
विष्णु ठाकुर शिव हरि सत्य लोक हो यदि नाम् पुकार,
आखिरि जन्म भइ गयो नरमा लोक हो गाल ता नपार ॥

१९६

जन्म छ नास कर्म यो खोटि लोक हो अब ता नभुल,
अनित्य खेल्मा मायाका जाल्मा लोक हो लौ अब नडुब ।
औसर पर्दा पालाले गर्दा लोक हो मनुष्य जन्म भो,
ईश्वरको भजन गरेनौं भने लोक हो यो जन्म इयर्थ गो ॥

१९७

तिर्थ जावे तिर्थ नुहावे मन की भ्रमण नहि छुटि आवे ।
बिना ज्ञान से भेद नहि पावे कैसे जनम छुटावे ॥
बिना दया से कौन सुख पावे ।
आशा नहि मारत फेर जग में घुमि आवे ॥
आशा मारा जोहो सो भक्त हमारा रस गुणले चीन ।
ब्रह्मा बिष्णु महे सतसङ्ग छु आये दर्शन दीन ॥
भेटि पुष्प कछु नहि चाहिये आसिर्वाद लिन लाई ।
अन्त्य काल्मा पर्ला विपत्ति रौला है मन पछुताई ॥
हरि हरि चरणको मङ्गलु गाई ।
भक्ति दिये ज्ञान बताई ॥
शिब शिव हरी हरी निस दिन भजना नहि राख्ना तु सक्यै ।
अनृत्य कोल्मा पर्ला बिपत्ति रौला है मन पछुताई ॥
माथमा मुकुट मोति जड़ावे ।
हिरा रत्न से सिर छपावे ॥
कानन कुण्डल कङ्गण लावे ।
जगमग जगमग ज्योति जगावे ॥
हूं हूं सदा शिव शम्भु आये ।
भक्तले दर्शन पाये ॥
ताल मृदङ्ग बेणु बजावे ।
चौसठ्ठि योगिनि मङ्गलु गावे ।
लक्ष्मि आफै चमर डोलावे ।
माहादेव में मिलि मिलि ध्यान लगावे ॥
मै माहादेव कि भक्ति संग मिलि जावे ।
फेर जग में कुछ नहि आवे ॥
जनम जनम का दुःख निभावे ॥

श्लोक

मेरा उपर ता दयालु हुनु भो आर्फै प्रभू देखियौ,
लोक्लाई पनि दर्शनै दिनु ह्वस, सब् ज्ञानका भेकि हौ ।
दर्शन बक्सनु भो हरे हजुरले यस्को काहाँ तक् भनू,
आश्चर्य पनि मान्छु यस् बखतमा मजा ब यस्तो हुनू ॥

१९८

कर्मै मात्र गरेर दुःख यिनका छुट्ला कसोरी याहाँ,
दर्शन बक्सनु होस् श्री सत्य रूपले भक्तादिका बिच् माहाँ ।
बिन्ती गर्छु शरण म पर्छु भगवान सत् शक्तिका हौ पुरा,
हे ज्ञानका चतुरा प्रकाश हुनु ह्वस, मेरा यिनै हुन् कुरा ॥

१९९

मेरा जन्म बहुत् बितेछ नरमा धेर कर्मको भोग् गर्ये,
मेरा दोष् सब माफ् गरी दिनु ह्वोस, यसमा शरणमा पर्ये ।
भक्त हौ कि अभक्त हौ म पनि सब् बुझ्नू हजुरले परो,
मेरा आशाय छैन केहि नरमा सेखि अघीको झर्‍यो ॥

२००

गर्नँ छैन म आश केहि अब ता सेखि ममताहरू
गर्नू केहि पर्‍यो भने पनि प्रभू यै तप् गर्ला बरू ।
गर्दैछु यहि तप् तपस् जति सबै दया भए पाउला,
ब्रह्मा बिष्णु महेशका हजुरमा यो अजि सब् लाउँला ॥

२०१

याह्रादेखि सिवाय दोस्रो अरू क्यै लाग्दैन लागोस् मती,
मेरा बिन्ति सुनी प्रकद् हुनु ह्वस् साचै भनिस् लौ भनी ।
ॐ श्रृष्टि उ० तर्फ पछाड़ी नभइ कन भयो पूर्वका कल्पनाले,
सत्का चित् बाच्य बाच क् अ० उ० म० स० हुँदा ब्रह्म शक्ती हुनाले

२०२

कुन् हो सत्ता बिचारून् बुध जनहरूले गोचरागो चरैको,
वाक्या तित् जो समाधि तिन गुण रहितें शुद्ध एक् चित् रहेको ।
हुँदामा जो भयाको नभए नभएकै एक दुइ देखि भिन्न,
जोहो सो सोहि होला अ० ह० म० बिच हुँदा साक्षि भूत् आफु भिन्न ॥

२०३

वदूका बाँणि बिचारून परम जनहरू भेद कुन् वेद को हो,
कस्मा कं भन्न सक्ला अगम पदबिको रूप् अरूप् सत्य कोहो ।
ब्यापक् अव्यक्त हुँदा सम रस सुख रूप् शान्ति निर्वाण जोहो,
सोहि हो सत्य साँचो अघटत घटना सचिदानन्द को हो ॥

२०४

यस्ता जो नाथका नाथ. अ० ह० म० त्रृपुटिमा स्वास निस्वास जोहो,
जानुन सब्ले बिचारी अगुण मय स्वरूप् शुद्ध चैतन्य जोहो ।
कस्मा कं गछे कस्ले गरिकन गरिनें कुन् कुरा कं कहुन् हो,
सङ्कल्पै छैन जम्मा कसरि हुन गयो यो लठारो फजुल हो ॥

२०५

सत्यै सङ्कल्प ईश्वर भनिकन श्रुतिको जो हुकुम् सत्य साँचो,
सङ्कल्पँ सत् स्वरूप् हो अझ पनि नबुझे भैं गयो कत्रो खाँचो ।
अन्तर्यामि प्रभू विना स्वरूपका के गर्नु तिम्रो बयान्,
शङ्करदेखि कृपा भयो र अहिले मेरा सुफल् भो नयन् ॥

२०६

यी सब् गुण मिलेका तपस्का सकस्ले ।
यी गुण पाउन सक्ला र सहज्मा कसले ॥

२०७

दोश्रो भाषा

भगवान्को इच्छा यो छ (कि) भक्तलाइ न चाँउने,
हरि वाँणि घेर उत्रलान् हुष्षि मच्चाउने ।
दुबो बन्सो इलामे सिरूवाले काने,
सम्झाइ दिन्छु सब्ले सुन्नून् दुःख पर्दा खाने ॥

२०८

कर्कलो र निगुरो सिस्नाहरूका मन्टा,
दुखिले खाँनु सुत्नु आनन्दिका गुएटा ।
माहाँजनका सम्पतिले चित्त पोल्दै ल्याउछ,
मन्मा सन्तोष् नहुनाले गुण्टा विजाउछ ॥

२०९

सन्तोष् दिने ईश्वर छन भित्र हेर्नु होस,
बाहिरि सन्तोष् नखोज्नु होस् बिचार गर्नु होस ।
बाहिरि सन्तोष् क्षिणमा नाश हुनेछ,
भित्र सन्तोष् लिन जाँने काम्ता हुनेछ ॥

२१०

घडि घडि इनै बाँणि हेर्नै गर्नु होस,
इ बाँणिको भेद पाये छुट्ला सबै दोष ॥
भ्रमत् गरि हेर्नु होला दुःख नमानी,
गर्ने छैन इ बाँणिले कोहि केहि हाँनी ॥

२११

कोलाहाल शब्द चल्ला सबै डराउला,
आत्यस् भइ बिचार नपाई त्यसै कराउला ।
यिनै वाणि बिचार गर्ने धैर्य हुने छौ,
हा हा नाथ शक्ति सत्य शरण हाम्रो लेउ ॥

२१२

निन्दा बेसि नहुनेको आत्मा डरोइन,
आफ्नु सत्य भजन पनि त्यस् ले छोड़ोइन ।
भगवान्को सुचन हुँदा भक्त जन्मा केही,
माल्लुम् हुँदा बिन्ति पत्र लेखेकै छौ एही ॥

२१३

बेसि कम्ति जो भएको माफ गरि दिनू,
जम्मैले यहि धर्म तिर चित्त धर दिनू ॥

२१४

(अवतारि भाषा)

लङ्गूर पारि लामा गांउ । ज्ञान ज्ञानैको इष्ट लांउ ॥
बक्षको मन्त्र झिकाउला । उड्डि जाने ज्ञान म सिकाउला ॥

२१५

पत्थर बृक्ष जङ्गल झार । भस्म हुन्छ भस्मै खार ॥
यो बिल्नेलाई बिलाइदे । सब सागरमा मिलाइदे ॥

२१६

कैलाशको ढोका खुलियो । दुनिया तो के मा भुलियो ॥
यहि धन जन्मका गुल्माल्मा । हामि त जाइ जांउ यहि हुल्मा ॥

२१७

मायार पास्को लहरो । रस्तालाइ पाच्यो पहरों ॥
चन्द्रमा सूर्य अग्नी जल । साखा त उज्यो सैन्य दल ॥

२१८

शक्ति ज्ञान छाड्दे गाल्नलाई । पृथ्वि ता दुल्लाइन पाल्नलाई ॥
शक्ति ज्ञान छाड्दे यो गाल्ने । पृथ्विले दुःख पाइन को पाल्ने ॥

२१९

पिता पुर्खा हाम्रो मरिगो । टुहुराको बथान भरि भो ॥
टुहुरा मध्ये को मै लाटो । मुक्ति पद पाउनु कुन बाठो ॥

२२०

मुक्ति पद्‌को रस्ता जान्दैन,
श्रृष्टि गुरू तप्‌ गर भन्दैन ।
सत्‌ गुरू साहेब महादेव,
मैथाङ्‌नेको शरण लेऊ ॥

२२१

पारस्मणि जस्तो ज्ञान मेरो,
गोब्रे च्याउ जस्तो धन तेरो ।
त्यही खर्च गरन त बिलोभ गर्छ,
कसो गरि तेरो पाप मर्छ ॥

२२२

लोभ पाप चुड्‌डि चढ़ाइदे
यहि शिव ॐ मा होम्‌ लाइदे ।
शिव शिव शिव ॐ शिव ॐ,
भय भ्रान्ति सङ्का गर्दे होम्‌ ॥

२२३

शिव शिव शिव खोइ शिव,
त्यहि शिव भित्र को मै जीव ।
कृष्ण कृष्ण कृष्ण खोइ कृष्ण,
सोर हजार राधेको एक तृष्ण ।

२२४

राम राम राम राम रामै,
रामायण को धुम धामै ।
राम राम राम श्री राम राम,
आत्मा भित्र बनो बिष्णु धाम ॥

२२५

चारै   भाषा   बोल्ने   भो,
अन्तर   कुरो   एउटै   हो ।
भाका   र   भाषा   घुमाउछ,
अभिमानि   मुढो   रमाउछ ॥

२२६

अठार   पुराण   नौ   ब्याकरण,
यहि   सचेत्   जिव्को   सबै   चाकर ।
ब्राह्मणको   छोरो   बेद   पढ्छ,
म   थाङ्ने   लाई   भेद   पर्छ ॥

२२७

पर्वत्   कि   छोरी   बाल्की,
यहि   सृष्टि   माया   जाल्की ।
अहिले   ता   भन्ने   सत्   खाल्की,
मेरै   ज्ञान   भित्र   देख्   रथ्   पाल्की

२२८

तेरा   काखको   मै   नानी,
मेरा   काखको   तै   नानी ।
दोस्रो   त   अर्को   होइननी,
तेरै   आँखा   भित्र   देख्   पानी ॥

२२९

त्यहि   पानि   भित्रको   मै   नानी,
दोस्रो   त   अर्को   छैननी ।
सब्   सागरमा   हेर   पानी,
दोस्रो   त   अर्को   होइननी ।

२३०

एकान्त सुन्ने माहाँ ध्यान्,
मागि राख बाबू लामा ज्ञान् ।
यहि लामाज्ञानको विचार गर,
बाहिर त नहेर भित्र हेर ॥

२३१

मुलुक् का दाशी रमाए,
राजाले धर्म कमाए ।
राजाले धर्म गरि दिए,
पैसा त धेरै छर दिए ॥

२३२

धन्य हो राजा तिन् सर्कार,
सलामि दिन्छु बारम्बार ।
माकुरो कपास्को कमाइ नलाउने,
धागै धागाले र उहि घर भर्ने

२३३

यो माकुरा भित्र को होला,
कति छ है माकुरा (धागै) धागाको (त्यो) पोला ।
यो बिचार गर्ने को होला,
चैतन्य जिव जो होला ॥

२३४

ॐ नमः शिवाय

सर्वार्थ योग बाणि भनेर जान्नू,
विदान्तका भेद पनि केहि ठान्नू ।
मिल्दैन सामन्य यि ग्रन्थ माहाँ,
मिल्ने छ पिछे सब शास्त्र माहाँ ॥

कसैले यसैलाई गिद् झइ मान्नू,
कसैले अगम तत्व भनेर ठान्नू ।
एक एक पद् ले गरि अर्थ बन्ला,
आउला यो धर्म युग नाम यसै को चल्ला ।

जो बन्तु पछ महिमा यसको बनावोस्,
लोक् ले पनि अब त झट्ट यो होस पावोस् ।
सर्वार्थ योग बाँणि छ नाम यसको,
लेखी समाप्त कन आज भइ गो ॥

(सर्वार्थ योग बाँणि)

प्रबन्ध

प्रर्थना

ब्रज झत्रो भयां रहदा तिमी,
स्थिर भई याहाँ श्री बसिन् जमी ।
हजुरमा लगी प्राण राख्तछाँ,
दरश बक्सियोस् नाथ खोज्दछौ ॥

हजुर कि कथा भक्ति जीवनी,
स्नेह मै लिदा पाप नाशिनी ।
श्रवण नित्यले शान्ति दायिनी,
ग्रहण गर्छ जो दानि हुन्तिनी ॥

अति मिठो बचन्दिव्य वाक्य झन्,
कविहरू पनी मन् पराउछन् ।
दीन दास हूं मोहमा परी,
अभय बक्सियोस् अमृते सरी ॥

—चिन्तामणि

स्वर्सेली राज्न परिपूर्ण चुरा
सुनिदिनुहोसनत हाम्रो कुरा
धर्मात्मी राज्न तिमि धर्म धाम
ज्ञानात्मी राज्न तिमि ज्ञान बिचार
बिबेकी राज्न बिबेक राखव गरिचोस
स्वराज्यमा धर्म अब भ्रट घरिचोस
स्वराज्यको धर्म ८ धर्म माहा
सम्पूर्ण न्यारा अब न म माहा
सम्पूर्ण सारा मि घोडेर ता हा
आनुभयो लौ अब देश माहा
नहोसन माहाराज्को राज्समा दुःख
पाउन दुःखीले कोहि चिज सुख

oral by Nainakala   provided by Mana Maya

मणि प्रेस, १० माइल, कालिम्पोंग ।

Index

www.ingramcontent.com/pod-product-compliance
Lightning Source LLC
Chambersburg PA
CBHW020902160726
47993CB00005B/1774